NIJINSKY IN AMERICA

Nijinsky in America

KINGA SZAKÁTS NIJINSKY GASPERS

NIJINSKY IN AMERICA
THE AMERICAN TOUR
OF THE
BALLET RUSSE
1916 – 1917

©1988 / 2013 The Educational Publisher Inc., Bilbio Publishing
Columbus Ohio

Nijinsky in America

I wish to thank Ms Professor Yunyu Wang for her dedication to Nijinsky's memory and for bringing the publication of this book to fruition. My thanks also goes to Mr. Jefferson Hsieh for his untiring labor during the editing of the manuscript.

Cover Design by Robert Sims

Edited by Mark G. Gaspers

Text copyright ©1988 / 2007 / 2013 by Kinga Gaspers. All rights reserved.

Published in 2013 by The Educational Publisher/Biblio Publishing

ISBN: 978-1-62249-067-7
Printed in USA

To my husband John – for his unwavering faith in me

To my mother Tamara – for entrusting me with this precious heritage

Much has been written about Nijinsky and the Ballet Russe on both sides of the Atlantic, not to mention the rest of the world. My one hope in writing this work is that it will prompt further research into this fascinating group of artists and consequently, the truth about them will be known. Then and only then will my grandfather's wish will be realized:

They are afraid that I shall tell the whole truth.
I shall tell the whole truth after my death because I shall leave heirs after me.
My heirs will continue what I have started. I shall write the truth.
(*Journal of Nijinsky*. 1919.)

Contents

Introduction 1

RHODE ISLAND, Providence – 30 October 1916 4
Providence Opera House

CONNECTICUT, New Haven – 31 October – 1 7
November 1916 – Shubert Theatre

NEW YORK, New York, Brooklyn – 2 November 1916 10
Academy of Music

MASSACHUSETTS, Springfield – 3 - 4 November 1916 13
Court Square Theatre

MASSACHUSETTS, Boston – 6 - 11 November 1916 16
Boston Opera House

MASSACHUSETTS, Worcester – 13 November 1916 26
Worcester Theatre

CONNECTICUT, Hartford – 14 November 1916 28
Parsons Theatre

CONNECTICUT, Bridgeport – 15 November 1916 30
Park Theatre

NEW JERSEY, Atlantic City – 16 November 1916 32
New Nixon Theatre

MARYLAND, Baltimore – 17 - 18 November 1916 37
Lyric Theatre

WASHINGTON D. C. – 20 - 22 November 1916 39
Belasco Theatre

PENNSYLVANIA, Philadelphia – 23 – 25 41
November 1916 – Metropolitan Opera House

Nijinsky in America

VIRGINIA, Richmond – 27 November 1916 44
Academy of Music

SOUTH CAROLINA, Columbia – 28 November 1916 47
Columbia Theater

GEORGIA, Atlanta – 29 November 1916 – Auditorium 52

LOUISIANA, New Orleans – 30 November - 2 December 1916 54
French Opera House

TEXAS, Houston – 4 - 5 December 1916 58
City Auditorium

TEXAS, Austin – 6 December 1916 – Majestic Theatre 62

TEXAS, Dallas – 7 December 1916 – Coliseum 64

TEXAS, Fort Worth – 8 - 9 December 1916 – Coliseum 69

TULSA, Oklahoma – 11 December 1916 – Auditorium 75

KANSAS, Wichita – 12 December 1916 – Forum 79

MISSOURI, Kansas City – 13 - 14 December 1916 84
Convention Hall

IOWA, Des Moines – 15 December 1916 – Coliseum 88

NEBRASKA, Omaha – 16 December 1916 –Auditorium 92

COLORADO, Denver – 18 - 20 December 1916 93
Auditorium

UTAH, Salt Lake City – 22 - 23 December 1916 99
Salt Lake Theatre

CALIFORNIA 102

CALIFORNIA, Los Angeles – 25 - 30 December 1916 104
Auditorium

The American Tour of the Ballet Rouse

CALIFORNIA, San Francisco – 2 - 8 January 1917 113
Valencia Theatre

CALIFORNIA, Oakland – 9 - 10 January 1917 117
Auditorium Opera House

OREGON, Portland – 12 - 13 January 1917 120
Heilig Theatre

BRITISH COLUMBIA, Vancouver – 15 January 1917 122
Vancouver Opera House

WASHINGTON, Seattle – 16 - 17 January 1917 126
Moore Theatre

WASHINGTON, Tacoma – 18 January 1917 134
Tacoma Theater

WASHINGTON, Spokane – 19 - 20 January 1917 138
Auditorium

MINNESOTA, Saint Paul – 23 January 1917 143
Auditorium

MINNESOTA, Minneapolis – 24 - 25 January 1917 147
Auditorium

WISCONSIN, Milwaukee – 26 January 1917 153
Auditorium

ILLINOIS, Chicago – 28 January 1917 – Cohan's Grand 156

INDIANA, Indianapolis – 29 January 1917 160
Shubert Murat Theatre

MISSOURI, Saint Louis – 30 January 1917 – Odeon 167

TENNESSEE, Memphis – 31 January 1917 – Lyric Theater 169

ALABAMA, Birmingham – 1 February 1917 172
Jefferson Theater

TENNESSEE, Chattanooga – 2 February 1917 – Grand 175

Nijinsky in America

TENNESSEE, Nashville – 3 February 1917 – Vendome 176

KENTUCKY, Louisville – 5 February 1917 – Macauley 181

OHIO, Cincinnati – 6 - 7 February 1917 – Music Hall 183

OHIO, Dayton – 8 February 1917 – Victoria 186

MICHIGAN, Detroit – 9 - 10 February 1917 – Lyceum 188

OHIO, Toledo – 12 February 1917 – Valentine 193

OHIO, Toledo – 12 February 1917 – **Valentine** 195

OHIO, Cleveland – 15 - 17 February 1917 – Colonial 197

PENNSYLVANIA, Pittsburgh – 19 - 21 February 1917 200
New Pitt Theater

NEW YORK, Syracuse – 23 February 1917 – Empire 203

NEW YORK, Albany – 24 February 1917 205
Harmanus Bleecker Hall

Conclusion 208

Epilogue 209

Works Cited 214

The American Tour of the Ballet Rouse

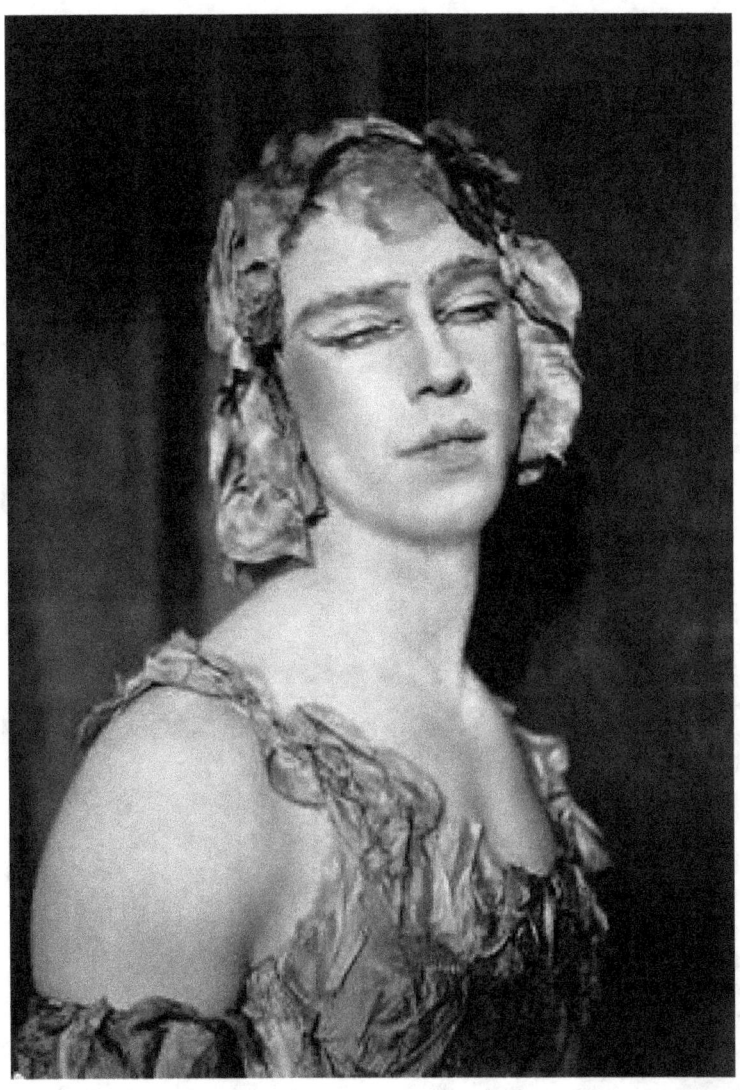

Nijinsky in America

The American Tour of the Ballet Rouse

Nijinsky in America

The American Tour of the Ballet Rouse

Nijinsky in America

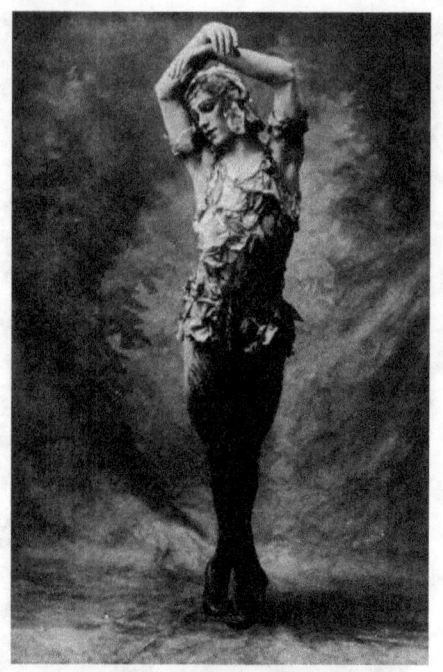

The American Tour of the Ballet Rouse

Nijinsky in America

The American Tour of the Ballet Rouse

Nijinsky in America

Nijinsky in America

The American Tour of the Ballet Rouse

Introduction

Imagine that on Monday, 30 October, you are in Providence, Rhode Island; Tuesday – Halloween – New Haven, Connecticut; Thursday, 2 November, Brooklyn, New York; Friday, 3 November, Springfield, Massachusetts; then Monday through Saturday, Boston, Massachusetts; the following week beginning with 13 November, a different city every night. This goes on and on for a period of not quite four months, through thirty-one States, for fifty-five cities in all. It is a tour, a group of performers consisting of artists, technical and support staff as well as family members – one hundred-fifty strong, crossing America, often stopping for only a single performance. The show requires much scenery, costumes, instruments for a full orchestra, in other words, tons of baggage. There is no big eighteen wheeler to precede the artists with their luggage, while they hop on an airplane or into a customized bus. This is no World Tour of a popular rock band, or an award winning musical. Everyone in the troupe, including its biggest star and box-office draw, commutes on a special train comprised of six baggage cars, three coaches, and a dining car. It is a home away from home for the months of October through February. They celebrate Christmas, New Year, birthdays, and anniversaries on the train, while covering roughly 12,000 miles. News of their coming fills the locals with excitement and the papers with glowing headlines. Their presence electrifies the air and no city is left untouched by the spectacle offered. They thrill, astonish and leave an indelible memory for all who see them, young and old, rich and poor, sophisticated, learned or not.

Historically speaking, America, along with the entire planet, grapples with political upheaval. War looms on the horizon. It is an election year in the United States, complicating an already tense situation. The incumbent's narrow win, sends a mixed message to the nation and the world. Important discoveries are made in the field of science and technology. There is a one hundred percent rise in food prices. Women demand and claim more equality with men. Congress passes laws protecting children and supporting education. The film industry is booming on both ends of the continent. Sounds like the end of the twentieth century? Perhaps the circus has come to town; well, not quite. The year is 1916. The remarkable journey we are about to retrace was accomplished by the Ballet Russe, with Waslaw Nijinsky was at the helm and was the main attraction; the reason why the tour came to be in the first place. Serge Diaghilev's Ballet Russe had come to perform in America in January of that same year, all the while promising Nijinsky. Nijinsky, however, was a victim of circumstance, detained in Hungary because of World War I. This seemed to be of little concern to Sergei Diaghilev, who did not wish to humiliate himself by asking Waslaw to return, having fired him in a jealous rage following Waslaw's marriage to Romola Pulszky. Otto Kahn, the director of the New York Metropolitan Opera, however, wanted it otherwise. The tour would be with Nijinsky or not at all; and so, the mad scramble began to try and extricate the distinguished dancer and his family from their involuntary bondage.

The performance dates, cities, and theatre names were taken from Romola Nijinsky's handwritten chronicle of the tour. Her account of the tour provides a unique perspective on America in the 1910s. The Ballet Russe had made an impact, yes, but by their candid and honest response to this exotic troupe, Americans made a statement about themselves as well. This story then is about America, her impressions and reactions; it is she who will regale you with the magnificent wonders of the Russian Ballet.

I offer this bit of Americana to my adopted homeland, in gratitude for all the opportunities she has afforded me and my family who came before, not the least of whom was my grandfather, Waslaw Nijinsky.

ON A PERSONAL NOTE

In 1853, Trubner and Company published a three volume work by Francis and Theresa Pulszky, *White Red Black. Sketches of Society in the United States during the Visit of their Guest*. This work was reprinted in 1968 by Negro University Press. Its authors, Francis and Theresa were accompanying the great Hungarian patriot Lajos Kossuth, on his tour of the United States on behalf of the Hungarian cause. Americans considered Kossuth the "Hungarian George Washington." Francis served Kossuth as aide and advisor.

The American Tour of the Ballet Rouse

The three volume work by Francis and his wife Theresa is a rich and detailed account of life in the United States, during the early 1850s. After their journey, the Pulszkys returned first to England (as they were in exile, just like Kossuth) and later to Hungary. They had six children, Gyula, Harriet, Agost, Gabor, Ployxena, and Charlie. Gyula and Harriet died in an epidemic. Agost became a prominent law professor. Gabor, godson of Garibaldi, fought along his side. Polyxena became a writer. Charlie, the youngest, founded the Hungarian Museum of Fine Arts and married the country's leading dramatic actress, Emilia Markus. They had two children, Tessa and Romola. Yes, Romola Pulszky, who later became the wife of the famed dancer, Waslaw Nijinsky.

And so, this book is dedicated to my son Mark, an American, with a heritage on his father's side that includes French, German ancestry as well as a Native American Princess; whose maternal great-great-great grandparents, the Pulszkys, traveled extensively in and wrote about this great land; whose great-grandparents, the Nijinsky's, toured America "from sea to shining sea"; whose grandparents, the Szakats lived in and were proud citizens of the United States; and whose mother had the great joy of giving him birth in a free land, having been once a refugee from communism. May he always love his homeland and cherish the memory of those who came before.

A NOTE ABOUT SPELLING

This writer has decided to keep whatever spelling found in the articles, as a result, the reader will discover a great a variety in spelling Russian names. Nijinsky's name appears as he signed his name: Waslaw Nijinsky.

RHODE ISLAND, Providence – 30 October 1916 – Providence Opera House

The smallest state in the Union, Rhode Island, had the singular distinction of being the number one stop on the tour. Rhode Island was prosperous during the turn of the century. Factories produced war materials, chemicals, and munitions. Shipyards built combat and cargo ships. Providence, the capital, boasted of an opera house. The Tilden-Thruber Corporation charged five dollars for floor and some balcony seats. Seats further back went for four dollars, while the family circle cost three. The ticket office accepted mail orders, and after October 26 one could buy unreserved seats for as little as two dollars to one dollar fifty cents at the door. In light of the artistic offerings at about the same period available at a fraction of the cost, tickets to see the Russians were outrageously pricey. One could see "America's Greatest Singing Comedienne, Blanche Ring," perform in the musical, *Broadway and Buttermilk*, in the same opera house. A mere twenty-five cents would get you in. The Hippodrome was even a better deal, of course it was mostly for those interested in silent movies, where one could see eleven reels, running continuously, for ten cents; on Mondays it cost "1 Cent Penny Copper." Pity the poor artist who happened to be scheduled during the same week as the Russians!

Providence Daily Journal advertised the Ballet's coming with great fervor: "Brought to America at a Cost of $500,000." "Greatest Artistic Sensation of the Twentieth Century," never mind that the twentieth century was quite young. The Sunday edition used photographs to entice the public. A full figure photograph of Nijinsky as Prince Igor graced the front page of the theatre section.

> At the Opera House tomorrow evening, for one performance only, the Metropolitan Opera Company presents "Serge De Diaghileff's [Diaghilev] Ballet Russe." The operas to be played are "Scheherazade," "Les Sylphides," "L'Apres Midi d'un Faun" and "Prince Igor." Mr. Nijinsky and his full cast with an orchestra of 60 musicians, conducted by m. Pierre Monteux, appear. The production is under the local management of Madame Hall-Whyteck. The description of the operas is as follows….

The American Tour of the Ballet Rouse

It is interesting to note that the ballets were called "operas." The members of the Ballet were well on their way, preparing for a Halloween night performance in New Haven, Connecticut, when the following review appeared in the 31 October 1916 issue of *The Providence Journal*, penned by an anonymous journalist.

RUSSIAN BALLET AT OPERA HOUSE

Remarkable Performance Witnessed by Large Audience.

MUSIC, MOTION AND COLOR

Striking Costumes and Daring Stage Settings, Together with Original and Graceful dancing, Combine in Picturesque Effectiveness. – Nijinsky and Lopokova in Cast.

At the Opera House last evening Providence was introduced to a new art. Music, rhythmic motion and color were blended in a most wonderful and striking manner by the famous Diaghiliff [Diaghilev] Ballet Russe. The eye was dazzled by the richness of the costuming and the gorgeousness of the settings, by the graceful and original dancing and the effective and ever-changing groupings, which moved to the measures of orchestral music. It was truly an unusual and remarkable spectacle....

Waslow Niginsky [Waslaw Nijinsky], Adolf Blom [Bolm], Mlle.Flore Revulles [Revalles], Lidia Lopokova [Lydia] and other celebrated dancers appeared in the four ballets or operas which composed the program. ...the settings showed color combinations of great originality. These were by the artist Leon Bakst. At the rising of the curtain the strangeness of their brilliant massed color seemed to usher the beholder into a new world where nothing was familiar. In "Scheherazade" against such a background the dancers in endless procession of graceful movements and postures, and costumed in an equally striking manner as regards peculiar color combinations, interpreted the story. "Scheherazade" is in fact, as given last evening, is nothing more than a one-act opera in pantomime. The interpreting medium is dancing instead of singing, with appropriate orchestral music, and with the assistance of a stage setting that in the way of daring color effects goes beyond anything hitherto attempted. The body of the company is wonderfully trained. Not a hitch marred the intricate evolutions and difficult modes of dancing displayed. The great Nijinsky appeared in "L'Apres Midi d'un Faun," in which his work was so slight and lacking in action that many in the audience were disappointed.

Nijinsky in America

American audiences were not aware that a few years prior, Waslaw's choreography of the "Faun", his first of four revolutionary choreographies, caused a riot at its world premiere in Paris. Parisian audiences did not object to the lack of action, rather, the total lack of classic steps and style, not to mention the sexually explicit nature of the work.

CONNECTICUT, New Haven – 31 October - 1 November 1916 – Shubert Theatre

"Voters! Step over to the polls looking your 'newest' in a Johnson Suit and Overcoat." The above is an ad found in a 1 November 1916 issue of *New Haven Journal-Courier*, for KUPPENHEIMER suits and overcoats that could be bought for twenty to thirty dollars. Connecticut, the "Constitution State," where you were encouraged to look your best when voting; after all, the Presidential elections were only a week away. Historic Connecticut claimed the first "Yankee Peddlers," who traveled far and wide in the 1700s and Eli Whitney, inventor of "mass production." People of Connecticut were equally proud of Hartford, the "Insurance City," and New Haven, home of the prestigious Yale University, founded in 1701, third oldest in the nation. Then there was the relocation of the U.S. Coast Guard Academy in 1900, the opening of a submarine base for the U.S. Navy in 1917, and the largest munitions factories supplying World War I, all located in Connecticut. Although the U.S. did not get involved in the world conflict until 1917, trouble was already brewing in the fall of 1916. From the above-mentioned issue of the *New Haven Journal-Courier*, the headlines warned of things to come:

> "SIX AMERICANS KILLED IN SINKING OF STEAMSHIP MARINA; WILSON DIRECTS ALL HASTE IN ASCERTAINING THE FACTS; SEC. LANSING ASKS GERMANY FOR COMPLETE INFORMATION."

It was not all gloom and doom, however. "News of Local Theatres," in 28 October issue of the *New Haven Journal-Courier* reported of coming attractions:

> Up to the minute in every respect the Hyperion Players will be seen all of next week in the newest of the theatrical treats, the breeziest and brightest of the latest batch of comedy efforts, the hit of the present season in New York...

What was this "bucolic comedy with song?", none other than *Broadway and Buttermilk* which competed with the Ballet Russe in Providence. It seemed that the Russians were getting second, actually third billing, as the article came last and was much more succinct and to the point:

> Aim of Serge Diaghileff.
>
> Our aim of the Serge de Diaghileff Ballet Russe, which with Waslaw Nijinsky is announced to appear at the Shubert, October 31 and November 1, is that its work is not confined to exploitation of the art of anyone nation. De Diaghileff has endeavored to secure the best wherever he has been able to find it. Bakst, the celebrated artist, who designed most of the scenery and general stage decoration, has found motifs in Japanese, Greek, Turkish and rococo designs; the music of Rimsky-Korsakov, Tchaikovsky, and Mussorgsky, is not devoted to national themes; and in the ballet itself, the ideal is to address itself to universal emotions and imagination. The scenery and costumes for two new ballets added this year were executed by Robert Edmond Jones, who is the first American to be so honored.

Next to a photo of *Broadway and Buttermilk* a picture of Flore Revalles could be seen. Since the Ballet performed for two nights, there was a change of programming on the second evening, *Carneval, Cleopatra, and Spectre de la Rose*. And how did this land of military prowess receive the Russian marvel? Judge for yourself, based on a review found in 1 November 1916, *New Haven Evening Register*:

> BALLET RUSSE MAKES WONDERFUL IMPRESSION AT THE SHUBERT
>
> At the Shubert last evening New Haven theatre goers were introduced to a new art. Music, rhythmic motion and color were blended in a most wonderful and striking manner...

Sounds familiar? It should; word for word, spelling mistakes and all, it is the same anonymous review given in the 31 October issue of the *Providence Journal*. The two papers most likely had the same owner, and definitely the same fine arts critic. On that same day, however, the *New Haven Journal-Courier* had a much more intelligent review. The critic, under the initials: T. M. P., considered the production "brilliant . . . a real revelation." It revealed how terpsichorean, musical, and theatrical art could be united so creatively, all the while producing results never before achieved even by the greatest artist to have come before.

The American Tour of the Ballet Rouse

It is a formidable array of dancers, which Serge de Diaghileff [Diaghilev] has gathered, with Nijinsky at its head, while the daring and graphic settings of Leon Bakst, with their bold sweeps and glow of color form an unusual background for the artistry of the dancers. Little less important and equally delightful are the costumes that sparkle and glimmer with bewildering color schemes and opulent beauty.

T. M. P. continued by giving an overview of the same program as the one in Providence, praised the choice of music, and then proceeded to talk about individual artists:

Waslaw Nijinsky ranks as the leading dancer of his sex, possessing wonderful technical skill, with rare originality and power of illusion, as shown in "The Faun," while in "Scheherazade" he gave a powerful impersonation of Zobeide's favorite.

It is evident that the New Haven public was not left "disappointed" by the "lack of action" in the "Faun." In summary, he had this to say:

Many pictures of rare beauty were presented last evening, rich and colorful, the product of a highly imaginative brain. The color combinations and gorgeous settings made a strong appeal to the visual sense; the music stirred the emotions, while both were evoked by the grace and beauty of the dancing. The company displayed unusual perfection in routine and the intricate figures moved along with consummate ease.

The second evening's performance was an entirely different program, "even more charming than the first; yet the audience was much smaller in size. Why, one wonders; was it the high-ticket prices? Who is to account for a fickle audience's taste?

NEW YORK, New York, Brooklyn – 2 November 1916 – Academy of Music

> Perhaps never was Nijinsky, in more captivating mood than yesterday afternoon, when he made his last Manhattan appearance in "Till Eulenspiegel," a comic-dramatic ballet of his own creation. This delightful fantasy was all too brief; it seemed as though the noted dancer had scarcely acquainted himself with his audience, when the fall of the curtain marked the conclusion of the performance. Nijinsky flung himself into his role with super abandon and his dancing portrayed in rapid succession a great variety of emotions. It was a fascinating "Till" that he offered yesterday: a Till so graceful and rhythmic he seemed more a will-o'-the-wisp escaped fugitive from "Midsummer Night's Dream" than a mortal.
>
> He was gay, dejected, wistful, and imperious. No two minutes saw him the same. With the rapidity of a lightning flash his whole demeanor changed and he would off one characterization, to assume one, the other extreme in its mood.

So reported the 29 October 1916 issue of the *Brooklyn Daily Eagle* on the occasion of the Ballet Russe's closing in Manhattan. Brooklyn, New York's most densely populated borough, had a right to its very own performance by the Russians. After all, they did boast of the renowned Academy of Music. Brooklyn residents did not have to go into the City for entertainment. There was plenty to do and see in their own backyard. The Brooklyn performance on 2 November was actually the third stop on the tour. The day before, under "AMUSEMENTS-BROOKLYN," some diversions, offered in the Brooklyn Daily Eagle were the BALLET RUSSE [top billing for a change], HIT-THE-TRAIL-HOLIDAY, THE THOROUGHBREDS With the FLYING SHERWOODS, AMERICANS, EDDIE FOY & the 7 Younger Foys, FALL CARNIVAL, THE SPORTING WIDOWS, THE SILENT WITNESS, THE MAN WHO CAME BACK, THE BIRTH OF A NATION, AND RICHARD KEY BIGGS in an ORGAN RECITAL. D. W. Griffith's masterpiece, *The Birth of a Nation*, had caused a major controversy, but eventually became a blockbuster, grossing $40,000,000. In addition, no less than sixteen movie theatres lured the public with such famed and tempting title as Jules Verne's *Around the World in 80 Days*. One

The American Tour of the Ballet Rouse

could also choose from Civilization, Slander, Romeo and Juliet, Rolling Stones, goes to show you, there is nothing new under the sun!

On performance day, ad for the Ballet Russe went to second place, with the top spot reserved for the Society of New York Symphony presenting selections by Saint-Saens, Mozart, Strauss and Wagner. Following the Ballet ad came the organ concert, still free, and then the movies: "WHERE FEATURE FILMS ARE SHOWN TODAY." Everyone of the sixteen theatres was showing a different film from the day before, including the STRAND movie house with the famous Lionel Barrymore in *Under the Gaslight*.

Brooklyn residents were sophisticated artistically, and did not take a back seat to Manhattan.

> The student Nijinsky in blackface as a small slave in *Petipa's Le Roi Candaule* was no more than a conventional black moor. In Fokine's *Cléopatre* (1909), Nijinsky supported the senior ballerina, Preorajenskaya, in a blackface slave duet. Le Pavilion d'Armide, his sensational solo as Armida's slave served no dramatic purpose except that of exuberant adornment. Slavery as a lyric metaphor, however, spelled ambiguous and provocative servility; ownership licensed willing or unwilling physical possession. The passionate and cruel harem queen's appetite for chair a plaisir, new flesh for enjoyment, was a traditional property of pornography.
>
> In *Scheherazade*, Nijinsky moved in three dimensions, muscle against lurid color on top of heavy-breathing orchestration. An old eunuch (Enrico Cecchetti), wheeled by his lascivious sultana (Ida Rubinstein), sprang her dearest human pet panther (Nijinsky) from its gilded cage. Fokine, in fresh security, freed from prim bureaucracy, could now compose without restraint. Bakst's hanging lamps and massive drapes framed orgy and massacre. Today the libretto sounds like an early silent film . . .
>
> *Schéhérazade* was the first massive explosion of Diaghilev's increasingly shrewd method for sending a smug or apathetic audience into shock.

Lincoln Kirstein wrote the above commentary in his 1975 NIJINSKY DANCING, a pictorial tribute to the Personification of Dance Perfection. In light of his thoughts, the following review

Nijinsky in America

from 3 November 1916, Brooklyn Daily Eagle will be all the more portentous.

BALLET RUSSE AT ACADEMY

Applause by Great Audience for Exotic Program

The Diaghileff Ballet Russe gave its one performance last evening, before a filled auditorium, at the Academy of Music, and there was, throughout, frequent applause for the wonderful skill of the dancers, and for all that went with the productions. And there was one hiss, when the "Scheherazade" number was in the height of its performance. The audience broke into applause at the wild actions of the dancers, in the orgy scene, and it was not evident whether the hiss was meant for the dancers or for suppression of the applause, so that there should be no interruption of the action, or, on the other hand, for reprobation of some features of the act. It would not have been out of place to express objections to the actions of the blacks, released in the harem, to join the women members, in the absence of the Shah; nor would it be anything but normal and natural to show abhorrence at the embraces and (stage) kisses that the harem women allowed to and gave the blacks. The actions were not merely suggestive; they were also expressive. They were, it is true, in keeping with the characters, but lasciviousness might have been left to the imaginations. It was art, but decadent art, "Art for art's sake," and all that sort of rubbish. No wonder that the police of London stopped the performance of it.

The good critic of this article, the name is unknown, continued for three more paragraphs, praising the troupe, claiming that they were better than when they performed "across the river," and stating that "'L'Apres midi d'un Faun' was tame.'" Considering the riot that the "Faun" caused at its premiere only four years prior in Paris, that was truly a curious declaration.

MASSACHUSETTS, Springfield – 3 - 4 November 1916 – Court Square Theatre

There are several cities in the United States named Springfield, but none has a more famous son than the Springfield in Massachusetts. In 1891, a physical-education teacher for the International YMCA Training School was asked to invent an indoor game for the winter months. Having come from Canada, he was no stranger to cold. The thirty year old took a soccer ball and for lack of boxes, made do with two peach baskets for goals. Presto, James A. Naismith gave birth to the American obsession, the basketball game! On a more serious note, Springfield had an armory as far back as the Revolutionary War. It was in this town that the Springfield rifle and the M1 Rifle were developed for World War I and II respectively.

Aside from "fun and games," "arms and ammunition," Springfield residents were well versed in the fine arts. In keeping with their military frame of mind, the preview in the 3 November 1916 Springfield Union began with:

Russians Invade Springfield

Springfield experienced a Russian invasion this morning, when Waslaw Najinsky [Nijinsky], conceded to be the greatest male dancer in the world, together with 186 other members of the Metropolitan Opera Company's Serge Diaghileff's [Diaghilev] Ballet Russe, arrived on a 12-car special. For two nights at the Court Square Theatre this sensational troupe of actor-dancers and musicians will reproduce here eight numbers of their repertoire, exactly as they have reproduced them in Paris, London and the Metropolitan and Manhattan Opera Houses in New York...

"L'Apres Midi d'un Faune," is to be danced by Najinsky [Nijinsky] himself. When first produced in Paris this ballet, because of its daring, brought down a storm of protest. Last year this was repeated in New York. Najinsky's [Nijinsky] concept of the faun is a spiritual one, and he has so defended himself before his critics...

Besides the 65 dancers in the troupe, including, Najinsky [Nijinsky], Adolf Bolm...

and Kachouba voted the most beautiful of Russian girls...

Nijinsky in America

There are 52 musicians, directed by Pierre Monteux, soldier-conductor; a technical staff of 20, four maids, three valets, six costume women and the families of many of those on tour.

The article featured Ekaterina Galanta in a photograph, and as usual the piece was surrounded by advertisements of all sorts. Thanksgiving was near and so the ads read:

THANKSGIVING GUESTS WILL SOON ARRIVE

Are the appointments of your home exactly right for the Thanksgiving festivities? The dining room, the living room, the library, the den; the guest rooms -are they all right? If not, - here are some special Thanksgiving needs at very Special Prices-

For $110.50 one could go home with a ten piece "Fumed oak William and Mary dining room suite," the set included: a buffet, china cabinet, six-leg extension table, 6 genuine leather seat chairs, and one arm chair. Consider then, that tickets to see the Russians went from one to five dollars. This was a lot of money when you could buy a package of pills to fight indigestion for 25 cents and see the Dartmouth vs. Syracuse football game for a buck. But it was worth every penny. The Russians' dancing was dubbed "supreme."

It is absolutely impossible to convey an impression of the beauties of the Ballet Russe. To many Americans the opportunity is given to learn a new language-the language of the dance. Thoughts too delicate, too subtle, for mere cumbersome speech are conveyed to audiences through the combined harmonies of Monteux, Bakst, Fokine and those consummate artists of the dance, Nijinsky, Bolm, Lopokova, Revalles, Spesiwtzewa, Gavrilov ...and the others of the ballet.

The critic, once again a person of mystery giving only the initials A. L. S. W., as identity, continued by retelling a conversation between Ralph Waldo Emerson and Margaret Fuller, while the two were watching the unrivaled Fanny Essler: "Ralph, this is poetry." "Margaret, this is religion," replied Mr. Emerson.

Scheherazade

Leon Bakst and Michel Fokine arranged this gorgeous ballet. The music is by Rimsky-Korsakow. It is a Nijinsky triumph....In addition to the exemplification of Nijinsky's art, *Scheherazade*

The American Tour of the Ballet Rouse

serves to illustrate the possibilities of realism in the dance. It is impossible to imagine a more realistic picture of animal passion than Nijinsky portrays in this ballet and it is impossible to imagine a scene of more abandoned sensuality yet such is the influence of the dance that these features, outstanding as they are, are subordinated to the exquisite realization of the dream of artists.

No "abhorrence," no "decadent art" for this critic. It seems that the Springfield audience, or at least its critic, was much more open minded about the performance of *Scheherazade* than the one in Brooklyn.

MASSACHUSETTS, Boston – 6 - 11 November 1916 – Boston Opera House

Boston needs no introduction, neither politically nor culturally. The largest city in New England has been dubbed the "Hub of the Universe" and the "Athens of America." The Ballet Russe was only one of many noted artists to come with the aim to amaze and astonish Boston's citizenry. In fact, the Russians had been there before, only ten months prior. Bostonians knew what to expect, they weren't easily mesmerized, yet the excitement was great. This time, for the first time in Boston, Nijinsky would be there too, he was coming not only to dance but to show off a brand new creation, premiered only weeks before in New York. A choreography by the unsurpassed genius of dance, who was willing to use and work with a little known New England scene designer!

The papers were filled with feature articles, interviews, and photographs galore with and about the Russians. Those who had seen the Ballet Russe in January did not think there was any room for further development or improvement of the company, but the opposite had been reported from New York...

> There is yet more to be seen, than was seen then, during the coming week. New York reviews of Mr. Nijinsky's spectacles and performances only echo the verdict given by Paris and London seasons before he appeared in this country. That he is probably the greatest artist as a dancer pure and simple, now known to the public, is a more or less accepted statement. But Mr. Nijinsky is also, by every report, an artist of supreme imagination and of a most amazing technique in the realization of ideas. It was he who planned the setting of Debussy's "L'Apres-midi d'un Faune" which the sculptor Rodin declared the most striking revival of the spirit of Greek art that he had witnesses in modern times. It is he who has recently put on the stage with the help of Robert Edmund Jones what reviewers of New York have hailed as a wonderfully intuitive interpretation of the spirit as well as the letter of Richard Strauss' tone-poem, "Till Eulenspiegel." (5 November 1916, ed. Downes Olin, "Russian Ballet Returns" *Boston Sunday Post*.)

Of the six performances scheduled for Boston, Nijinsky was slated to dance five times. Lydia Lopokova with the Ballet Russe on its

The American Tour of the Ballet Rouse

premiere season in Paris, had been working as an actress in the States when the Russians came in January. She joined the tour along with Specewtzewa who came directly from Russia with the Czar's permission.

Even so, Boston audiences had a plethora of entertainment choices; for instance: Herbert Beerbohm Tree was appearing in the Merry Wives of Windsor; the incomparable Sarah Bernhardt and Ignace Padarewski were coming to Boston the following week; and at the Shubert, "Robinson Crusoe Jr. with complete original cast of nearly 200, including the far-famed beauty squad of dainty, darling, dashing, dimpled, Dresden doll divinities, and Al Jolson."

With a photograph of Nijinsky and Lopokova, the headlines read: "Muscovite Host Invades Back Bay, Twelve Carloads of Ballet Russe Unload - Names, Temperaments, Snake and All." Never mind that they were not "Muscovites," but from St. Petersburg. Likely the editor of the Boston Post found that "Muscovites" had a more intriguing resonance to it. And about the snake:

215 OF THEM

Two hundred and fifteen strong, the Muscovite army of artists and all their baggage and brilliant Bakst impedimenta flowed from the 12 cars of their all-steel special train through a shifting delta of press agents, photographers, porters and reporters. [They were staying at the Hotel Lenox and Copley-Plaza.]

Flore Revalles, who has done her part to make Cleopatra famous, appeared muffled in black furs such as never, graced the burnished barge of Egypt's queen.

About her fingers curled and twined a tiny snake from which she says she learns the sinuous movements of her Cleopatra dances. Immediately the girls of the ballet scattered away from her chattering terrified Russian. The reporters and photographers rushed toward her, chattering their best Boston English.

Snake under Glass

Press agent Bernays from the Metropolitan Opera came tearing up with Mark Anthony's little glass house. (Mark Anthony is the snake's name and he runs out a black tongue in poisonous anger if one so much as mentions Julius Cesar.)

Nijinsky in America

The article continues with more juicy tidbits about the Russians and then:

> Finally a small man in a cap and a big, fuzzy overcoat alighted. Nijinsky had arrived - and the photographers and press agents staged another skin-tackle play which gained about six yards and scored a series of photographs of the famous dancer and Mrs. Nijinsky.
>
> Faun is for Wear
>
> One zealous cameraman, seeking more nature studies to go with the Flore Revalles' snake, asked if Nijinsky's faun could be photographed in its crate. It was disappointing to learn that the famous faun of Nijinsky is not an animal, but a costume which startled Paris, and which can be sent parcel post from here to Artesian, North Dakota, for 3 cents postage. (6 Nov. 1916, *Boston Post*)

The *Boston Post* wasn't the only paper to get excited about the snake. On the same day, the Boston Herald reported of bystanders with their eyes bulged when they saw Revalles "with her pet snake coiled about the fingers of her right hand." And although the reader could discover that Mark Anthony [the snake] lives in his cage lined with sawdust and is kept "night and day, on the dressing table in her room in the Copley-Plaza," [pity the poor hotel maid assigned to that room!] All in all, the Herald was more interested in Nijinsky. Several corrections have been added to the text.

> NIJINSKY THINKS GENIUS NO BAR TO WAR SERVICE
>
> Distinguished Star of Ballet Russe, Who Arrived in Boston, Yesterday, Discusses the War with Herald Man at Copley-Plaza-Accompanied by His Wife.
>
> GREATEST MALE DANCER HAS RETIRING NATURE
>
> A quiet little man, retiring in manner almost to the point of shyness, descended from a special train at the Huntington avenue station yesterday afternoon and walked along the platform toward a waiting taxicab...
>
> Income, if not the test of greatness, has been said to be the criterion of earthly success. If you wish to judge Nijinsky's place in the sun by this standard, consider the figures which are said to measure his salary - $1000 a night, $5000 a week. When a sprained ankle rendered him temporarily unable to dance the loss to the management

The American Tour of the Ballet Rouse

of the Diaghileff [Diaghilev] Ballet Russe, of which he is the star feature, was estimated at $50,000 a week.

At the hotel Mr. Nijinski, [French spelling] who is at present the subject of international diplomatic complications because the Czar of all the Russia's desires his services in the trenches, discussed the war.

With Mrs. Nijinski, he was in Bohemia, [actually Hungary, not Bohemia,] when the conflict broke out. As Russian subjects, [Romola was Hungarian by birth and Waslaw had a Russian passport although he had not been back to Russia since 1911, and would become stateless at the end of the War,] they were interned for 18 months in Prague, [not Prague, but Budapest] where they were not permitted to leave their house [a touch of drama on the part of the journalist - they were not allowed to leave the country, but could move about otherwise]. Finally, through the intercession of United States Ambassador Penfield; they were permitted to go to America, Mr. Nijinski giving his word of parole that he would remain in this country and would not fight against Austria. Now he has received notice that his class of recruits has been called to the colors, and the diplomats are wrangling over the question whether he shall be permitted to keep his promise to the Austrian government, or shall give up his work here and return to Russia. "Some writers insist that a man of genius should not be forced to serve in the trenches," said the Herald man yesterday, "because he is worth more to his country in the line of his art than he is on the battlefield."

All Should Fight.

"I believe," replied the dancer, "that such a man is under the same obligation as any other to fight when called upon." He declined to discuss the present state of the negotiations over his possible return to Russia and the prospect of having to fight. "That is a personal matter between the Russian ambassador at Washington and me, "he explained.

He said that he found Americans quite as appreciative of talent on the stage as are Europeans. An adequate introduction to the public is necessary, he said, on both sides of the Atlantic, given that; the response of the public is enthusiastic.

Mr. and Mrs. Nijinsky spent the summer at Bar Harbor and both were delighted with the New England coast. The dancer speaks very little English and his wife acts as interpreter.

Nijinsky in America

The big night arrived, many notable people attended to see and to be seen. The social column had a detailed list of who came with whom and what they wore, including an exhaustive description of silks and brocades adorning the ladies

> Mr. Nijinsky made his first appearance here as Till in his own comic-dramatic ballet "Till Eulenspiegel, "a choreographic illustration of the orchestral rondo by Richard Strauss. The roguish Till plays pranks with market women, mocks the priests, plays the part of Don Juan, has great sport with the learned. At last his insolence is unbearable. He is tried, convicted, and hanged. Then the people mourn his fate. "After all he was a merry rascal, and we shall miss him." Now, according to some, Till really lived and was not hanged. But this is immaterial. The Till of the legend mounted on the gallows, and the court scene and the execution provided rich material for Strauss and Mr. Nijinsky.
>
> This ballet was very interesting in many ways. The scenery and costumes designed by Mr. Robert E. Jones, a New Englander, showed a wildly artistic fancy.
>
> The market place with the nightmare houses and the mediaeval costumes, especially those of the chatelaines, might have been invented by Gustave Dore for one of Balzac's "Contes Drolatiques." Mr. Nijinsky acted Till with infinite humor, and when occasion offered, which was seldom, proved himself to be the lightest and nimblest of dancers. The Ballet, however, showed chiefly his pantomimic skill. Mr. Anselm Goetzl conducted for Mr. Monteux, here as in New York, as he was unwilling to conduct a work by a German who has expressed himself since the war as a foe to France.

Boston audiences were quite taken with Nijinsky, but missed the bravura of his amazing ability to leap – a facility which made Waslaw famed, but which he passionately abhorred. Often he remarked that he was an artist, not an acrobat. But people came to see spectacle and could only be consoled when there was a glimmer of hope that Nijinsky's famous "leap" might be seen on Thursday night. By then, the foot injury Waslaw suffered in New York was expected to heal. Even the critic of the Boston Evening Transcript, amidst a full page article and pictures, bemoaned the fact that although very good, Gavrilov [who replaced Nijinsky in Le Spectre de la Rose)] could not "quite cleave the air as does Mr. Nijinsky."

The American Tour of the Ballet Rouse

By the token of the performance last evening, "Petrouchka" has been thoroughly restudied under Mr. Nijinsky's masterful and quickening hand while Mr. Monteux's notion of Stravinsky's music differs materially from that which Ansermet exemplified last winter. If memory does not slip, the newer conductor has rehearsed the piece aforetime with the composer and so more exactly fulfills his purposes. As it was and hampered here and there by an orchestra a little short of Stravinsky's requirements in the number and variety of the instrumental choirs. Mr. Monteux gave the music a somewhat coarser texture . . a fuller clangor, a more intense rhythmic life. He slapped Stravinsky's tingling dissonances and scarifying chords upon the listening ear. He multiplied the din of the fair...As with the music, so with the action of the fair, far excelling in graphic simulation, running animation and ready variety that of last year. The folk-dances better rhymed, more technically expert and much more spontaneous and exuberant. The action of all concerned teems with lively little details...

All this is to give the first and last scenes of "Petrouchka" a savor, and a force of Illusion; a tang of place, time, folk and festival: a pleasure of the theatre that the expertly composed and more tamely executed ensemble of last year missed. Plainly Mr. Nijinsky stimulates as well as exacts. Indeed it is praise enough of Miss Lopokova's hard and perverse little minx of a ballerina that he is content with Mr. Massine emphasizes the fantastic, ironic, piteous substance of "Petrouchka." Mr. Nijinsky does not neglect it, but stresses in his turn the pictorial and amusing envelope. (8 November 1916, *Boston Evening Transcript*)

THE HIGH SINCERITIES OF HIS FAITH AND PRACTICE

An Epitomized Conversation in Which He Tells of His Beliefs, Experiments and Ambitions with the Arts of the Dancer and the Mime - The Field That He Would Ever Widen - Example from Precept in His Own Till and His Share in "The Enchanted Princess" - Another Day of the Russian Ballet

Seen on the stage in the illusion of personating, costume, action, Mr. Nijinsky seems a tall, even a substantial, figure. Seen in his own person, in the quiet of his rooms or across a dinner table, he is actually no more than medium height and of slender contours. A Slav unmistakably in the smallness of his head, the fineness of his features, the brightness of his narrow eyes, the mobility of sensitive mouth and chin. A dancer or at least a personage of the theatre in a flowing ease of carriage that has become as second nature. A man of the cultivated world not only in the intonations of his speech, which is French when it is not Russian, but also in the plasticity of his mind and manner - all three mirrors as it were, of a quick sensibility to many varied interests. (Mr. Nijinsky may dwell and work apart, except when he is before his audiences, but he follows none the less the ways and the concerns of the immediate mankind about him: even to the conditions that make slow the accounting of the vote of California and Minnesota.) A man, finally who is no mere dancer and mime by natural aptitudes, arduous training, assiduous application and the general applause, but who kindles his artistries, faiths and ambitions out of a keen and meditative mind and a finely touched and unquenchable spirit.

For Mr. Nijinsky is no contended technician of the dance, superlatively as may exemplify the older virtuosity in such a piece for the display of it as "The Enchanted Princess" or, in a measure the quasi-idyllic "Phantom of the Rose." He was schooled in it for nine years, as is every Russian dancer; he practiced it for years afterward in the imperial theatres of Petrograd and Moscow before a public more expert and insistent with these technical felicities and feats than any other in the world. He still makes use of them daily in mimed impersonation and graphic suggestion, remote indeed from the ends for which the elder French and Italian ballet masters designed them. They conceived the art of the dance as self-contained, self-sufficient, absolute, reward enough in its own agilities, graces, subtleties for those that practiced and those that watched and applauded it. Obviously it asked little of the mind; it gave as little room for the play of the spirit. Yet for the dancer and the mime of these later and newer days who would ply his intellect and set free his fancy and feeling in all that he undertakes, this old virtuosity provides often the apt and ready means - a shading here, a happy stroke there, a luminous point upon an implication that might otherwise be dark, a persuasive suavity that ingratiates and kindly disposes the spectator. The alertness, the patience, the dexterity, the endless quest for exactitude of the elder virtuosity have their uses in the new freedoms. In itself it may be no more than a relatively paltry goal: yet without it the dancer and the mime of these days lacks his tested tools.

So Mr. Nijinsky in amiable wisdom, retrospective and present, clear-minded and exactly phrased always, about the art of the dance. As

The American Tour of the Ballet Rouse

lucidly and with a like gentle confidence and conviction, he is ready to link the present with the future. He recalls the repertory of the Russian Ballet: on the one side the pieces that exemplify the dance, pure but hardly simple - "The Sylphs," "The Enchanted Princess," "The Phantom of the Rose," "Butterflies," "Carnival" - ballets of atmospheric and poetic suggestion as well as of the skill that they exact; on the other side, the melodrama -- "Cleopatra," "Scheherazade," "Thamar," seeking illusion by acting that should be only more graphic because it is wordless and using the dance in itself as a means and aid to dramatic impersonation and narrative...

Even "Petrouchka" widened the field only by the setting of a fantastic and ironic tale without the busy and realistic action of the booth and the fair...

Yet in "Petrouchka" - as Mr. Nijinsky proceeded with brightening eye and nervously graphic fingers, intent now upon that which kindles his mind, warms his heart, and is to him faith, work, ambition- yet in "Petrouchka" was the germ of the idea that first persuaded and finally conquered him. .... He touched his audience by what it felt about him rather than by what it merely saw him do. Why not, then, go forward to a ballet that should depend much more upon this static suggestion, a ballet that should not be full of dynamic emphasis, a ballet almost - to put an extreme case - without movement...

In "The Afternoon of a Faun," Mr. Nijinsky first worked out his idea of a ballet that should be intrinsically static, impersonal, so to say, of spiritualized atmosphere and illusion, of reticent means and of means newly devised or employed. Studious always of pictures and sculptures, the old Greek bas-reliefs suggested the simplicity, the directness, the sparing ness, even the rigidity of line in pose and gesture that he sought...

So Mr. Nijinsky designed and accomplished his version of "The Afternoon of a Faun." So he went forward to Debussy's "Jeux," to Stravinsky's "Sacre du Printemps," to the present "Till Eulenspiegel," and the future "Mephisto Waltz." In "Jeux" he sought to simplify and spiritualize light fancy until the audience should forget that it was looking upon youth that might be on their way to or from tennis, yesterday, today, tomorrow and feel only the play ever renewed young moods, caprice, pastime and affection. He pursued a distilled illusion; he used a distilled and concentrated means. So far as he could accomplish his end, the piece - half mimed, half danced and sometimes merely a still projection - characterized. In "Le Sacre du Printemps" - spring rites of a primitive and pagan Russia - he returned to static suggestion, to rigid, sparing but always clearly rhymed pose, gesture, movement, to this intensified projection by subtler and keener means than action, of the beliefs, the emotions, the ceremonies of primitive folk and faith. Already he had persuaded Stravinsky to his experiments and they worked upon "Le Sacré" in a common courage and loyalty. Then for a year or two pause for the nursing of new ideas, for the shaping of new designs, for the fresh opportunity. It came with "Till" and therein Mr. Nijinsky would have the choreographic theatre flower in the dénouement of character in this Eulenspiegel, in the graphic concentration of a place, a time, a folk, their moods and their manners, in hint withal at a social philosophy. The stage of the mime may thus match, may outdo, the austere stage of the spoken word. Who shall say that he has not succeeded? So Mr. Nijinsky ended, but not until he had lifted once more the expository, the graphic finger: "Mois, souvenez-vous bien! C'est pour le Beau, en maintes formes, aspects, visages, que je travaille."

Thus ran an hour or two of rambling and stimulating theorizing, a vision, as it were, into the designing and directing mind, and the prompting and the inventing spirit of the artist, whose work the world sees in result but not in process. (H.T.P.)

The article continues, but to reprint it here would be prolix. Suffice it to say that Nijinsky had won Boston's heart and affection

But we did wonder earlier if Boston audiences had an opportunity to be awe-struck by Nijinsky's well documented athletic/acrobatic feats? Readers of the Boston Evening Transcript could save for their grandchildren pictures of Nijinsky the "sensuous" in the "Phantom of the Rose" as they called Le Spectre de la Rose, and right next to it for dramatic effect, [Nijinsky] "In the Rigid Pose and Angular Gesture of the New Version of Debussy's Faun and Nymphs." Bostonians were not left disappointed; on 9 November Nijinsky gave irrefutable proof that everything written about his genius was true.

Two-Fold Nijinsky

So far the evening had been the vivid, various and vigorous Mr. Bolm's. Now, in contrast, it passed to the more subtle, artful and finely tempered Mr. Nijinsky. At last he danced before Bostonian eyes the phantom of the young girl's dream over the rose and the pleasure her first party has brought her. Out of the mists and roses of

The American Tour of the Ballet Rouse

the moonlit garden it came in one swift light bound, like soft gust of the night wind, in the leap that is as the bridge between magic fancy and seeming reality. With a bound like to it and even ampler in its span and airier in its lightness, the phantom vanished - the dance done - into the misty mystery whence it came. Between, the long circling about the stage that Mr. Nijinsky accomplishes in lines of a perfect symmetry with the contours of Weber's music, the exquisite pirouettes that seem less feats of agility and exactitude than the eddies of an inner elation; the entrechats that cleave the air for the flash of an instant as foot meets and parts from foot in gossamer contact; the lovely and adroit play of arm and hand and body in flawless and flowing harmony and rhythm, the aroma of fancy distilling from the whole - a dance of the vapors and the gleams of the misty night, a dance of as sublimated a sentiment in girlish fancies. [Lopokova was awarded a single sentence of praise:] The white sparks kindled Lopokova too. (H. T. Parker.)

Mr. Parker does go on, or should I say gushes, with a description of Nijinsky as the Faun. Before we take our leave of the "Athens of America," two very important observations are in order: critics considered the Russian Ballet under Nijinsky "inspiring" rather than "dulled, " as they found it under Diaghilev in January. Secondly, the Russians were to return the following spring in order to "seal its present conquest," President Wilson had other plans. America's entrance into World War I sealed Waslaw's fate, the tour stopped abruptly and he had to leave the country, never to return.

MASSACHUSETTS, Worcester – 13 November 1916 – Worcester Theatre

Worcester, Mass. is a hop, skip and a jump, a mere forty miles West of Boston. With a little effort, residents of this largely industrial and manufacturing center of New England could have attended performances in Boston. Thanks to "public-spirited guarantors of Worcester," however, the city had its own night with the Russians. Boston was a tough act to follow, the company had settled in, so to speak, for a week and now they were on the road again, with the prospect of a number of one nighters. The thirteenth was a Monday. The troupe had Sunday off; well, not really, they had to move to Worcester. Back to living on the train. It is fascinating to note how the original number of personnel changes with each reporter. According to the *Worcester Daily Telegram*, the Ballet Russe came with two trains, comprised of six Pullman and eight baggage cars. The *Worcester Evening Gazette*, however, reported of two trains with twelve cars. For "the bigger the better" minded Americans, the ads tried to lure by stating that it would be "The Greatest and Most Costly Performance Worcester Has Ever Seen." Possibly true, nevertheless, it was not that easy to win over Worcester's citizenry. Only 700 attended the performance, but then it was a smaller venue.

Nijinsky, once again, passed the "Spectre" role to Gavrilov, owning to the New York foot injury. And what's more, the critic doubted if Nijinsky could have "done more" with the role than his "artistic successor." The *Worcester Evening Post* critic complained that Monteux "was at time oblivious of the fact that he was not in a large auditorium." On the other end of the spectrum was the review in the *Worcester Evening Gazette* who did not mince words:

> But when all is said and done, that which will be remembered of the coming of Serge Di Diaghileff's [Diaghilev] Ballet Russe will not be the sprightly agility of Nijinsky, the fairy daintiness of Lopokova, but the magnificent orchestral accompany provided under the direction of Pierre Monteux and more than all else, the fantastic, barbaric splendor and weird fanaticism of Prince Igor. (14 November 1916)

The American Tour of the Ballet Rouse

The one, truly noteworthy comment came from the critic of the 14 November 1916 issue of *Worcester Daily Telegram*:

> Nijinsky has remarkable grace of movement for one of such splendid physical development. The calves of his legs and his thighs are full and muscular, but one associates his arms and the peculiar sensitive qualities of his face, more with the attributes of woman. It is quite marvelous, therefore, with what delicacy of poise he holds himself and with what grace and freedom of movement he bounds here and there upon the stage.

And with that, the Russians bid adieu to Massachusetts, but not to New England. They were not going far, only across state lines, back to Connecticut and the "Insurance Capital of the World."

CONNECTICUT, Hartford – 14 November 1916 – Parsons Theatre

Hartford received the Russians with unabashed enthusiasm. As a prelude to their arrival, The *Hartford Courant* gave a short synopsis of each ballet to be seen. This is noteworthy because "Mephisto Waltz" was among those listed. Set to Liszt's music, Nijinsky choreographed it in Vienna. He continued to work on it during the summer he spent with his family in Bar Harbor, Maine. Due to the foot injury and lack of rehearsal time, however, the ballet was never produced. Romola gives a detailed account of Waslaw's concept in her book Nijinsky. The Hartford Times not only told the "Mephisto" story, but stated that it will be "produced for the first time on any stage." [Here's a challenge for a diligent graduate student to find out whether it was ever performed on the tour or not!] The four ballets performed in Hartford were "Carnival," "L'Apres Midi d'un Faune," "Prince Igor," and "Le Spectre de la Rose."

A humorous article, with a different slant, appeared the day before the performance, in the Courant:

PARSON'S THEATER.

Ballet Russe Here Tomorrow...

Waslaw Nijinsky, premier dancer and artistic director of the Serge de Diaghileff [Diaghilev] Ballet Russe . . . walked about the streets of New York during the three weeks' rehearsal of the ballet and three more weeks of performance without being recognized by a soul. This is because Mr. Nijinsky does not look like Paul Swan or Vernon Castle. Instead, he resembles a half grown Cossack without a beard, and in New York he might pass for a shipping clerk or a plumber's apprentice. Taking Padarewski or Caruso as standards of comparison, Nijinsky looks like a rough person. He talks business mostly in Polish, gossips in Russian rests up with small struggles in French and thinks mostly in rubles. The little English he has picked up does not interfere with his dancing at all. A reporter walked down Broadway with Nijinsky and while several people recognized the newspaper man, the greatest dancer in the world passed unnoticed. No one turned around and gaped at him; no one cried "there he goes." He threaded his path through the Great White Way's parade of comedians, songwriters, piano players and chorus folk without getting a single glance of recognition.

Of course, the ladies were not ignored and American women found Lydia Lopokova a fashion trendsetter. She had a wardrobe that could be "the envy of a debutante."

... the rose colored evening wrap, made of taffeta, lined with the softest tea-rose charmeuse, whose very ruffles and ribbons breathe dainty femininity ... (11 November 1916, *Hartford Times*.)

In the adjacent column was an article about Fritz Kreisler, who was slated to appear with the Hartford Philharmonic the following week, in the very same theatre, and who had spent time with the Nijinskys at Bar Harbor. Hartfordians took note of the expensive tickets, but felt that it was worth it: "While the price of seats may seem high, one should consider that they are no higher than in New York." All in all, the Ballet was found to be gorgeous, opulent, brilliant, unique, unusual and a genuine treat. And with that, we move on to our last stop in Connecticut.

CONNECTICUT, Bridgeport – 15 November 1916 – Park Theatre

Bridgeport took the "Russian invasion" in stride. No gushing, no sentimental reporting for this city, just level headed matter of fact details. Not that this city's residents weren't delighted at the prospect of seeing "The greatest and most costly performances Bridgeport has ever seen." It's just that perhaps they were used to big productions, colorful advertising, publicity stunts, and exaggerations. As you recall, in my introduction, I suggested that the circus may be in town - well, Bridgeport's claim to fame was the founder of *The Greatest Show on Earth*. Yes, Phineas T. Barnum, although born in Bethel, Connecticut, twice served the Connecticut legislature and was Mayor of Bridgeport in 1875 and 1876. Seaside Park has a statue of its famous citizen, who helped shape and build Bridgeport. It is understandable then that one of the first, major articles about the Russians deals with the enormity of the company:

BALLET RUSSE CARRIES IMMENSE ORGANIZATION

One Hundred and Eighty Seven People - Two Complete Trains with Necessary Paraphernalia.

When the Diaghileff Ballet Russe troupe left New York for the tour Sunday morning it was the largest organization, outside of circus, ever taken on a coast to coast tour. There will be fifteen productions and one hundred and eighty-seven people taken en route. It will take two special trains: one, of six baggage cars and engine, the other, engine, eight coaches and one Pullman, to move the troupe.

The dancers will make up sixty-five of the aggregation. Then there will be a managerial and a technical staff. The managerial staff will consist of one manager and his assistant and four advance men with executive offices at the Metropolitan Musical bureau in New York...

The orchestra will consist of fifty members and one property man. The technical staff will consist of one American technical director, one chef machinist, one Russian property man, five stage carpenters, three electricians, one technical advance man, three property men, and two transportation men. There are six costume women with the troupe, two valets and four maids.

This resume does not include the families of some of those who will accompany the troupe.

The American Tour of the Ballet Rouse

Forty trucks, forty by six feet in dimensions will be required to move the productions. One hundred and twenty hangers the largest ever used in the country, some of them seventy-two by fifty-five feet in dimension will be carried.

It will be most interesting to see that Bridgeport is very much favored by being allotted four ballets in the wonderful performance to be given here by this colossal organization when it appears on Wednesday evening, November 15 at the Park theatre, following is the repertoire: Les Sylph ides, La Princess Enchantee, Papillion's and Prince Igor, four entirely different ballets showing the strength of the organization from every angle. (2 November 1916, *Bridgeport Evening Post.*)

The review was brief and concise, giving only a glimpse of the colossal production the night before. The most telling statement about the locals was that the Russians found the "Bridgeport audience so entranced that for once there was no shuffle to get home before the curtain dropped."

NEW JERSEY, Atlantic City – 16 November 1916 – New Nixon Theatre

The fifth smallest state in the union, New Jersey, is the most densely populated too. Atlantic City, where the Ballet Russe was slated to perform on 16 November, was a well-known seaside resort. The fame of its Boardwalk is known far and wide. It is a structural marvel when one considers its dimensions and the age in which it was built. Originally, the Boardwalk was completed in 1870 and rebuilt in 1896. Still standing today, it spans a four and a half mile stretch along the Atlantic coastline, with a sixty foot girth of wood, steel, and concrete. It then continues on for another two miles along Ventnor City, just south of Atlantic City.

The arrival of the Ballet Russe was just one of the many opportunities for diversion, offered in the *Atlantic City Daily Press*. Each day for a week preceding the performance, ads were extolling the wonders produced by the Russians. They were brief little articles, focusing mostly on the magic of Bakst's settings and designs. One had to look hard for the ballet amongst such important topics as: "Lionel Barrymore in Brand of Cowardice," "Ruth Roland At Court Theatre," "Dancers Clamor for New Steps" [had nothing to do with the Ballet Russe], "Girl Without a Chance" at the Apollo, and such mundane, but nevertheless important matters as the promotion of "Pape's Cold Compound," that will "end a cold or grippe in a few hours."

The following day, 9 November, "The Music of the Ballet Russe" was featured. Once again, it was a short little article that emphasized the fact that even without the ballet, the concert alone would be worth going to and predicted that the musical numbers featured would become favorites among concert goers. And again, the brief, three paragraph piece was surrounded by matters of much greater importance, for instance, "Big Ball Room Steam Heated." The article encouraged patrons to visit Young's Million Dollar Pier to go dancing or see a picture show. It guaranteed adequate heating for the most severe "atmoshperical" conditions. Friday night's feature was a tango contest, dancing classes and exhibitions were also slated.

The American Tour of the Ballet Rouse

The following day's paper, once again had an assortment of ads and brief clips of interest, not the least of which was a Chaplin revue at the Cort Theatre, "a five reel laugh," according to some, the best work Chaplin had ever done; and all this for the regular admission charge of a dime to fifteen cents. A bargain compared to the Ballet Russe's one to five dollar prices. Interestingly, Nijinsky later in the tour met Chaplin in Los Angeles as they shared a mutual admiration for each other's work. The ballet topic of the day was concerned with the jewelry found on the costumes:

> The barbaric splendor of the costumes designed by Leon Bakst...is achieved to a great extent through the use of jewelry. As such lavish use would not permit stones in heavy settings; and this it was that gave rise to the arts and crafts movement. One of his costumes...was hardly seen in Paris before it was almost entirely reproduced in American shops - designs, jewels and all. (10 November 1916, *Atlantic City Daily*)

Five days before the sole performance in Atlantic City, its residents were reassured that "Nijinsky Will Positively Appear." This was necessitated by the numerous inquiries at the box office to that regard. The tiny article is barely worth mentioning, dwarfed by the ads for the "Grand Promenade Dance," the "Tango Contest," and Bull Montana, champion fighter, demanding $2.00, $1.50, $1.00, 75 cents and 50 cents seats. The movies shown beforehand were still ten for the balcony and fifteen cents for first floor seats. Coffee houses have become all the rage in the late twentieth century, but actually, there is nothing new under the sun, and here is proof:

> The big night of the week is naturally Saturday night, and to provide for the entertainment of the throngs who attend this popular Boardwalk cafe, [Dunlop Cafe], Manager Bowman offers his big and successful revue, with Billy Cullen, Spiff Stevens and ten of the sprightliest show girls, direct from the Broadway cafes.

On 14 November, the Atlantic City Daily Press printed a picture of Adolph Bolm next to a minuscule, 9 line article about Nijinsky in "Les Sylphides," a truly forgettable piece of journalism. And again, fashion won the spotlight:

> There is one phase of the "good old times" that always returns. The girls of yesteryear and the flowers of yesteryear may fade, but the

styles always come back. Fashion authorities always concede that the fashions of 1916 will revert to those of 1840. Just why this is true will be understood when the Serge de Diaghileff's [Diaghilev] Ballet Russe with Nijinsky, is seen for the first time in this City at the New Nixon Theatre, Thursday evening Nov. 16.

The fashion world has been well shaken up the last six years by the effect of Leon Bakst's costumes for the Russian Ballet. His daring colors and bold designs and Oriental effects have revolutionized styles, Parisian, English, German, and American. But one quiet little ballet had to wait its turn. This was "Les Papillons," a romantic episode of the '40's. And now, having had their fill of the more sensational aspects of Bakst's genius, designers are declaring for the full skirt, tight waist and flat bodice which are characteristic of the costumes in the 1840 ball.

Didn't I tell you there is nothing new under the sun? On 15 November, one could read all about the "Ten attractive show girls, directly from Broadway and the cafes of the Gay White Way..." The girls were a hit. And at the Cort, not to be outdone, "Valkyrien, the Baroness de Vitz, premiere danseuse of the Royal Danish ballet, who, out of sixty thousand contestants, was voted the most beautiful maiden of Denmark, heads the bill of photo-plays at the Cort Theatre on Boardwalk today." [Note the term for film, "photo-play."] So what does the paper talk about when it comes to the greatest dancer in the world? You guessed it, fashion! The title is misleading: "Nijinsky in the Ballet Russe." Then it continues with an interview with Bakst that took place in Paris.

The big day had finally arrived, even if the ads and articles remained small; credit must be given to the journalist who had summed up the Russian Ballet in a succinct manner:

> What must at once appeal to art lovers - and there are many at Atlantic City - is the fact that the ballet is not merely a production, but is in itself an artistic movement. It brings the message of Russian culture to the new world, and finally dissipates the absurd notion that Russia is a benighted nation of darkness. The Russian Ballet breathes light and color such as has not been seen in America. The Ballet Russe, as we shall see it, represents a co-ordination of all the arts...For Mr. Louis Cline of the Atlantic City Daily Press, Nijinsky was good enough, but he was not reluctant to offer criticism:...

The American Tour of the Ballet Rouse

Another feature of last night's performance was the first appearance, as a member of the Ballet Russe, in this city, of Waslaw Nijinsky, who is second only to the incomparable Mordkin, the peer of all male Russian dancers. The graceful agility and muscular nimbleness of Nijinsky, with his balloon jumps and whirling spins, together with his amazing skill and ability as a pantomimist, was quite a revelation. Nijinsky is not a comely of feature as Mordkin, nor as magnificent in body, nor can he stride with the same grace, but he is satisfying and his technical equipment is supreme. It is upon the latter that he has attained his success. However, one has to dissociate Nijinsky's touch of effeminacy before his performance can be thoroughly enjoyed. (17 November 1916)

History was not as kind to Mr. Mordkin as was Mr. Cline.

Waslaw did not take kindly to being called "feminine" and in an interview given earlier in New York; he refuted statements of the above kind.

A TALK WITH NIJINSKY

Warslav [Waslaw] Nijinsky, the star of the Diaghileff [Diaghilev] Ballet Russe, is sensitive about being termed "feminine." The epithet was applied to him by severe critics, when he appeared as Narcissus, the mythological Greek...

The artist-inventor of ballets, in an interview, denied fervently that he is feminine in any of his portrayals, but insists that he interprets and follows the atmosphere of each character enacted by him. When he acts as a youth, he remembers that youth is simple and innocent - but never feminine. When he acts a Greek role, he must, and does, sink his own individuality...

Nijinsky continued: "I step forth on the stage. Before me is the orchestra, supplementing my interpretation; behind me stands the scenery, lending color, shade and background to my movements, while all about me is the rest of the troupe, with whom I must co-operate. I must consider all these elements, for I do not act alone - I am part of an ensemble. I must convey not only the spirit of the dance proper but of the scenery, the music, the age in which I am placed.

To forget any of these constituents would mean the disruption of all unity. My work is, therefore, not limited to movement, but comprises a devotion to various fields of related art. Of course, all this means hard and trying effort."

Nijinsky in America

"But surely," said the interviewer, "you must have had considerable training to perform those gymnastic feats that have caused so much admiration."

"Of course, all that was fundamental, but you must not suppose that this is all implied in the dance, as many people do. I have often heard remarks made that my greatness lay in the agility of my limbs. But nothing could be further from the truth. They would have me perform acrobatics and nothing more. I could easily satisfy them. I could leap higher, I could do more twists and turns, like the clown in a circus."

In a succinct, straightforward manner, Waslaw answered all his critics and encapsulated his vision as an artist. Often he protested that he was not a circus acrobat, but an artist. Waslaw was legendary for totally immersing himself in the character he was portraying. Little wonder then, that audiences the world over waiting to see cheap spectacle were astonished when they were gifted with more than they bargained for.

MARYLAND, Baltimore – 17 - 18 November 1916 – Lyric Theatre

Friday Night, Nov. 17th, at 8:30 – Serge de Diaghileff's Ballet Russe – *Orchestra equally as good if not better than ballet. Was splendid. Monteux a marvelous conductor. Ballet not worth $5.*
CARNAVAL – *Fairly good.* [Nijinsky danced the Harlequin.]
PRINCE IGOR – *Very good. Music finer.*
La Princesse Enchantee – *Short – nil.* [Nijinsky danced the Prince, Lopokova the Princess.]
CLEOPATRE – *Very good. Best after Scheherazade.*
Saturday Night, Nov. 18th, at 8:30 –
LES SYLPHIDES – *Music Excellent.*
LE SPECTRE DE LA ROSE – *Wonderful dancing by Nijinsky.* [The young girl was danced by Spesiwtzewa.]
LES PAPILLONS – *Music beautiful –*
SCHEHERAZADE – *Best in repertoire.*

And so wrote a patron on his or her program, which the author did not feel was worth the five dollars, but nevertheless, went both nights.

We did not travel very far; Baltimore is practically around the bend from Atlantic City. The Lyric Opera House is still in existence, ninety years later; and one of the oldest public library systems in the United States, the Enoch Pratt Free Library, holds the afore mentioned Ballet Russe playbill. Constructed in 1814, the first building in the United States built specifically as a museum is here. Baltimore abounds in culture and history. Here, Francis Scott Key was inspired to write the national anthem. The John Hopkins University and Medical Center is world renowned as well as the Peabody Conservatory of Music. The first Roman Catholic archdiocese in the United States was established here in 1789, and consequently, one of the country's first major cathedrals was built – the Basilica of the Assumption of the Blessed Virgin Mary. Town notables include Babe Ruth, who was born here, and Edgar Allan Poe, who was buried in the city.

Nijinsky in America

Now that we heard from a private individual, let us see what the papers had to say.

BALLET RUSSE UNIQUE

Novel Color Effects in Bakst Scenery and Costumes.

SPIRITED DRAMATIC DANCING

Nijinsky Not At His Best in First Appearance – Flore Revalles Striking In "Cleopatra."

Serge de Diaghileff's Ballet Russe featuring Nijinsky appeared for the first time in Baltimore last evening at the Lyric. There was a large audience, the entertainment proving one of great interest not merely because of the spirited and unusual dancing but also because of the fine opera orchestra, under the direction of Pierre Monteux, which played the music with great brilliance....

The ballets last evening of course merely served to suggest the greater choreographic dramas produced in Paris, for only the smaller works are being carried on this tour, the most important interpretative ballets being too heavy for transportation...

Nijinsky, who did very little last evening, suggested his particular prowess in his very witty portrayal of Harlequin in the Schumann "Carnival" – the set was Bakst at his very worst and was entirely out of key with the costumes, which were of Boheme period – a bit of pantomime that made one eager to see him in one of the great Stravinsky roles which won him fame and distinction. He is, of course a magnificent technician.

There are moments when his entire body seems to flutter, his control of the muscles being quite astonishing... (18 November 1916, *Baltimore Sun*, Sunday Morning)

WASHINGTON D. C. – 20 - 22 November 1916 – Belasco Theatre

The nation's capital needs no introduction, not in the United States or abroad. It is and was, even in 1916, a cosmopolitan city teaming with international residents. The Ballet Russe had performed there earlier that year, but without Nijinsky. There was a sophisticated, if somewhat guarded enthusiasm for this second appearance by the Russians:

> A symphony designed to charm the eye and the ear, a production in which the grace of the dance, the coloring of master artists and designers, and the music of Chopin, Schumann, Tchaikovsky and Borodin are blended to delight the audience, is the entertainment offered by Serge de Diaghileff's [Diaghilev] Ballet Russe, which made its second appearance in the National Capital at the Belasco Theatre last night. The production here is by arrangement with the Metropolitan Opera Company and will be continued tonight and tomorrow night. To those who had seen the ballet last year, the chief interest in the production last night was the appearance of Waslaw Nijinsky, who has been regarded in the capitals of Europe as the leading exponent of the dancer's art and who was unable to take part in the ballet here during the first engagement. Nijinsky is a marvel of grace and of power, trained to the last notch in the school, which is responsible for the Russian ballet. He appeared in two of the four parts of the program. First, in "La Princesse Enchantee" with Mme. Olga Spesiwtzewa, a pas deux, [should be pas de deux] in which the art of the ballet is brought to a high pitch by Michel Fokine and enhanced by the scenery and costume designed by Leon Bakst, whose mastery of color and line won him a Nobel prize. Mme. Spesiwtzewa's grace and beauty vied for honors with the premier dancer.
>
> Nijinsky's second appearance was in "Carnival" as Harlequin. His rendering of the pantomime, comic, and at the same time full of grace, was a sample of the dancer's art, which proved a real delight to the audience. (21 November 1916, *Evening Star*)

The article continued by discussing the other artists, all of who had been seen before. What then made this particular stop on the tour interesting for us in 1996? Once again, we are fortunate to have a cherished copy of a Washington D.C. program in the Martin Luther King Memorial Library archives. That, more than the

Nijinsky in America

review, gives a picture of the lives and times of Washingtonians in 1916. The Belasco Theatre, where they performed, was located on an incredible piece of real estate:

> The Belasco Theatre was situated opposite the White House and Lafayette Square, the most beautifully situated and appointed theatre in America, presenting on its stage at all times only the foremost foreign and native artists and attractions. A Washington landmark, which none should fail to see...

Naturally, ticket prices reflected this prestigious site, not to mention clientele. Subscription for the entire season for a box ranged anywhere from $75 to $200; orchestra seats were $35; balcony - $12, $9, and $6; and gallery - $3. For a single performance, the box was anywhere from $75 to $25; orchestra - $6 & $5; balcony - $4, $3, and $2; and gallery - $1. We must once again recall the cost of living in those days; for instance, a "Deer Head" cigar was 10 cents. A fashionable boot for women "made from calfskin and buckskin" cost $8.50, but other smart styles could be purchased from $3 to $22 a pair. Man's coats and suits were $25, hats with "style, quality and value" $2 & $3; and a Wardrobe trunk with drawers and hangers could be yours for $18.50 and up. But perhaps the biggest eye opener, when it came to prices, was an advertisement, soliciting donations for the Red Cross. Consider that World War I was already raging in Europe since 1914 and it would be only a matter of time before America got involved.

> WHAT OUR RED CROSS CAN DO WITH YOUR MONEY.
>
> 1 cent will buy iodine to disinfect a wound; 1 cent will pay for enough gauze for one dressing; 5 cents will buy a bandage; 8 cents will pay for a temporary splint; 10 cents will provide chloroform for an operation; 25 cents expended as above may save a limb or a life; $2.40 will pay for 100 yards of gauze; $19 will pay for 100 pounds of absorbent cotton; $21 will pay for 1,000 sterilized bandages; $35 will deliver a case of surgical dressings or a case of hospital clothing, $40 will purchase 100 lbs. of chloroform; $2 will send a baby kit; $8 will send a child's kit.

PENNSYLVANIA, Philadelphia – 23 - 25 November 1916 – Metropolitan Opera House

The City of Brotherly Love – Philadelphia. This Quaker City has so many notable titles and such rich heritage; the topic could fill a separate chapter, better yet, a book. It is a center of U.S. culture and education. More importantly, Philadelphia is the birthplace of the United States of America. It was the capital during the Revolutionary War, and both the Declaration of Independence and the Constitution were adopted here.

Aside from well-known historic sites such as the Liberty Bell and Independence Hall, one can find in Philly the oldest art school in the United States, the Academy of the Fine Arts founded in 1805; the nation's oldest art school for women founded in 1844, the Moore College of Art; the Walnut Street Theatre, the oldest active theatre in the country; the oldest U.S. art museum run by the Academy of the Fine Arts; and the first library to circulate books, established by Benjamin Franklin. Franklin was also responsible for some publishing firsts, namely, the *Pennsylvania Gazette* and *Poor Richard's Almanac*. The first magazine and the nation's first daily newspaper were published here in 1741 and 1783 respectively.

Of great interest to us is the oldest opera house in the United States, opened in 1857 and still in use. Philadelphia's Academy of Music is the home of the famed Philadelphia Orchestra, the Pennsylvania Ballet and the Philadelphia Opera Company. Furthermore, it is where the Ballet Russe performed in 1916. The Free Library of Philadelphia, compliments of Benjamin Franklin, houses a number of programs and playbills from the 1915 and 1916 seasons of the Ballet Russe. They first performed there on March 27 through April 1, 1916, and although Nijinsky was not among them, his name appeared on the program as the choreographer of *L'Apres-midi d'un Faune*. The title role was performed by Leonide Massine. Although the review describes rather than evaluates the ballets, it is interesting to see the perspective from which the "Faune" was viewed in 1916 Philadelphia:

Nijinsky in America

> "The Afternoon of Faun" is given to the poetic and melodious Debussy music familiar to patrons of the Philadelphia Orchestra, which several times have offered it as a concert number. The ballet depicts a faun resting on a huge rock, against a typical Bakst background. Several nymphs enter with undulating grace and entice him to join them. He does so, and one of the maidens lures him, only to leave him, after enslaving his passions, with but her floating scarf as a memory of her charms, and he, fondly caressing it, returns to his original reclining posture on the rock. Leonide Massine gave a remarkable characterization of the faun, and the nymphs were quaintly attractive in their attitudinizing, particularly in the use of hands and arms, posing like some of the figures seen on Egyptian vases and urns. (1 April 1916, *Evening Bulletin*.)

Although the Russians had returned to Philadelphia in a little more than seven months and some of the pieces were repeats, the enthusiasm for their art had not waned. Large audiences were attracted for all performances. Nijinsky made his debut and farewell performance in the Till. The audience's only base of comparison was *Le Spectre De La Rose* which in March was danced by Gavriloff.

> The Ballet Russe gave the last performance in its present engagement at the Metropolitan Opera House yesterday afternoon when it appeared in the most attractive program of the season. First on the list came "Till Eulenspiegel," in which the famous Nijinsky made his local debut last Thursday evening. As his remarkable impersonation has already been the subject of extended comment in these columns, it is enough to record a repetition of his previous success. Nijinsky's clear and intelligent conception of the prankish Till is visualized and vitalized with an astonishing elaboration of graphic gesture and illuminative pantomime and the act in its entirety reproduces with a singular effectiveness the substance and spirit of the story which embodies and of the medieval era to which it relates.

> The other number in which Nijinsky participated was the "Spectre de la Rose" based on a poem by Gauthier and set to the music of Weber's well known waltz, in which Lydia Lopokova was his associate, and here the grace and agility of the dancer were charmingly displayed. (26 November 1916, *Inquirer*)

Philadelphians were clearly sophisticated when it came to the arts. They had anticipated future appearances of the Russians, which of

The American Tour of the Ballet Rouse

course we know by now, would never materialize. The Ballet did return however, to Pennsylvania at the end of the tour.

VIRGINIA, Richmond – 27 November 1916 – Academy of Music

The *Mother of Presidents and States*, Virginia was not above a little commercial venture. One wonders if magnifying glasses were provided to the patrons to help discover who was dancing. Obviously, noting the two blank advertisement slots, the promotion office did not do its very best. Mr. Leo Wise, manager of the Academy of Music in 1916, must not have been pleased. The building burned to the ground in 1925.

If time permitted, Waslaw would have been able to see Richmond's oldest house, built around 1754; it now houses the Edgar Allan Poe Museum. The great American author lived in Richmond as a child, and later was editor of the *Southern Literary Messenger*. Poe and Waslaw had much in common as we shall soon find out.

The week of 27 November, Thanksgiving week, held much promise for entertainment at the Academy: Monday night the Russians, then Blanche Ring in "Broadway and Buttermilk," and finally, Franz Lehar's operetta "Gypsy Love." Tickets for the Ballet Russe ranged from one to six dollars, and box seats from eight to ten.

NIJINSKY

We shall say nothing about the orchestra, for it was most excellent.

We shall say nothing about the danseuses in the solo parts: all of them were amazingly well drilled and reasonably comely (except for their muscular backs).

We shall say nothing of the scenery, for while it was bizarre it was at least interesting in novelty and was in keeping with the spirit of the various dances. We shall admit that all these things were most admirable and presented with a fine regard for those unities which RICHARD WAGNER, and not the Russians, laid down generations ago.

We are chiefly interested in this M. NIJINSKY. He is, perhaps, the most "tooted" artist in America today, and has actually usurped a part of the place held by MR. CARUSO. He has been described as "the embodiment of grace," as the "consummation of art," and as "living rhythm." His "prodigious bounds" are decreed marvelous and at his

The American Tour of the Ballet Rouse

"faultless artistry" the edict is that one must be "enraptured." Very naturally, we were anxious to see this paragon and to compare his dancing with that of lesser lights, expecting in the contrast to see something truly astonishing.

What we saw, in common with some 1,200 Richmond theatre-goers, was a man of about 35, perhaps five feet ten inches tall, tolerably well-formed and primarily conspicuous for a yellow shepherd's wig and a pair of legs that "STRANGLER" LEWIS or any other heavy weight wrestler would have envied. To be perfectly frank, from his waist down he reminded me more of ZEYAZKO than any other notable.

Waslaw was not quite 35, but rather 26 at the time. He wore "white tights over his muscular legs and a black jacket with white sleeves."

What he did was just this: he posed for a while upstage, with a group of hard-working ballet women around them, he came down stage with LYDIA LOPOKOVA, lifted her a few times into the air, went off, came back, leaped about, manhandled MLLE. LOPOKOVA again, took a rest, posed the ballet about him, felt six times at the right-hand side of his wig, went off, came back still again, bowed several times and called it a day.

Now, MR. NIJINSKY may not have been feeling at his best. He may have been the victim of his own selections for the evening. He may have thought it was not worthwhile exerting himself in the provinces. But whatever the reason, he did nothing last night to make his performance stand out above that of any of the other men of the ballet. M. GAVRILOW and M. BOLM both outshone him; a dozen women in the company, in our opinion, did work that was more artistic in every sense of the word. In fact, if the truth be told, four-fifths of the audience had to take the latitude and longitude of the program really to be convinced that the man dancing with MLLE. LOPOKOVA (and only two distant from the tall young woman with a bad "run" in her stocking) was really MR. NIJINSKY. And that raises a very interesting question: do we see art with our own eyes or with those of others? Do we look at actors or at names? Do we applaud performances or reputations? (28 November 1916, *The News Leader*, Richmond VA.)

Nijinsky in America

So much for Nijinsky astonishing everyone. Even the "god of dance" is permitted an off day now and then! Nevertheless, it is refreshing to read that not everyone was "awed" by the great Nijinsky, which, more than empty flattery, affirms his humanity as well as his renown. There were however, other opinions voiced too, in Richmond.

RUSSIAN BALLET PRESENTED ON MAGNIFICENT SCALE

So often and so brilliantly has that many-sided art-form, known as the Russian ballet, been exploited in Richmond within the last four or five years that little need be said now of the qualities that make it stand apart from, and above all other dancing known to us. The Russian ballet has come to mean not only dancing to musical accompaniment, but music itself, and acting - not to speak of settings that enhance the value of all three. At its best, these are indivisible parts of the whole, and where any one is lacking, the whole is to that extent incomplete.

Considered, it is understood, the foremost man dancer in the world, Waslaw Nijinsky was featured as the head of the principal dancers. He appeared in only one ballet, and as this was devoted to what may be called pure dancing, it was impossible to judge of his pantomimic ability. In "Les Sylphides," he danced several times, and with the same exquisite grace that distinguishes all the masters of that school...let it suffice to say that Volinine is the finer figure of the two, and if Nijinsky has the higher technique, it wasn't discernable last night. Indeed, Mr. Gavrilow...also quite outshone Mr. Nijinsky, certainly in popular favor. And also did Adolf Bolm, the artist who virtually headed the organization during Nijinsky's absence...

On the whole, the performance given by De Diaghileff Ballet Russe was just about twice as "big" as anything of the kind seen here before. (Douglas Gordon, 28 November 1916, *Richmond Times-Dispatch*)

SOUTH CAROLINA, Columbia – 28 November 1916 – Columbia Theater

Nijinsky Plans All American Ballet

Waslaw Nijinsky, whom critics the world over have declared to be the modern super genius of the dance, likes America. Nijinsky, who will be seen here at the Columbia theater on Tuesday night...has an absolute faith in the possibilities of American art as far as its offering material for the ballet is concerned. Mr. Nijinsky demonstrated this fact when he selected the American artist, Robert Edmond Jones, to design the scenery and costumes for his two new ballets this year.

His latest excursion into the realm of American art for stuff on which to build his ballet dreams has resulted in his deciding that Edgar Allen Poe's famous short story, "The Masque of the Red Death," will make a wonderfully dramatic ballet. Poe's story will be remembered, deals with a mediaeval masked revel...

The opportunity which the fantastic horror of Poe gives to a man of Nijinsky's quick understanding of pantomimic possibilities and ensemble effects can be realized immediately.

Nijinsky will undoubtedly again call upon the services of Mr. Robert Jones whom he considers the equal of Baskt [Bakst] as a scenic genius. It is a happy coincidence, in view of the nature of the story, that Mr. Jones has gained his reputation to a very great extent through his understanding of the color red as applied to stage decoration.

The above column appeared as the last segment of a full page article about the Ballet Russe in the 26 November issue of *The Columbia Record*, Columbia, S. C., along with pictures of Nijinsky as the "Spectre," Flore Revalles in "Scheherazade," and Ekaterina Galanta, "The prettiest Girl in the Corps de Ballet." Following this splendid article was a bit of unrelated trivia, separated by a single line: "A key for police patrol boxes has been made of non-conducting material to guard users from possible electric shocks." Possibly there was just enough room on the page so the typesetter felt inclined to put it there! Nevertheless, the above quoted piece of journalism had other interesting bits about the Russians as well as some astute insights:

Nijinsky in America

The Coming to Columbia of the World's Greatest Interpretive Dancers an Event of Supreme Artistic Importance.

In the Serge de Diaghileff Ballet Russe which will visit Columbia on Tuesday, the 28th, many people in this region will have perhaps their only opportunity to witness a performance which will pass into the history of the art of dancing and the ballet and hold there a position excelling in brilliancy anything that has preceded it. How many of us, reading the authors of early Victorian days, have regretted that we could not have seen the incomparable art of Marie Taglioni, Fanny Ellsler, Carlotta Grisl and a few others of their compeers who made dancing and the ballet so popular in the "forties."

It will be the same when the days come in which the history of the wonderful Ballet Russe is seen in retrospect, with this distinction, however, that whereas the individual stars of the old days glittered against a background of very mediocre dancers, who served only to provide an ensemble, the Ballet Russe is an aggregation of premier dancers. It is true that Waslaw Nijinsky, Adolf Bolm, Flore Revalles and Lydia Lopokova are the bright particular stars, but every member of the organization is like-wise an artist of interpretive ability and finished technique.

The writer of this particular preview was nothing short of a prophet. He/she continued by discussing the fact that dancing is a serious art and the importance of ballet in Russia. Two days later this same paper featured a short piece entitled:

RUSSIAN BALLET HEAVY MOVEMENT

A "movement," as the railway officials term it, of no small consequence was the transportation of the Russian ballet troupe...The troupe had two special trains. These were brought from Richmond and arrived in Columbia early in the afternoon.

The Southern railway handled the company. J. W. Wassum, superintendent of the Columbia division, went to Richmond to assist in the transportation. The trip was made in good time and in good order.

After playing here the company moves to Atlanta, via Southern railway, and from there another road will carry the troupe to New Orleans.

"Not quite as heavy as a circus movement, but quite a good job at that," said a railway official Tuesday.

The American Tour of the Ballet Rouse

Consider that the troupe performed on the 27th in Richmond, on the 28th in Columbia and moved on to Atlanta for one night on the 29th. Quite a feat when one thinks of the logistics of setting up and striking the sets, costumes, instruments and moving 150 plus people, including temperamental artists, some of whom speak only Russian! But everything was done in the great, efficient, American way, and the Russians were received with enthusiastic anticipation. It is also note worthy to mention that once again someone wrote about that elusive "second" new work [*Mephisto Waltz*] choreographed by Waslaw in America and designed by Jones. And now to the matter of Poe's poem. Edgar Allen Poe (1809-1849), great American poet and writer, considered by many a genius, a man of mystery; his parents - touring performers, much like Waslaw's; what attracted Waslaw to his work? Waslaw, who was considered by many the genius of dance, but otherwise an insignificant, certainly not an eloquent, articulate man

> I am come of a race noted for vigor of fancy and ardor of passion. Men have called me mad; but the question is not yet settled, whether madness is or is not the loftiest intelligence - whether much that is glorious - whether all that is profound - does not spring from disease of thought - from moods of mind exalted at the expense of the general intellect. They who dream by day are cognizant of many things which escape those who dream only by night. In their grey visions they obtain glimpses of eternity, and thrill, in awaking, to find that they have been upon the verge of the great secret. In snatches, they learn something of the wisdom which is of good, and more of the mere knowledge which is of evil. They penetrate, however, rudderless, or compassless, into the vast ocean of the "light ineffable" and again, like the adventurers of the Nubian geographer, "*agressi sunt mare tenebrarum, quid in eo esset exploraturi.*" We will say, then, that I am mad...(Edgar Allen Poe, Eleanora)

So wrote Edgar Allen Poe, but it could just as easily have been Waslaw Fomitch Nijinsky, "*Je suis un fou qui aime l'humanité, Ma folie c'est l'amour de l'humanité...*"

A Tipperary Hat From Pershia.

It's a long, long way to the top of the Tipperary hat which set the fashion for all other Tipperary hats. And it's a long, long time since

Nijinsky in America

it first was worn.

When "Scheherazade" is presented...tonight the spectators will see in the costume of an adolescent, designed by Leon Baskt [Bakst], Russia's master colorist, a model of the ancestor of all the Tipperary hats. Baskt [Bakst] always turns back to Persia, more or less, for his flaming colors and exotic designs. For "Scheherazade" he must have done so also of necessity, as the ballet is the tragic story of love in a Persian harem. The headgear of the adolescent which Bakst designed is a tall blue inverted waste-basket, in the front of which are two wings clasped with a huge pearl ornament. From the older art of Persia, this headgear was carried over to the newer civilization in the British Isles, and was abbreviated into the popular Tipperary hat, which finally traveled across the ocean to America. The hat, however, is not the only part of this costume which has finally percolated to America. The blue girdle, looped over in front with the long ends hanging down, is the direct grandfather of recent styles in sashes. The long, pointed blouse is the direct grandmother of that fashion in recent years. The breast ornament is the own mother to the la valierre; the trouserette, the harem skirt and various other styles are off springs of these pantalettes. Bathroom slippers undoubtedly sprang from this Oriental style of footwear. Altogether, this costume has a large progeny which has been at home on this side of the ocean.

Such was the enthusiasm and anticipation of Columbia's populace, how disappointing for them then that Nijinsky did not dance that night! Politically as important as the other Eastern Seaboard States in the Union, a land of famed gardens filled with magnolias and cypress along with five hundred different varieties of flowers and trees, the rugged beauty of the Blue Ridge Mountains, all of this, and much more, is South Carolina, the Palmetto State. Columbia is its capital and largest city. In 1916, Columbian's felt very privileged to be one of the few towns in the South to book the Russians.

COLUMBIA ART CAPITAL WITH BALLET REIGNING

Wonderful Russians Made This City Center of Stage.

Southern Conservatism Rewarded With Most Pleasing and Graceful Interpretations.

Columbia was a city last night to a brilliant, moving "society" sense of the term and the city's center was the Columbia Theater.

The American Tour of the Ballet Rouse

Automobiles filled the whole block from Lady street to the capitol plaza, smartly dressed people slighted from car after car and when the automobiles were emptied the theater was filled with a larger and more fashionable audience than perhaps it has ever before assembled...

Columbia was hostess to all the State for an occasion extraordinary - the appearance of the famous Ballet Russe...

And so people from every section and corner [of the South] came for it.

A Spice of Disappointment.

And well worth anyone's coming from anywhere was the performance. It brought its disappointments, of course. What much heralded, long awaited and high costing event or occasion in life does not? The disappointments of last evening were these: That the magical Nijinsky, premier danseur of the whole troupe, did not appear here and that all the big, super-artistic, impressionistic and ultra-dramatic numbers were eliminated from the program. The conservatism of the South was given as the reason for the selection of the most conservative offerings in the repertoire of the Russians.

(29 November 1916, *The State*, Columbia, S.C.)

And a good thing too! One can just imagine the reaction to Scheherazade, which was objectionable at best in Brooklyn, in the State that was first to secede from the Union and where the Civil War began, all on account of abolishing slavery. What Columbians did see, they liked. Credit must go to Waslaw, who, as artistic director, had the final decision of program offerings.

GEORGIA, Atlanta – 29 November 1916 – Auditorium

The *Empire State of the South, Peach State, Goober State*, are some of the monikers Georgia is known by; another conservative, Southern State, very much involved in the Revolutionary and Civil Wars – a state of lush vegetation, fertile valleys, tobacco fields, cotton, coastal plains, Appalachian plateaus, Blue Ridge Mountains and the Savannah River. The Ballet Russe arrived in Georgia a day before Thanksgiving. Atlanta's name is connected to railroad history. Terminus, a town founded at the southern end of the Western and Atlantic railroad became a trade and transportation center. In 1845, a railroad engineer renamed the town Atlanta. It was a bustling business center as early as the turn of the century. Coca-Cola had established its headquarters there and the city's population increased by leaps and bounds, close to 90,000, by the early 1900's. Atlanta was not the only one with growing pains. The US Census Bureau estimated that by January 1, 1917, "113,309,285 people would be under the American flag."

The Ballet Russe once again, presented a conservative program, including: *Les Sylphides, La Princesse Enchantes, Prince Igor and Cleopatra*. The single performance was under the auspices of the Atlanta Music Festival Association. To this day, residents of Atlanta may enjoy the Atlanta Arts Festival. According to the Louise Dooly, who reviewed the Russians for the 30 November 1916 issue of the Atlanta Constitution, the Russians "scored a triumph."

A triumph of modern art is the Russian Ballet as exemplified in "Cleopatra" last night...an art which stands not on the heights that men must raise their eyes to see its glories against the heavens, but an art which comes down from its pedestal for admiration, clothed with such glamour of obvious appeal that the tickled senses of the beholder happily fool themselves that Parnassus has been materialized for one-night stands in the smaller cities and longer engagements in those three hundred thousand inhabitants or more...
"La Princess Enchantee," a vivid idyll by Tchaikovsky, introduced the leading artist of the company, Nijinsky, with the lovely Lopokova. Like rare pieces of fine bric-a-brac, galvanized into the posture and action of a pair of fairies, their interpretation was a

The American Tour of the Ballet Rouse

supreme expression of technical delicacy and perfection, one of those art manifestations so facile as well nigh to conceal the art, which makes it.

And with that stop, the Russians began their US tour in earnest. Ahead of them were the curious and waiting to be mesmerized audiences of forty more cities. The route was determined partly by the railroad lines available; also, by wealthy promoters in each city, willing to put up the necessary funds. So, if your state does not appear, don't take it to heart, there was probably no way of getting there or not enough inhabitants to warrant a stop. We should also remember that aside from Alaska and Hawaii, which joined the Union much later; Arizona and New Mexico were brand new states at the time, having ratified statehood only in 1912. Much of the country was still the wild, unexplored West or North, where daily existence was as much of an achievement as one of Waslaw's famous leaps!

LOUISIANA, New Orleans – 30 November - 2 December 1916 – French Opera House

Thanksgiving! Football is in the air! Why not a jersey for Waslaw with a big # 1 on it? Why not use up-to-date football methods and put numbers on the dancers of the Russian ballet so that if the management should desire to have two or three substitute Nijinskys, or might care to run in Miss Jones or Miss Oppenheim in place of Miss Lokosokoplova, (Lopokova) the trick might be turned without violating all the ethics of the game? After all it is the quality of the dance that counts, and if No. 8 performed well perhaps none would care in the least whether No. 8 was the same who wore the numeral a week before. On the other hand, when a spectator is foolish enough to pay his money to see a name and a personality and the name only is given, he is apt to feel "stung." Furthermore a stung spectator is not the most desirable of sandwich-men to advertise the apian entertainment.

> Friday night witnessed the second performance by the Ballet Russe with an almost complete change of program. The only feature repeated was the remarkable "Prince Igor" dance, which both in setting and in Terpsichorean art still remains the most thrilling event of the engagement...
>
> Cleopatra herself was done with great charm by Flore Revales. (The dancer did not have her name engraved upon her so that if her true cognomen should chance to be Smith or Watkins The Times-Picayune disclaims any blame.)...There had been some preliminary complaint about the slope of the opera stage but in spite of the pitch the dance went on. The stage setting for "Les Sylphides" was again a Bakst design - unless here too there has been some misunderstanding and the thing should be credited to Humperdinck or Doolittle. It was in "Les Sylphides" that the person tagged as Nijinsky danced. He had grown taller and thinner since Thursday, was more agile and not quite so emotional. (2 December 1916, *The Times-Picayune*.)

Obviously, the above quoted journalist was not amused by the Russians. Did the management switch dancers and replace Nijinsky? Possibly. Or was the critic so enraptured by Nijinsky's dancing and his extraordinary ability to become one with the role that he thought it was another dancer? The night before, Nijinsky danced the "Spectre," a ballet with a completely different pathos.

The American Tour of the Ballet Rouse

Perhaps we will never know, because the journalist's name is as much a mystery as his innuendo. Clearly, two nights before a different critic, whose name we also don't have, had the floor, so to speak:

> BRILLIANT AUDIENCE ATTENDS PREMIERE OF THE BALLET RUSSE
>
> Socially Thursday night's debut of the Diaghileff Ballet Russe took the place of a premiere of the opera season, so off the stage as well as on the spectacle was extraordinarily brilliant. Long intermissions allowed for society's intermingling, and the curtain fell at 11:20 o'clock after a memorable evening when the arts of the dance, stage setting and costuming reached the highest point yet touched in New Orleans. Individually Pavlowa at her best passed beyond any individual female dancer of the present troupe, and Mordkin touched a different note as high in its way as any given by Nijinsky, but the ensemble of the arts, including the immense symphony orchestra and the latest development in the stage painting of Bakst, raise the present combination to supremacy.

You may recall the "touchy" subject matter of "Scheherazade" from earlier cities, well; it seems the Russians found a solution by the time they reached New Orleans:

> In one respect only the Ballet Russe, and more particularly the ballet" Scheherazade," reached New Orleans too late, for one had but to look across the audience to realize that though the ballet itself had just arrived, its influence already was with us. The costume and effects that Bakst created out of pure color and the wealth of his imagination were quick to permeate the fashion fabric of all civilization, so that here, there and everywhere one sees reflexes and scintillations of the great Russian's art in the costumes of our assembles. It was for this reason perhaps, that one could not feel the full force of novelty and originality that so startled the world when Bakst ideas were freshly dripping form his wonderful palette. Even those who went to "Scheherazade" expecting, dreading or hoping to be shocked by its audacity scarcely found any cause for flutter, gasp or blush. ...
>
> In the correct version of the dance the slaves of the harem are blacks, but, for reasons obvious enough in Southern regions, the negroes have been paled into brownness. The result is a distinct loss, as the

contrast falls and the real thrill of the situation is dulled. (1 December 1916, *The Times-Picayune*)

Well, so much for the "abhorrence" experienced back in Brooklyn. But, how does one explain the relative nonchalance exhibited towards the Russians? New Orleans was a cosmopolitan town from the first, by nature of its beginnings. Louisiana was purchased from the French in 1803, nearly doubling the size of the United States. Having been named after the French king Louis XIV, a great part of Louisiana's populace was either French or had French ancestry. The Ballet Russe, having come to fame in Paris, should have felt right at home in New Orleans, with street and structure names like Hotel Dieu, St. Louis, Bienville, Lafayette Square, Le Petit Théatre and the sight of their venue, the French Opera House. Built in 1859, it was the cultural and musical center of New Orleans. The Russians were only one in a long list of international stars to appear there. In addition, many of the well-to-do had seen the Ballet Russe in Paris, therefore, the imitation of the Bakstian costumes and effects. It is understandable then, that perhaps the enthusiasm was not as animated as in some other cities. Nevertheless, Nijinsky had once again proved that everything written about his artistry was true.

> ..."The Rose Impersonation" by Nijinsky. Wherein lies this dancer's art? That problem is as difficult as the art itself, for it is all subtlety, demi-teinte it would be called in music. Often he has the softness and voluptuous grace of a woman, and again, as when he raises his partner high in the air, there is an iron vigor that is as astounding in turn as the tenderness had been. As the spectre one almost fears at times that the artist will, in very fact, swoon, so real does his emotion become.

Perhaps Waslaw did dance both nights and the previous journalist was totally overcome by his artistry?

Waslaw Nijinsky, with Diaghilev's Ballet Russe, came to the French Opera House on 30 November 1916. The troupe, complete with symphony orchestra, arrived in New Orleans on a special train of two sections with fifteen cars each. Although there was little advance publicity concerning the appearance, Lelia and Mrs. Urban, a friend of her mother, were in the audience that happy Thanksgiving to see the great dancer perform. The original program called for *Carnaval, Prince Igor, Le Spectre de la rose*, and *Scheherazade*, but *Cleopatre*

The American Tour of the Ballet Rouse

was substituted for *Scheherazade* because of local opposition to the white-black romance in the latter story. Also, the program announced that Flora Revalles would dance with Nijinsky in *Cleopatre* and that Olga Spessivtzeva would perform with him in *Le Spectre de la rose*. However, as Lelia recalls, Karsavina performed these dances with Nijinsky.

The above quote is from the book *Lelia: The Complete Ballerina* by Harold George Scott, published in 1975 by Pelican. Tamara Karsavina was in Russia at the time, not in America, although invited, she could not be a part of the tour. It is a biography of Lelia Haller, and according to a New Orleans' source, "this city's most prominent ballet mistress."

TEXAS, Houston – 4 - 5 December 1916 – City Auditorium

In 1914, Houston became an ocean port by enlarging the Houston Ship Channel. There was an industrial and shipping boom that turned it into the largest city in Texas. As a thriving metropolis, there was much that occupied Houstonian minds, yet, they were unabashedly enthralled at the prospect of seeing the Russians.

The entire page was dedicated to the preview of the Ballet Russe. It not only described the ballets and the company but delved into the aesthetic of the Russians' art:

> The programs set by the Russian ballet for presentation in Houston Monday and Tuesday nights at the City Auditorium is one of rare interest and perfect balance. Comprising some eight of the incomparable themes of the Diaghileff [Diaghilev] production, it combines in those eight all the wide range of feeling and passion, of beauty and witchery, of sadness and joyous abandon, that has made the Ballet Russe the sensation of the Old and New Worlds alike, and placed the name of Nijinsky, Bolm, Revalles, Gavrilov, and the rest of the company above the high stars in stage land.
>
> The feeling that runs through all the ballets is essentially Russian and fundamentally Oriental. That is, the basic chords struck by the emotion of each piece is of a height and depth, of an exceeding brightness or of the weirdest gloom, moving always to swift passion and to strong contrast - a gamut of sentiment unknown to the Western mind, but infinitely fascinating. It will be hard for the spectator to experience in his own breast, for example, the cold passion and cruelty of Cleopatra, or of Scheherazade, but the spectacle of their enactment is sure to hold him breathless and sway him to every nuance of feeling, however delicately oppressed, that is created by the combination of the indescribable Bakst scenery, the unearthly Slavic beauty and grace, and the surpassing technique of the artists.
>
> Programs slated for the Houston performances were "Les Sylphides" with Waslaw, "Scheherazade" with Gavrilow, "La Princess Enchantee" once again with Waslaw, and also, "Thamar," and "Till Eulenspiegel."
>
> As for Tuesday night, those who have been fortunate as to secure tickets for the ballet Russe may anticipate the climax to which the

The American Tour of the Ballet Rouse

first engagement leads. It is Cleopatre, the most profound, and the most impressive of all the ballet's repertoire.

Not to be outdone, Houston's other large daily also ran a feature article. There was picture of a "figure by Bako [Bakst] from "Daphnis et Chloe," at the Ballet Russe," and a list of the program, which differed somewhat from that of the Chronicle. But the Houston Daily-Post: Sunday Morning edition devoted space to other events too. One could find a detailed program listing of vaudeville at the Prince and a list for the Liberty, where for one day only, Douglas Fairbanks would be seen in "The Habit of Happiness." Side by side with the Ballet Russe was a photograph of two football teams, the South End and the North Side "that clashed in annual contest of high schools last Tuesday." Who won remains a mystery! Then there is a matter of "there is nothing new under the sun," as I have stated before. The pastor of the First Methodist Church, Dr. Hubert S. Knickerbocker, invited local newspaper men to take part in a special service and sermon: "Houston Institutions and Professions and Their Spiritual Needs." The good pastor invited "representatives from all the city dailies to be on the program and they have accepted....I am going to preach on 'The Bible and the Newspaper.' One of the sections of the sermon will be a demonstration from three local dailies showing how much spiritual truth is illustrated every day in the pages of our newspapers." One wonders how today's journalists would fair under Dr. Knickerbocker's scrutiny. And finally, a bit of fascinating trivia:

ROOM FOR ALL EUROPE

It's Area Nearly the Same as That of Western United States. The United States can swallow all of Europe - area, population and all. The entire combined computed area of the foreign countries and the area of the Western United States are very nearly the same, says the Popular Science Monthly. The discrepancy is bare 15, 00000 square miles on Europe's side. At the same time, however, Russia in Europe would spread over the whole western part of our country, crowding it to the doors with its 111,000,000 of people, being the largest of all the European countries.

Nijinsky in America

> The State of California has ample quarters for seven European countries, but its population is only a little over 2,000,000, whereas little Rumania alone harbors just about 7,000,000 inhabitants.
>
> Austria-Hungary fits rather tightly across the shoulders in Texas, which has scattered population of nearly 4,000,000 whereas Austria-Hungary has more than 51,000,000 of people accommodating within its boundaries.
>
> More striking, however, is corpulent Idaho with its 325,000 inhabitants living in an area sufficient to quarter 16,000,000 of Europeans living in four large countries. Then there are Montana and North Dakota with their 900,000 of people enjoying enough room for Spain and Portugal's 25,000,000.

No wonder Americans felt invincible! But let's get back to the Russians. Nijinsky as "The Spirit of the Rose" was pictured in the *Chronicle's* article which reiterated the preview: "Remarkable Extremes in the Strange Dances Show Wide Versatilities of Artists From Land of Slavs Now in Houston on an American Tour." Houstonians were pleased: "Never has so rich a feast for the eye and ear been offered in Houston…"

> Together they circle away, threading the mazes of a dance as intricate, as unreal, as lovely, as dreams of summer nights, and a light as blown rose petals on the sweet winds of June - and here description must stop. The Spirit in Le Spectre de la Rose is too delicate and too intangible for mortal words; it is a dance that is danced not on the stage, but in the hearts of those who watch - and remember. It is Nijinsky, master of the spirituelle and interpreter of things half seen and wholly dreamed…
>
> Finale is Very Fitting
>
> Les Sylphides et Papillons, Nijinsky and the Chor de Ballet, is the best realization of the classic spirit in the dance. Set to the music of Chopin and Schumann it struck a responsive chord and formed a fitting finale to the offering of the evening.
>
> ("Russian Ballet Glory of Color, Music and Motion, Red Blood and Savagery." *The Houston Chronicle* 5 Dec. 1916: 6.)

At this juncture, I would encourage you to reread Richmond's reaction to Waslaw, but first, a final word from Houston – a Mr. Upshur Vincent to be exact, critic for the *Daily Post*: "This dancer

The American Tour of the Ballet Rouse

[Nijinsky] is a wonderful specimen of manhood. He is remarkable in his strength and his agility, but there were many among his company who excelled him in the art terpsichorean if the first performance may be taken as a criterion of his work."

TEXAS, Austin – 6 December 1916 – Majestic Theatre

Don't You Want to Get Away from the Annoying Features of Catarrh?
C. E. GAUSS TELLS YOU HOW
He Offers to Take Any Case of Catarrh, no Matter How Chronic or Deep Seated It has Become, and Prove That It can be DRIVEN OUT.

Mr. Gauss has been manufacturing this Combined Treatment for years, during which time over one million have come to him for medicine and advice. The medicine relieves the disease by first removing the cause, and produces results where all else has failed.

Write him today for a free package of GAUSS' COMBINED TREATMENT FOR CATARRH and you will be happily surprised at the results.

FAMED BALLET RUSSE WITH EXOTIC MUSIC DELIGHTS AUDIENCE
Dancers Are Incomparable Color Is Overwhelming Orchestra Is Splendid

The Ballet Rusee, dancers Incomparable, made the boards ring with the exotic music of the orient at the Majestic theater Wednesday nihgt. Of the score or more gigantic spectacles in the repertoire of the company, the four played last night stood out like beacon lights in a colorful "Bakstian" scheme. To the union of wonderful physical strength and grace, came the wildly romantic music of the Russians.

With springing and leaping and dancing never before equaled, the Ballet Russe astounded Austinites and wove for Them a fairyland of miracle and love.

Framed on the right side by an article entitled "Jack Rabbit Dinner Is an Occasion for Eulogies of Bunny," Austinites were openly jubilant about what they had seen the night before. For them, Waslaw had lived up to his reputation for being the most "illustrious dancer of his day." In *Les Sylphides* he "gave to the languorous and misty beauty a flawless and poetized version. He was a keen mimic, alike in perception and projection, a dancer of sinew and spirit, with muscles and legs of iron, (no wrestler's physique for this critic), a manifold artist." Austin audiences were won over, "The Ballet Russe came to Austin, heralded as

The American Tour of the Ballet Rouse

masters; they went away a conquering host." Many in the audience had come from San Antonio. Advertisements for the Russians with their "bewildering wealth of costuming, music and dancing," had begun nearly a month before. The one night event was locally sponsored by the Austin Musical Festival Association. As in many cities, the music and its performance under the baton of Pierre Monteux were heralded as much as the dancing. It is a fitting insight into the fabric of the city's history as Austin is now known as the "Live Music Capital of America." We are off to the Dallas-Fort Worth area. Two cities that have grown into one huge metropolis, but each of which claimed their very own performance by the Russians in 1916.

TEXAS, Dallas – 7 December 1916 – Coliseum

Dallas, the cultural center of the Southwest, boasts of the Dallas Opera Company, the Dallas Symphony, a Civic Ballet Society, the Metropolitan Ballet, a Civic Chorus and a Chamber Music Society. In addition, the New York Metropolitan Opera visits yearly, performing at the Music Hall of State Fair Park, where popular musicals can be seen in the summer time. It was in this same park, some ninety years ago that the Ballet Russe appeared to great acclaim – little wonder, knowing of Dallas's love for the arts. Dallas's history gives us a hint of its cultural foundation: "In 1855, a group of French scientists, writers, artists, and musicians settled near Dallas to form a cooperative community. The community failed and many of its residents moved to Dallas." Dallas was incorporated as a city in 1871, in direct result of the arrival of two railroad lines: the Houston and Texas Central, and the Texas and Pacific. A mere forty-five years later, the Russians traveled on those lines.

They might have journeyed on the "dependable" Santa Fe, I. & G. N. Line, which ran between Dallas and Laredo, stopping in Austin, San Marcos, New Braunfels and San Antonio. The company proudly advertised their "oil burning engines" which produced "no dust, no dirt, no cinders." One could go from Dallas to San Antonio overnight, a journey that would be twelve and a half hours long, for a distance of approximately two hundred-seventy miles. There were stops along the way of course, but even so, it was a lengthy trip. As we recall, the night before the Russians performed in Austin, about two hundred miles south of Dallas and seventy miles north of San Antonio. Realizing that the Ballet Russe's special train did not make as many stops as a passenger train, it nevertheless, gives us an idea of the strenuousness of train travel in those days. There were other lines promoted in the 1916 *Dallas Times Herald*: "Hours Saved [on the MKT] Texas Special to Kansas City" and on the "Cotton Belt Route" one could experience "Lone Star Comfort," when traveling from Dallas to Memphis, a fourteen hour overnight trip, with "observation cafe car and unequaled service." This information could be found along side Will A. Watkins Company's heralding of the Ballet

The American Tour of the Ballet Rouse

Russe's arrival. The music store sold pianos, players and phonographs, where one could hear and purchase the Ballet Russe's records as well as other Columbia records played on a "Grafonola $15 to $350 -- SPECIAL CHRISTMAS TERMS." The *Times Herald* and the *Dallas Morning News*, two papers writing about the Ballet Russe are still in existence today. Here is a sampling of what they wrote in 1916:

> Serg Diaghileff's great Ballet Russe -215 artists, [amazing how the numbers change with each reporter!] musicians and mechanicians - will appear at the Coliseum in Fair Park Thursday evening, under the management of Mrs. Jules D. Roberts and Mrs. John Priestly Hart. [a coup for women's suffrage.] The aggregation arrived in Dallas Thursday morning and during the day the Coliseum was put in order for the magnificent production....
>
> Waslaw Nijinsky heads the ballet - a man declared by authorities to be the greatest dancer of his sex in the world. Other stars include Lopokova, Revalles, Bolm and Gavrilow.
>
> What the Ballet Russe is.
>
> "The Ballet Russe is not a mere production," said a well known patron of the arts Thursday. "It represents an artistic movement, and unfortunately many people are not familiar with that movement.
>
> "The thing that people do not seem to understand is that the ballet as conceived by Diaghileff and carried out by his own troupe is far in artistic advance of grand opera. It is the next step in the fore of opera not only for America, but for the world at large.
>
> "This is true because the ballet has achieved what has long been the ambition of grand opera, but which has never yet been realized - a complete co-ordination of the arts. Operatic performances, as a rule, are something wonderful to hear, but very ordinary and uninteresting and conventional to look upon.
>
> "The ballet is something to see and hear, and it carries distinct literary and dramatic significance. The perfection of the dancing is combined with drama, with haunting music, with bizarre and weird combinations of color in scenery and costumes. The leading performers of the ballet, if women, are always strikingly beautiful, because beauty and youth are made the prime requirements for members of the ballet corps. It is the magic of ensemble which grips the attention of the audience at a Diaghileff performance.

Nijinsky in America

Opportunity May Never Repeat.

"It is not at all unlikely that the opportunity given to come in contact with beauty will be the only chance ever accorded here. New York is the American home of the ballet, and it is so thoroughly appreciated there that tours will be inadvisable. The Diaghileff [Diaghilev] organization is in this country practically through exigencies of war, which makes its foreign performances impossible. The ballet will probably return to Europe at the close of the war, and never visit this country on tour again. New York is probably the only place where the ballet can be seen in America after the present tour." (7 December 1916, *The Dallas Daily Times Herald*: 14)

The prediction of the patron quoted in this article was frighteningly accurate. The trumpeting of the Ballet Russe in the *Dallas Morning News* was equally elaborate: "artistic sensation of the century brought here at a cost of $500,000." Tickets were $1.50, $2, $3, $4, $5, and box seats $6. The Box Office was located at "Marvin's Drug Store." Curtain was at 8:30 P.M. Houston's critic for the Chronicle was quoted to say: "The dancing was simply marvelous, while the scenic effects were magnificent and the great orchestra is in keeping with the whole." Dallas was well "in the saddle" for what they were about to see.

Serge de Diaghileff's Ballet Russe was given at the Coliseum last night. Those that were lucky enough to be present - saw a performance that kept them spluttering around for new adjectives and left them a little dazed when it was over. It was something new. It was not the kind of dancing that this country has seen much of. It was pantomimic grand opera, yet it was not like grand opera. The splendid orchestra that gave the interpretation was, of course, operatic, and pantomime is nearly all the acting there is in opera, but there is nothing in grand opera to give the fluidity, the plastic kaleidoscopic tableaux, and the choreographic subtleties that were so prodigally displayed last night. The symphony orchestra which did all the talking, all the singing, all the interpreting and gave the atmosphere to each dance…all its perplexing beauties were brought out by the finish of its rendition.

The first ballet "Les Sylphides," by Fokine, was a romantic reverie, like a pastel in color, dreamlike in movement, and with Chopin music, like a landscape of Wateau come to life…It was no dance of chorus girls, there were nineteen on the stage, but all were artists.

The American Tour of the Ballet Rouse

The second ballet was "Carnival." In this appeared the two supreme artists Lopokova and Nijinsky, as Columbine and Harlequin. There was much humor in this pantomime with, of course, the pathos of Pierrot. The music by Rimsky-Korsakow and Glazunow was electrifying and full of the whimsical. Nijinsky is extremely versatile and this ballet gave him opportunity to show his humor, his vivid ability as a pantomime, and his dancing which was rhythmic acrobatics. He created a Harlequin not to be forgotten. There was a vigor, a certainty, a masterfulness that is only attained in the highest art. There were many who wished that he would remove his mask, which he did not, even when he was called before the curtain, and there were some who could not realize that this amusing clown was the greatest dancer in the world. To most people greatness must come in a solemn garb, and the wild mimic in his circus costume, upset the conventional idea of a great dancer...

The last ballet was "Scheherazade," much more easily written than pronounced. This Persian fable has been the talk of the country since it was first presented in New York...

When the curtain went down it left an amazed and somewhat bewildered audience. It was not ballet, nor opera, nor tableaux. It was a musical exploitation of a moving picture of the Arabian nights made real. There was a story told – partly by pantomime, but mostly - by music - that was clear and direct. The music was Oriental, with metallic raspings and wooden thumps, with no shock absorbers. It was no imitation music, it was the real thing. It was carried to a point where the human voice would have been an intrusion. It was pantomime carried to the n'th power.

This ballet made clear that there are some windows of the western mind that have not yet been opened, perhaps on the fourth dimension, or the sixth sense, or even come eleven, that left the audience applauding but not sure just what they were enthusiastic over...("Ballet Russe Scores Big Success in Dallas" 8 December 1916, *Dallas Times Herald*)

Enthusiastic they were, perhaps exuberant would be a better word for it:

> Gorgeous in the splendor of its settings, beautiful by reason of the dancing of all its artists...

> The work of Waslaw Nijinsky, the world's greatest male dancer, stands as a matter of course above the rest...

Nijinsky in America

All in all, the whole performance last night was one that will live for a long time in the minds of those who were privileged to be there...

The various episodes of "Le Carnaval de Schumann"...

All the characters...were there eager to transport the audience, by means of ironical romantic episodes, into a land of dreams where Waslaw Nijinsky reigned supreme.

The outstanding feature was, of course, the dancing of the world's greatest male terpsichorean artist, Nijinsky. It was the only time he appeared during the evening and that the people appreciated him was seen by the great applause they gave him. Nijinsky is a dancer, who not only dances with his legs, but also with his brains; his personality infuses whatever he approaches with his own spirit and his own enthusiasm. As a dancer, pure and simple, as an interpretive artist, as an original personality, he stands alone. His movements flow one from another without effort and without break in a sort of musical legate. His lightness of limb is controlled by a tremendous muscular power, so that when he leaps into the air he seems to float and when he touches the ground and is about to bound upward again it seems as if his feet spurn their natural resting place. His sense of rhythm is almost unexampled; he dances with legs, body and arms, melting into the music or controlling it, as the case may be. He has the face of a child and the frank smile of a boy and despite his power; his movements have the grace of a woman. ("Diaghileff's Ballet Russe Is Splendid" 8 December 1916, *Dallas Morning News*)

TEXAS, Fort Worth – 8 - 9 December 1916 – Coliseum

A mere 30 miles west of Dallas, Fort Worth has had to endure an age old rivalry with its sister city. Fort Worth began its existence as an army post, named after Major General William J. Worth, a hero of the Mexican War. In 1916, this "Cow town" did not take a back seat in welcoming the Ballet Russe. As a matter of fact, they garnered two performances. If you thought that Dallas audiences were overly jubilant about the Russians, then, just read what Fort Worth had to say!

The promotion of the Ballet Russe began a month before their arrival. Prospective Fort Worth audiences were kept informed of the Ballet's triumphs: "Nijinsky Wins New Yorkers on First Appearance," "Nijinsky Will Dance Here Dec. 8 and 9," "Libretto to Read Dancing Will Be Work of Nijinsky," "Nijinsky Creates Spiritual Response to His Art," "Ballet Corps to Arrive on Special Trains." Obviously, Fort Worth had more than a passing interest in the Russians. Daily articles entitled "Legends of the Ballets," featured the synopsis and history of ballets to be presented. Then, on the day and the day after the first performance, the Russians became front page news: "Big Ballet Russe Here Tonight at Coliseum," and "Big Russian Ballet Delights Large Crowd at Coliseum."

We are indebted to the *Fort Worth Record's* detailed information about the travel arrangements. The Metropolitan Opera Company had an advance agent in the person of Ben Stern, who always arrived ahead of the troupe in order to make sure of a smooth transition from town to town. In this case, the 30 mile trip from Dallas to Fort Worth was organized with the help of George Pentecost, general passenger agent of the Rock Island Line. Moving the Ballet Russe was compared to setting up a three-ring circus. By this time, it became clear that there were two trains, one carrying the scenery, costumes, and so on and a seven car, standard Pullman, housing the artists. The paper also reported that by special arrangement, the baggage cars, two of which were one-of-a-kind constructions for the unusual Bakst's settings, will be unloaded "at the north side station." Details, such as heating the enormous Coliseum had to be attended to well in advance and a contingency plan devised in case the weather turned colder. Every little item was of interest for the Fort Worth audience, but it was Waslaw who earned the greatest attention.

The article concerned with the New York appearance focused on "Till Eulenspiegel" and how the "Noted ballet dancer delights his audiences at Manhattan Opera House with interpretation of Strauss masterpiece." On November 8, the *Fort Worth Record* proudly announced that under its patronage, the "world's greatest male dancer, former prisoner, comes here with Ballet Russe . . . " The long article that followed was about Waslaw, his life and art.

> He has composed some ballets, including the famous "L'Apres Midi d'une Faune" which is the result of his ardent studies in ceramics, as he has always had a passion for archaic decoration. In addition, he is, this year performing in two new ballets of his own conception. "Till Eulenspiegel" and "Mephisto Valse." [Once again this mysterious, elusive work appears in print]. Off the stage Waslaw Nijinsky is in no way conspicuous, being an average sized man with bronze brownish hair, and a Slavic countenance. He was paying a visit at his father-in-law's [Charlie Pulszky] home in Budapest that he was caught and interned by the military authorities, owing to the outbreak of the present war. Nijinsky is very much wrapped up in his art. He never tires of emphasizing that his conception of a part is inspired, and that it is a spiritual conception founded on a mental impression.
>
> "Every movement which I made upon the stage," he recently said to an interviewer, "commencing with the posture of my little finger on my left hand is the result of mental study. I have studied sculpture, painting, music, poetry, tragedy and have taken as my special province the works of Michael Angelo and Leonardo da Vinci, which portray strength and grace at the same time.
>
> "If you look at a sculpture by Michael Angelo and DaVinci, you can almost see the movements which a dancer should perform in order to portray force and beauty. You can see the strength and the grace. This has to be mentally digested and then again from my brain it is transferred into my own body and thrown across the footlights to the public.
>
> "In the same way that an actor portrays a role and studies certain movements incidental to certain phrasing, the dancer must study all of his movements beforehand, but in a much more detailed form,

The American Tour of the Ballet Rouse

because having no words to utter and having only movements with which to portray all the emotions, these movements have to be worked out in more detail and at the same time along broad enough lines for the audience to understand. He is like a great conductor such as Toscanini, when he conducts an opera like "Tristan and Isolde" which embraces all the emotions human beings experience, worked out in great detail, and at the same time co-coordinated into great lines." (8 November 1916, *Fort Worth Record*)

Waslaw is known for his revolutionary choreography as much as his exalted leaps. He has been dubbed the father of modern dance. All this with only four extant choreographies: ""L'Apres Midi d'une Faune," "Le Sacre d'un Printemps," "Jeux," and "Till Eulenspiegel." Of the four, only one, "Afternoon of a Faun," is truly known. Waslaw had devised a system of choreographic notation and transcribed the Faun into this method. The original manuscript is housed in the British Museum. The other three had been "reconstructed" by a number of people in this century, but they are not the "real McCoy." These works unfortunately, have not been notated by Waslaw and consequently, the reconstruction is based solely on photographs, reviews, interviews and the reconstructors' imagination. Sadly and unjustly, many claim these reconstructions to be Nijinsky's choreography. Waslaw's legacy lives on in spite of this, but how much the world of dance would have benefited, if his dream had been realized:

> Idea of Great Ballet Leader is to Evolve System of Symbols to Transcribe Dance to Paper
>
> Local experts of the fox-trot and the tango will be interested to learn that Waslaw Nijinsky, premier danseur and artistic director of the Serge de Diaghileff's Ballet Russe...has by long and patient effort gotten his muscles so that they operate after the fashion of the scales of music. When he wants to move the muscles that correspond to A or B flat he gives himself the proper pitch and gets bulging results which correspond to the desired scale. Every day he practices these scales going, up and down between hip and torso until he is anatomically in tune. Then when he rehearses a dance just the right muscles are called into action to interpret precisely what the programme calls for.
>
> How utterly simple this makes the old tango seem. Going forward, with the muscle scale . . . Nijinsky is now working to reduce every

dance to a systematic record so that one trained to the art may follow the notations. Just as a person at the piano follows a score, to be sure he is dancing according to note. When the eminent dancer perfects this new system he means to hand it to posterity in what might be called and, in fact, is just about to be called "a new choreography for choreography."

Book to Be Lifework

"This book is to be my lifework," related the dancer recently, "and my detention abroad on account of the war gave me the chance I needed to begin writing it. But the project has been in my mind for some years. "The idea is to evolve a system of symbols by which the choreography of dance can be transcribed upon paper, just as music is recorded through the medium of notes. I claim no priority to the conception of this idea. For a century or more, projects tending toward this end have claimed the attention of dancers. No end of labor has been expended, but thus far fruitlessly. The collage of the numerous experiments has been due only to persistent failure to discover a system which was sufficiently comprehensive and thorough. Too much complication and too little directness and explicitness have defeated these aims. I feel sure that I have overcome those obstacles.

Believes Method Simple

"Although I cannot yet make public my discovery, I believe it is superlatively simple and lucid and analogous to musical notation. Not only will it be easy to record a complete dance, as it is now to record a symphony or a sonata, but as one musically trained is capable of hearing a symphony mentally by merely reading the score, so will it now be possible for the mind's eye to conceive the whole ballet by perusing what I might call its score, which will be set forth by the symbols I have devised.

"Just as the layman may now be able to make some practical use of a treatise on piano technique, he should similarly be able - so far as physical attributes permit - to acquire a certain terpsichorean facility of his own."

Casual jotting in the new symbols which Nijinsky created were almost his undoing while a prisoner in Austria [actually, Hungary]. His notes on new dances were discovered and as no one could decipher their meaning, he was accused of being a spy and narrowly escaped arrest. No amount of explanation on his part could dissipate their suspicions and many complete dances which he had written out at full length were seized and destroyed.

The *Fort Worth Record* had done a great service not only to the art of dance by sponsoring the Ballet Russe, but to the memory of Waslaw Nijinsky, by publishing the above and the following articles, which gives us, and all future generations, a deeper insight into the man behind the mystique:

Nijinsky Creates Spiritual Response to His Art

In flowery phrases the French poets have told why Nijinsky distinguished leader of the Ballet Russe…is the greatest dancer in the world. They liken him to a…tongue of flame, to a jet of water spurting from a fountain. They have also said, "half man, half god."

Nijinsky is great, to put it in plain English, however, because he possesses the supreme faculty of creating a spiritual response to his art. No art is great until it can give you more than color or sound or form or motion. In a great picture you feel more than color and line.

It is not enough that a dancer be graceful, charmingly costumed, with a background by the great Bakst and music by Debussy or Stravinsky. All those things are delightful and appeal to the eye and ear, but the great dancer must do more. He must give you an expression of the emotion he experiences as he dances. But few dancers have ever been able to do this.

Secret of Nijinsky's Success.

The magnificent success of Nijinsky, surpassing all other ballet dancers, is accounted for through his extraordinary power of giving out his spirit through his dancing. He is able by the most simple means to bewilder and overwhelm his audiences with a genuine realization of beauty.

To Nijinsky dancing is far more than technique or color. He says," The idea is the great thing in all dancing." He rarely considers technique, he speaks of the new movement in the theater as if it was a thing of small importance, and he accepts music as the handmaiden of the dance. But of the idea which creates the dance, of the spirit which endows it with beauty, he cannot speak enough. "It is," he says, "a spiritual art."

Spirit is Impressive

Nijinsky in America

Nijinsky is a great spirit, whether in his dancing, the most beautiful ballet dancing in the world, or in meeting him quietly as a social human being, whether in his own home with his beautiful and charming wife [Romola] or in the park in New York playing gently and happily and sympathetically with his own adorable baby [Kyra]. Always Nijinsky is more than the person you meet, more than the man who talks with you or who plays with his children or who creates and constructs fine ballet art. You feel always that wonderful glowing spirit which animates all of life for him, which infuses into his art richness and exquisite subtlety impossible to describe, and which marks the boundary between great art and charming presentation of music and motion...

The article continues: "Nijinsky reigns supreme in his art not only in the dance itself, but in the creation of the dance, the selection of the music, the stage setting and the designing of the costumes," followed by a chronicle of Waslaw's exquisite portrayal of the faun. There was much more that was written about Nijinsky and the Ballet Russe in the Fort Worth papers, but repeating it here would be superfluous

TULSA, Oklahoma – 11 December 1916 – Auditorium

Sunday, the 10th of December was the company's time for travel and rest. Rest in particular for Waslaw, who made an unusual concession to Fort Worth audiences, and performed two nights in a row. The critics took note of his magnanimity, declaring that an artist of Nijinsky's genius is "apt to be very temperamental and object to consecutive appearances." One might think that Waslaw's generosity was only in compliance with the request by the general manager of the tour, Max Elser Jr., who was a one time Fort Worth resident. However, it was more than that; Waslaw, as we have seen and Tulsans soon discovered, was a kindhearted, noble human being, with a tremendous sense of humor and an interest in numerous other things in life, aside his art.

Nijinsky, the World's Premier Dancer, Is Amazed at the Tulsa He Finds.

A WONDERFUL ORGANIZATION

Convention Hall, Where Ballet Will Be Held, Is Revelation to Artists.

Occupying a special train of twenty coaches, [it has grown to 20?], the battalion of artists and musicians who will appear before Tulsans tonight . . . arrived here yesterday at 4:15 o'clock.

A journey from Fort Worth, Texas, starting at 2 o'clock in the morning, and marked by one minor accident after another, had put the visitors in anything but a cheerful mood, but as it was Sunday, with no performance in the evening, the outlook, from the artistic standpoint, was not so bad. They arrived here more than two hours late.

Waslaw Nijinsky, ranked far above all other male dancers of the present age, and the brightest star of the score of celebrities in the company, climbed into one of the many waiting automobiles at the station and requested (in French) to be driven to the theater where the ballets were to be presented. As Tulsa is by far the smallest city in which the dancers will appear on their transcontinental tour, he naturally had expected that the accommodations here would be, at the very best, rather limited.

Gets First Surprise.

Nijinsky in America

What was the surprise of M. Nijinsky's escort when the noted dancer gave an ejaculation of combined wonder and delight when he stepped on the deep stage at Convention hall?

Thru the attending member of the company who was serving as interpreter M. Nijinsky informed those in the party that the reason for his pleasure was the Convention hall stage. He explained that the sloping stage, which Tulsans had feared would be a drawback to the ballets, was most desirable. The stage, which is about twenty feet deep, inclines approximately 18 inches. M. Nijinsky expressed great pleasure. He said the stages in practically all the leading theaters of Europe built for ballets were inclining, but that the one at Convention hall was the second of the kind he had found during the tour of the United States. The other was in a New Orleans theater.

Some one in the party suggested that M. Nijinsky should give "a good exhibition" Monday night with this advantage.

Always Good

To this, without the slightest appearance of braggadocio or boasting, M. Nijinsky replied with a smile that he "always gave good exhibitions."…An interviewer expressed surprise that the dancer did not even pretend to speak English.

"The truth is, I never had time to master the language," he answered thru the interpreter. "It seems I'm always busy. If it's not one thing it's another - a massage, a ride thru the city, or something else. And there are so many cities." M. Nijinsky could be described as just what one would expect as the world's greatest dancer.

He is of medium stature. His head is small and the features are Russian - high cheekbones and wide set Slavic eyes. It is the face of the Russian aristocrat. The hands are beautiful and well shaped and the whole body appears to be what the body of the premier dancer ought to be. This sunshine of the southwest in the midst of winter is a marvel to him, coming out of the colder north and east.

Many of the visiting artists displayed great interest in this section of Oklahoma because of the myriad of oil wells that they saw from the train windows as their special rolled thru the Mid-Continent field toward Tulsa. It was the first time that many of them had seen such a sight. Not so M. Nijinsky. The Pennsylvania and Texas fields, as well as the Rumanian and other fields in Europe, have been viewed by him.

The American Tour of the Ballet Rouse

Shrine is a fraternal organization that has its roots in the Scottish Rite Masonry or the Knights Templar in York Rite Masonry. Two Americans, Walter M. Fleming, a physician, and William J. Florence, an actor, founded the Shriners in 1872. To this day, Shriners do charitable work, supporting hospitals in North America, specifically, and providing free specialized medical treatment for crippled and burned children. In Tulsa, a number of Shriners played host for the Russians:

> Several Shriners had their automobiles lined up at the station when the special train pulled in. Many members of the company were conveyed in the autos to their hotels and afterward given a spin around the city. All of them seemed to be much interested in Tulsa, her streets, her homes, her nearby oil wells, and most important of all, her marvelous progress.
>
> One of the Shriners discovered after he had driven a short distance that some very distinguished visitors were his guests. In the car with him were Mr. and Mrs. Fradkin and Mr. and Mrs. Waslaw Nijinsky. The former is the concertmaster of the company and the latter is the world's greatest male dancer.
>
> "I found both of the gentlemen delightful," said this representative of the Shrine afterward. "My conversation with them was extremely interesting to me. They evinced a genuine interest in everything I told them about Tulsa. I took them to the old Indian council tree on the Sinclair estate and they asked many questions about the Indian history of the city. Mr. Fradkin was especially interested in the commercial aspects of Tulsa and indicated that he might return here some time and make investments."

Fradkin had with him his prize violin, an instrument that he values at $20,000. No small change even today, but then, when indigestion could be alleviated with a 10 cent purchase, ladies fine coat could be bought for $25, a $5 ticket to see the Russians was expensive and when for $16,450 a Mr. Carl Stern could buy 140 acres of land, then, $20,000 was a small fortune.

> Treasures Violin.
>
> "He told me that he never lets it get away from his person," [I bet!] said the Shriner. "He takes it to bed with him, on the train and everywhere he goes. He had it with him today, in a little black case."

Nijinsky in America

> Fradkin spoke English quite well, and interpreted for M. Nijinsky, who talked French.
>
> They asked their host not to divulge the name of their hotel. They seemed to be very unassuming...

The above story appeared in the *Tulsa Daily World*. Today, over ninety years later, the *Tulsa World* is still in business. Speaking of business, the Russians were a tremendous artistic success in Tulsa, but not so financially:

> Two thousand persons sat spellbound in Convention hall last night while the world's greatest dancers presented three wonderful ballets. The Ballet Russe is to dancing what the Ellis Grand Opera is company was to operatic art. The Ellis Company drew $27,000 into the box office here in two nights. Serge De Diaghileff's Ballet Russe attracted barely enough money to pay the $5,000 guarantee and other expenses.
>
> Akdar Shrine temple stood sponsor for the affair. Like many other organizations here that has assisted in making Tulsa the musical and artistic center of the state, Akdar has become a martyr. But in spite of the fact that the financial gain was nil, Noble Lee Levering, who bore the brunt of the details of the promotion, smiled throughout the evening. It was a wonderful performance and he believed that the Shriners, good, loyal citizens that they are, would feel amply repaid for all their efforts. (12 December 1916, *Tulsa Daily World*)

Tulsans and the Shriners are to be commended for their valiant effort to raise the cultural awareness of the city. It was truly a courageous attempt since Oklahoma was a very young state then. Tulsa, in 1907, the year of statehood, had a population of only 7,298 souls.

KANSAS, Wichita – 12 December 1916 – Forum

We have arrived right, smack in the middle of the country. *Sunflower State, Wheat State, Breadbasket of America* is only some of the monikers Kansas is known by. It is Midway U. S. A. The Geodetic Center of North America, found in Osborne County, is the reference point for all maps of North America, Canada and Mexico. Kansas is linked to such famous names as Wyatt Earp, Wild Bill Hickok, Bat Masterson and Dodge City. President Dwight D. Eisenhower called it home and it became his final resting place. Wichita, its largest city, is linked to Beech, Cessna, and Stearman, all pioneers in the airplane manufacturing industry. Just like Tulsa, Houston, and other places in Texas, Wichita too, had benefited from the discovery of oil.

The Forum received a face lift in 1954, only to be demolished in 1965. But on the 12th of December, 1916, the place to see and be seen was the Forum... Both the *Wichita Eagle* and *Beacon* reported heavily on the comings and goings of the Russians. Today, these two papers have joined forces to become the sole daily newspaper, the *Eagle - Beacon*. Wichitians of 1916 were eager to know all there was to know about their illustrious guests. One single issue ran all of the following articles:

"Ballet Russe Is Animated Art Exhibit - Famous Diaghileff Troupe Looks Like A Display And A Menagerie, Too; Came About Noon On Special Train From Tulsa; Scenes Like A Tower Of Babel At The Union Station - Stars, Wives, And Many Pets, Including A Live Alligator," "Russia's Three Most Beautiful Girls Make The American Tour," "Ballet Tour Is A Long One," "Nijinsky At Football Game," [we'll get back to that one!], "Won't Play German Music," "Morgan With Orchestra," "Always Ready To Explode," "It's Not Lacking In Music," and "Like An Exhibit Of Art." But perhaps the most illuminating as well as intriguing article was one entitled: "What A Reporter's Ears and Pencil Picked Up."

> Andre Bartseure, a member of the Russian Ballet, which arrived at noon today, exhibited knowledge of other than Russian dances. As he was standing on the platform, hopping around to keep warm, one of the colored porters came along, whistling an Irish jig. The

Nijinsky in America

Russian danced with such skill that the Negro could not whistle; his mouth popped open with surprise.

The mascot of a ballet dancer must be a poodle dog. There were 17 white, curly dog heads looking out of the car windows as the train came in today.

As a group of girls passed down the platform it was noticed that one of them was limping as though in great pain. Her feet and ankles were wrapped in heavy cloths and these bandages were reinforced by leather braces. "She sprained her ankle about a week ago," said one of the men, nodding toward her. "I expect, though, that she'll dance tonight. This is going to be one of the biggest performances on the trip, and we'll nearly have to use her. She isn't a solo dancer, but she can help put a lot in the company's appearance."

I assume by biggest, the gentleman meant the size of the audience, and the Forum had capacity to seat a great number of people. In fact, later I'll tell you about the "Odd Mixture of Emotions the Ballet Russe Excited in 3,000 Persons Who Saw It at the Forum."

Fred Courry, "just a plain American" and a member of the orchestra, as he put it, dashed out of the car door as the Pullmans were being backed away from the station. He had a collar, coat and vest in one hand, a suitcase, overcoat, roll of music and hat in the other. "Gee! I had to hustle," he said as he fastened his collar. When told that a joke had been played on him, he said that some of the boys must have bribed the porter to tell him that the train was going to the edge of town. As he attempted to get a nice looking knot in his tie, between shivers he vowed vengeance on the other members of the orchestra.

Twenty-five special men were needed to unload the scenery and other props. The delicate machines for the different scenic effects were as carefully packed in big steel boxes as a shipment of jewelry, and were handled with as much care as though they were made of plate glass.

The American Tour of the Ballet Rouse

A great deal of trouble was caused by the 65-foot curtains. After much experimenting a combination of wagons was hooked up so that the curtains could be taken to the Forum, without danger.

Noon seems to be an early hour for the ballet dancers to arise. A great many were still in their berths and only a few complained of being hungry for breakfast, as they passed down the incline at the Union Station.

Now to the matter of Waslaw and football. Perhaps you recall the suggestion made earlier in the tour that Waslaw be given a football jersey? Well, let's see what Waslaw thought of this very American sport:

Thru an Interpreter He Tells of It in Wichita Today.

...Nijinsky...said today that he had almost seen football practice at Yale a week or two before, when the Ballet was in New Haven. Unfortunately the doors were closed as the Yale team was holding secret practice so that the entire dancer saw was a long line of more or less damaged heroes pouring out of the locker rooms under the bowl after practice.

He Can't Speak English

In Springfield, however, the entire company had a chance to see an entire game. As Nijinsky speaks only French and Russian, and Mrs. Nijinsky . . . was not very well acquainted with football, he had some difficulty in understanding the game, but his enthusiasm was none the less intense.

"The thing that appealed to me about the game," he declared to a reporter, "was the fact that it was the whole team which seemed to count rather than any individual player, no matter how brilliant he might happen to be. In a way that reminds me of the spirit which pervades the Diaghileff Ballet. With us, as with your football players, it is the entirety of effect which counts rather than the superlative excellence of any individual among numberless dancers."

There were other equally intriguing questions asked of the troupe; for instance, whether they'll be involved in moving pictures? One Ballet Russe manager's witty remark explained the financial realities of backing a group of this magnitude:

Nijinsky in America

You understand of course, that it would necessitate bringing the entire organization to Los Angeles, and any aggregation of dancers that can play up to $100,000 in two weeks would most assuredly demand all the money that I have, my right eye and left hand, in addition to any hopes that I may have for a future life, in return for their services.

The comment on Los Angeles was strange since it was part of the tour's itinerary. As you can imagine, touring the Russians cross country must have been an organizational nightmare. We're talking about 150 plus people, many of them speaking only Russian, in an era when long distance communication was uncertain at best and travel was problematic. Mind-boggling would be an apt term to describe the undertaking. A journalist for the Wichita Beacon was astute enough to address the problem.

Keeping the Ballet Together and Calm Is no Task for a Nervous Person

To provide for the eccentricities of 65 temperamental Russian dancers is not a job to be coveted. No matter what it is, the salary is not half enough. But taking a train with 65 volatile, explosive Russians, along with an equal number of excitable musicians and a third large contingent consisting of wives, babies and pets, to say nothing of the mechanical staff, is a job to be compared only with taking Verdun - with - this difference, however, that it is accomplished somehow.

Getting the Train Off

The dispatching of the scenery, settings, props, mechanical equipment and costumes, is said to be nothing compared with getting the dancers, themselves off. Nijinsky's faun rides in a crate in the first baggage car. Flore Cleopatra Revalles' pet snake has luxurious quarters all to himself in a glass cage, and Adolph Bolm's olive wreath is always brought down in a hand box shortly before the train leaves.

The day the madhouse burned was dignified and orderly compared with the scenes of confusion as the hour of departure approaches. It is like "Igor," "Eulenspiegel," and "Petrouchka" combined without the music.

Names Stump Irish Lad

The American Tour of the Ballet Rouse

When only a few minutes remained at Tulsa, where the company was last night, and two of the principal dancers and the chief machinist had not arrived, Nicholas Kremneff, stage manager began to get nervous, so he called a messenger boy. "Go in the station," he told the red-headed Irish lad who responded, "and page Mlles. Spesiwitzewa and Wasilowska and M. Michel Tschaoussovcik -- and you might ask for Miesczysias Pianowski also."

"I'll chuck up me job before I even try it," the boy said.

A few minutes later Waslaw Nijinsky and Adolph Bolm came walking arm in arm, as rival premier danseurs so often will, and the train pulled out.

People came from out of town; special trains brought audiences from Arkansas City and Winfield. The *Eagle* critic considered words quite inadequate to describe the spectacle: "a harmony of mime and dance and symphonic music in which words, which have no part in it, can have but a trifling force in its description." He called the dancers: "of clumsy name but graceful muscle glow with exceeding brilliance ..." The journalist chose to divide his review into three parts: music, scenery and dance. He found the music "at once terrible and fascinating," "haunt the spectators and lash them into a mood." "...an evening of music such as Wichita has not heard in years, fairly gurgled with the palpitating tones of harps and of reed instruments." Bakst's work was considered nothing less than the "passions of a pent up soul [which] came out on canvas and on cloth." Then there was the dancing of course, especially the dancing by Waslaw.

> ...As Arlequin in Le Carnaval, Mr. Nijinsky's feet seldom are visible in one position and one wonders if at any time, even when not on the stage, his heels ever touch the surface. His dancing with Miss Lopokova as Columbine brought from the audience of three thousand odd a spontaneous manifestation of approval.

The article continued with a critique of the final number, Le Spectre de la Rose, danced not by Waslaw, but Gavrilov. The journalist ended it this way: "...Mr. Alexander Gavrilov, who in a day not so distant should cause Mr. Nijinsky's pedestal to totter - perhaps to fall." Did Gavrilov succeed? You be the judge...

MISSOURI, Kansas City – 13 - 14 December 1916 – Convention Hall

"How different," writes H. T. Parker in the *Boston Transcript*, "is the Russian Ballet under the exacting and inspiriting Nijinsky, eager that it do its best and fullest for its new public in America, from the Russian ballet under the careless and chafing Diaghilev, dulled rather than stimulated by new conditions!"

Although Boston never had the trying experience of Kansas City, in waiting for hours outside locked doors while Mr. Diaghilev rehearsed his dancers, they are still aware of the shortcomings that unfitted the former director of the ballet for an American tour.

It is Waslaw Nijinsky who brings the dancers to Kansas City today...

"The Phantom [Le Spectre] of a Rose" has been requested by so many Kansas City persons that it has been substituted for "The Enchanted Princess."

Waslaw was more than willing to demonstrate to the good people of the *Show Me State* in the *Heart of America*, where one of the busiest rail centers in the country converge, why he was the greatest dancer the world has ever known. In the countless books written about Nijinsky and the Ballet Russe, Waslaw's intelligence was often questioned; not to mention the wisdom of Otto Kahn to name him director of the cross continental tour. The above quote, as well as the absolute success of the tour more than supports Kahn's decision. By now, we realize the inherent, logistic and artistic difficulties an undertaking of this magnitude incurs. Yet, Waslaw was sensitive to the needs of his audience. He was not only willing to change the program at a moment's notice, but perform more than his contract required. Clearly, he enjoyed America, its people and its customs. A few years later, he will write in his now famous "notebooks" about his love for America. How sad then, that America was not willing to take him back for treatment of his mental illness.

Waslaw Nijinsky's name could have been well included in this political cartoon found in a rebellious "little magazine" called *The Masses*. Its reason for being was clearly stated:

> This magazine is owned by its editors, has no dividends to pay, and nobody is trying to make money out of it. A revolutionary and not a

The American Tour of the Ballet Rouse

reform magazine; a magazine with a sense of humor, and no respect for the respectable; frank, arrogant, impertinent, searching for the true causes; a magazine directed against rigidity and dogma wherever it is found; printing what is too naked for a money-making press; a magazine whose final policy is to do what it pleases and conciliate nobody, not even its readers. MAX EASTMAN-EDITOR

The creator of the revolutionary "Faun" and "Rite of Spring" would have whole heartedly agreed with its editors.

But let's return to Kansas City and its reception of the "superhuman genius, Waslaw Nijinsky, who not only comes as the chief artist, but as artistic director of the performances." The Russians were there about nine months earlier, minus Waslaw. *The Kansas City Times*, still in existence today, considered Waslaw's directorship and presence a definite plus.

THE REAL RUSSIAN BALLET IT WAS ENJOYED LAST NIGHT WITHOUT LAST YEAR'S ANNOYANCES

Nijinsky, Bolm, Lopokova and Revalles the Great Stars in a

Setting of Rich Color and Poetic Action

The Russian Ballet, which came rather stumblingly to Kansas City last season, made its re-entry last night and fully justified its claim to be called the most significant contemporary movement in the theatre.

It is as natural for the Russians to dance as it is for the Welsh to sing, the Scotch to preach, the Irish to fight, or for children to play. It is impossible to think of these floating, flashing creatures as other than spontaneous, creating at the moment their swift flights and soft descents. Their dancing bears out the compelling rhythms of their music in testifying to the rhythmic genius of the race. It doesn't matter that Nijinsky knew beforehand every move he was going to make in the dream phantom of the rose, nor had that Adolf Bolm learned from Fokine the perfectly ordered action of the barbaric "Prince Igor." What really matters, and makes of the Russian Ballet an art full of fresh, warm impulse, is the fact that the dancers love it.

Because there is in Russia a race genius for dancing, the art of their ballet may never extend to other countries save only as it is taken there by native Russians.

THE INDIVIDUALITY OF NIJINSKY

Nijinsky in America

But there is the ballet and there is also Nijinsky. We are told that he is the directing force of the entertainment produced last night in Convention Hall. And yet he is as distinct from the group as the spirit of poetry is different from the spirit of prose. His art, achievement, performance -- perhaps it is more correct to say his imagery -- is so subtle and at the same time so simple and direct, like a tree branch in a Japanese print, a lyric by Sappho or a picture by Meissonier, that he seems at first incidental -- obvious. Not until he returns to the stage again and again does the creative force of this dancer's art make itself felt.

...Bolm gives the impression of belonging to the ballet -- of being a great dancer merely because of the greatness of the Russian ballet.

It is the same with little Lydia Lopokova, embodiment of charm, and with stately and impressive Flora Revalles. But with Nijinsky it is different. Only he can seem to run lightly upon air without apparent effort and alight like a bit of thistledown. There is magic in Nijinsky's dancing....

MORE OF NIJINSKY

Waslaw Nijinsky danced in "The Phantom of a Rose" and in the "Carnival." In the first, his incredible lightness and delicacy of motion were admired. In the "Carnival," in which he disclosed a humorous bent, there was miming as well as dancing -- delectable, elusive pantomime -- and an expression of personality that awoke the audience at last. In spite of the steady flow of Schumann's music, there was much applause.

Throughout the program the influence of Mr. Nijinsky was felt. Smoothness, nicety of detail, evidence of an all-pervading sense of beauty may all be traced to him. To appreciate the inspiration of his presence, one has only to note the difference between the dancing of Lydia Lopokova this year and last. (14 December 1916, *Kansas City Times*)

The article continued with an evaluation of the orchestra, which, in the critic's opinion was fine, but Monteux "could not equal the impression made by Anselmi [Ansermet] heard last year." The local management under Miss Myrtle Irene Mitchell went as far as reducing 1,500 tickets to a dollar on the 14th. It is interesting to note that in a number of cities along the tour, the manager was a woman. There goes the argument that women had no voice during the early part of this century!

The American Tour of the Ballet Rouse

The *Kansas City Star* continued to follow Nijinsky's fate. In an 18 April 1950 issue, a long article with photograph of the now elder Nijinsky and his wife, paid homage to him. Waslaw had died the week before. But it was not only the news media who remembered him. During the early 1980's, this author had gone on a quest to find people who had seen Waslaw dance in America and record their memories. Obviously, these people were very young in 1916, yet the impressions left on them by Nijinsky were nothing short of the sublime.

Dear Kinga,

It was a long time ago and I hope my memories are accurate.

A group of Camp Fire Girls were taken back stage to meet Waslaw Nijinsky .It was the first time I'd ever saw ballet dancing and that I remember it still shows how very impressed I was.

This was in Kansas City, Mo...I'm not sure of the dates, but I'll always remember the dancing.

I hope you had the opportunity to see him dance. This man making the regular stylized turns in support of the girl, then when it came time for his solo work suddenly became as a bird. Great graceful leaps where he seemed to be suspended, the whole performance smooth and fluid. Light and graceful yet there was a feeling of authority.

You can easily see I know very little about the dance. Not even the proper terms. But his performance at the matinee for children has been one of the special memories.

Best wishes –

Marion Scott

(6 February 1980, Marion Scott, Letter written to author)

Ms. Scott had no need for apology, her remembrances tell it all.

IOWA, Des Moines – 15 December 1916 – Coliseum

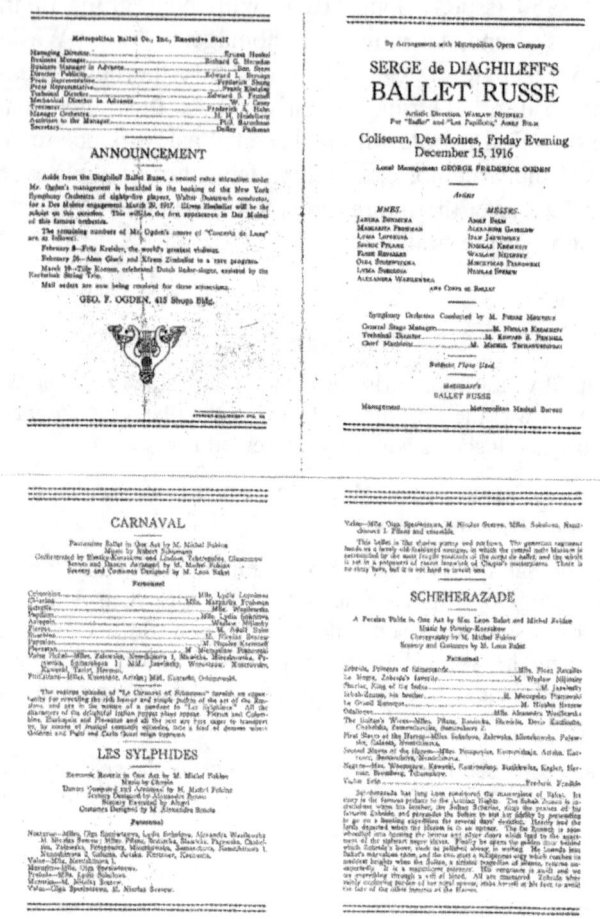

Figure 1.

We are half way through our journey. All in all, it has been relatively trouble free; no major set-backs or problems. And so it should be in the Corn State, Iowa, one of the great farming states of the country. The place that provides seven per cent of the nation's food supply. One cannot help but wonder what the French speaking members of the troupe thought when hearing the American pronunciation of Des Moines (duh MOYN), named by

The American Tour of the Ballet Rouse

French explorers Moin after the river, la riviere des moines. But welcome the Russians they did, and when some of the dancers decided to go on strike, a noble Des Moines resident came to the rescue!

Sundry splinters in the floor of the temporary stage brought on a flood of troubles incident to the performance of the Ballet Russe at the Coliseum last night. The grief most apparent to the spectators was low temperature, it was 64, although hours before the atmosphere in that neighborhood was warm to a degree, which the revered haunt of art and commerce seldom has attained. At that hour, the two Lydias, Mlle. Lopokova and Mlle. Sokolova, described as "light as thistledown in a breeze" put their feet down unlightly and announced they wouldn't put them down on the stage.

A Strong Russian Offensive.

It was a happy hour for art in Des Moines when Ralph Bolton happened to go to his office at the Coliseum at 5 p.m. Instead of going home, according to custom. But for that there would have been no Ballet Russe.

The Russian horde already had withdrawn its impedimenta that are the baggage and the scenery. The men, including the great Nijinsky, didn't mind the arrangements but they were routed by the women. The assembled "ovas" and "inskys" were going away and they didn't intend to say goodbye.

The Lydias Call a Strike

Sitting in his office Bolton called one of his workmen to direct him about some supplies.

"Won't need 'em," the man announced. "Ain't going to be no show."

"Why not?" demanded Bolton.

The reply of the workman was brief and, one might say, pointed.

"Splinters," he said.

Bolton advanced to the northern front of the Coliseum, finding it in the hands of an Amazon enemy. The two Lydias were surrounded by a group of be furred nymphs. They were chatting in Russian.

Where the Bakst Settings Went

A team and wagon were going out of the north entrance with the last of the scenery. The critics of the dance who wondered later where the Bakst settings were might have found them in the railroad yards.

"What's the idea?" or words to that effect, suavely inquired Bolton of the deadliest of Russians.

A small, harassed man got himself out of the group and introduced himself as manager. He pointed at the stage, which it may be admitted, was no hardwood floor.

"Splinters!" he said. "She (pointing to one of the Lydias) say she get them in her toes."

Bolton into the Breach

It was here that Bolton saved "the phantasmagoria of color and motion," which later was to leave "an impression that will not soon fade, of lightness, power and a fierce splendor."

"Well. I'll build a new platform." he said.

"But you can't do it," the manager protested.

"Watch me!" said Bolton.

For want of nails and lumber the Russian kingdom might still have been lost to us, for lumber yards were closed at that time. Bolton persuaded a manager to open up and presently 2,000 feet of lumber, without splinters, was delivered.

A New Stage in Two Hours

Ten carpenters went to work. In two hours and ten minutes the new stage was ready. The Lydias tried it out without damage to their toes and the ballet began on schedule time as Bolton sank into a chair in his office and reflected upon the ways of artists. [A great lesson for Europeans on American know-how.]

The balleteers apparently had not believed Bolton could get the stage built and they didn't get all of the scenery back. This will explain the appearance of this paragraph in the morning review of the production.

"The principal deficiency due to poor staging facilities was in the omission of heavy draperies in "Scheherazade." The green of the background was in consequence a little too glaring and there was not the full effect of oriental richness."

The American Tour of the Ballet Rouse

Too Late to Warm Up

And now to explain the temperature.

In removing the Bakst and other settings, the north entrance of the Coliseum was open for half an hour and in getting some of them back, the door was open for another period. Prevailing north winds the while swept into the building and all Bolton's firemen couldn't get the temperature back again.

The average highs and lows in Des Moines, during the month of December are 34 & 18 Fahrenheit. It is a small wonder then that they managed to heat the place up to 64F, with the doors ajar. Cold, splinters, missing scenery notwithstanding, the Russians performed "brilliantly" and enjoyed magnificent praise. Everyone, including the two "Lydias" shared in the accolades, but once again, it was Waslaw who captured Iowans' heart. According to the critic, it was needless to say that Des Moines had never seen the likes of Nijinsky. The better question to ask was "whether there will ever be such another. Nijinsky is more than a dancer. He is a revelation of human nature. His appearance as Harlequin...was necessary in order to assure the audience that he is really human..." It was in "Scheherazade" that Waslaw really vowed his audience as the dusky lover of the sultana...he is not human, but a lithe and powerful animal. Slipping like a panther about the stage...he draws all eyes after him. ...Nijinsky is the one definite figure, the incarnation of something terrible in human nature...

In this ballet, Nijinsky scarcely touches Zobeide, despite the voluptuous character of the dance. Crouching beside her, springing away, gliding in a crouching attitude clear across the stage, and now and again with a swift movement touching a necklace or a loose bit of drapery, an effect is produced which is as if a panther had taken human shape and become filled with human desires.

This wild animal effect is seen again when the lover is slain by the sultan. Nijinsky is hurtled half across the stage, falling prostrate, and writhing in a death struggle, which stand him on his head without the support of his arms. Then his legs contort and he falls in a twisted heap. Those who have seen Carl Akeley's moving pictures of big game hunting in Africa will remember the scene in which a lion is shot to death in the middle distance before the camera. Nijinsky's death struggle is like that of the lion. (I. N. B., 16 December 1916, *Des Moines Register.*)

NEBRASKA, Omaha – 16 December 1916 –Auditorium

We now turn our sights West. Although when Hosiah B. Grinnell heeded the noted editor of the *New York Tribune*, Horace Greeley's advice to "Go West, Young Man, go west and grow up with the country," he ended up in Iowa. The Russians were now heading west in earnest. On their train ride from Des Moines they continued to see farm after farm, as well as acres and acres of corn; for they had arrived to the Cornhusker State. It was a natural for the Ballet Russe to follow that route, as Omaha has one of the busiest railroad terminals in the country. As a matter of fact, they traveled on the famous Rock Island railroad and the city had hired "all of the big transfer wagons…to haul [scenery]…and more than half a hundred stage hands will be on hand to take in the show." The *World-Herald* that reported such tid-bits for those who were "lovers of the choreographic art," is still in existence today. Like Iowans, the majority of Nebraskans worked the land. It is understandable then that the Russians did not play to a full house, nevertheless, the "spectacle of extraordinary beauty…[was] fairly well attended." Critic Borgium called it "a collaboration of fantastic figures and rhythmic movements, accompanied with forms in the realm of music, which made the scenes intensely realistic." This was an audience very much taken with Waslaw's technical skills, "Mr. Nijinsky, who has been called the god of the air, seems to escape the law of gravitation and by his marvelous vaulting and aerial movements fairly took the breath from his audience. He sustained with ease the wonderful reputation that preceded him." It seems that Waslaw was very much in tune with his audience, no matter where he performed, and was able to transcend all barriers, be it social, cultural or artistic, and communicate with those who saw him, on a higher plane. He must have particularly enjoyed this leg of the trip as his fondest dream was to be able to return to his homeland and have a small farm.

COLORADO, Denver – 18 - 20 December 1916 – Auditorium

Linking the Denver Pacific Railroad to the Union Pacific at Cheyenne, Wyoming in 1870, made Colorado's first rail connection to the East. In spite of the close proximity of the two cities, Cheyenne was not one of the stops for the Ballet Russe. Denver, however, warranted not one, but a three night stay by the Russians. Denver, the "mile high" city, was an important center of commerce as early as 1910. The U.S. Mint issued its first coins there in 1906, and Denver was on its way to becoming regional headquarters for the U.S. Government. Political and financial importance aside, Colorado's greatest claim to fame is its breathtaking scenery. The Continental Divide runs through the Rocky Mountains, which have been called the "Roof of North America," due to the 50-60 peaks that reach 14,000 feet (4,270 meters) being the tallest in the chain that runs from Alaska to New Mexico.

According to Denver's oldest newspaper, the Rocky Mountain News, first published in 1859, Denver society was more than ready for the biggest social event of the year. Many of the "smart set motored up" from Colorado Springs, no small feat, considering the weather, which had kept others away from the Auditorium. Denver is some 50 miles north of Colorado Springs and the weather late in December is between 18 and 45 degrees Fahrenheit, with lots and lots of snow. Ms. Sara Farrar, a critic for the *Rocky Mountain News*, had this to say about it:

> ...The audience was surprisingly small. The boxes were empty on one side of the house and only an occasional one was occupied on the other, but the balconies and parquet were moderately filled. A storm always has a devastating effect on a performance in Denver and even the great Russians were not able to overcome the prejudice against bad weather.

But first, let us get back to those valiant members of society who braved the elements. It was considered a "fashionable event." The 19 December 1916 issue of the *Rocky Mountain News* featured a number of articles about the Ballet Russe, but centered was a large photograph of "Denver society folk" who attended the performance the night before, including such dignitaries as "Mrs.

Nijinsky in America

Alexander Craig, R. Alexander Craig and Miss May Wilfley, Mrs. Arthur Warner and Mrs. Clarence C. Campbell, Mr. and Mrs. J. Foster Symes." [You might wonder why I bother to list these names? In the hopes that someone, somewhere, reading this book will have the joyous discovery of some long lost ancestor and consequently enrich this fascinating story even further.] The following day there was a photo of Nijinsky and Lopokova too. Speaking of photographs, members of the troupe took time to assemble for a group picture, in front of the auditorium, I assume. Some 129 of them, with Waslaw in the middle, all bundled up in winter wear, braved the cold and smiled for posterity.

The article continues, describing in great detail what many of the ladies wore and giving an extensive list of other "fashionables" noticed in the audience. We know by now that there were those critics who strongly disagreed with the general consensus that Waslaw Nijinsky was the greatest dancer that ever lived. For us, ninety years later, it only proves that Waslaw was human, with good and not so good days, but more than that, it gives credibility to the overwhelming praise he received throughout this country and the world. And so it happened in Denver that out of three critics from three different papers, there was one less than enthusiastic about Waslaw. The *Denver Post*, still in existence today, ran the following review on 19 December 1916 by a certain F.W.W.

> Someone has said - I think it was Owen Meredith - that there is a caressing and exquisite grace - never bold, ever present - which just a few women possess.
>
> One naturally thought of this last night when watching the fairy-like creatures, especially Lopokova, Sokolova and Wasilewska, dance in the opening "Les Sylphides" at the Auditorium. It was radiantly delicate and beautiful; full of poetic charm of refined femininity.
>
> It was Lopokova who carried the "reverie." It was she who showed the fine artistry of Pavlowa, plus the essential quality of youth. And to think that three years ago Lopokova was doing "a turn" at the Orpheum, when you might have seen her for a quarter, while last night, I am told, it cost many folks $5.00!
>
> Even then, critics got in free!

The American Tour of the Ballet Rouse

Lopokova is a human delight. She is uncommonly good to look upon, for, as the late Mr. Shakespeare said -

"There's language in her eye, her cheek, her lip;

Nay, her foot speaks."

Perhaps Mr. F.W.W. was infatuated with Ms. Lopokova? There was not the same fetching interest in Nijinsky. In fact, the audience was a little bewildered, as to that rare acrobatic artist. The crowd didn't know him and when he first appeared, for that reason there was no reception.

As if anyone could forget those knotted boilermaker legs, famous when he danced with Pavlowa after the retirement of Mordkin several years ago! But true it is they were forgotten; indeed it was well along in the romantic episode when it passed from mouth to mouth, "That must be Nijinsky." Then the applause became generous, if not judicious...

The violent Bolm is perhaps the best male artist of the group as a dancer. In this respect he outdoes Nijinsky, although the latter is a wonderful director.

But Bolm is the beloved of an audience that revels in his warm impulses, in his genius, his dramatic intensity...

It remains to be seen whether Bolm is the beloved of the audience. Mr. F. W. W. ends his review by admitting that he had seen Bolm in New York and London and that the good people of Denver were getting their money's worth as far as the Ballet Russe was concerned. And now let's hear from the other two. Notice, the Rocky Mountain News critic dared to sign her full name and she was a woman!

> Trappings Wonderful, Nijinsky and Lopokova Entrance Audience with Dancing
>
> ...The art of the Russians has become familiar to Denver thru the genius of Pavlowa and her troupe and the present organization is superior only in numbers and in the magnificence of its pictorial features. There is none among them that reaches the heights of the incomparable Pavlowa unless it be Waslaw Nijinsky, and it is impossible to compare the feminine and the masculine dancers...

Nijinsky in America

...

Nijinsky Is Outstanding Figure.

"Waslaw Nijinsky, outstanding figure, who is the directing genius of the ballet, is also the outstanding figure of the dance. One feels his great ness in his stillness and repose as much as in his swift flights and bounds.

...

It was in this spot (Princesse Enchantee) designed by the color magician that Nijinsky and Lopokova were most wonderful. The magic of their twinkling feet and hands trembled like dewdrops were the most extraordinary performance of the evening. Nijinsky floated and bounded, it seemed, as no thing of flesh and blood could, and departed, flashing high thru the air...

On the same day, Jack Barrows of the *Denver Times* wrote:

...Nijinsky is a marvel of grace, a powerful being with muscular legs that tell ponderously the story of incessant exercise. His leaps and bounds demonstrate what many other men try to do...

The following day's performance was the one poorly attended because of the storm; nevertheless, the above critics and audience were pleased once again. The most insightful article in Denver, if not on the tour so far, however, was not what happened on stage but behind it.

BEING A RUSSIAN BALLET GIRL IS A HARD LIFE; FOOD DENIED FROM 2 P.M. UNTIL THE SHOW IS ENDED

BY RICHARD MILTON

What all those pretty girls are doing while the audience is clapping its collective hands madly in summons to return is - pulling up their stockings and smoothing down their diaphanous skirts, mostly. They also are striving to regain sufficient breath to spring back upon stage, pirouette, smilingly on toes and bow with seeming gratitude for the applause. It's hard work being a ballet girl. It's harder work, perhaps, being a principal - only the principals get more for it.

Back behind the scenes, on the un-idealized side of the stage settings, one finds that out. Here they are, limbering up shapely legs in a series of twists and turns and hops and jumps, while they all chatter away in French and Russian - and the crowd waiting impatiently on

The American Tour of the Ballet Rouse

the other side of the curtains. Tired they look - they've been doing that twisting and turning and hopping and jumping at intervals throughout the day, for in the ballet there are many rehearsals. Rouged lips droop at the corners, shoulders sag somewhat. And then - a sharp signal from the technical director. That great orchestra, controlled by the baton of Pierre Monteux, soldier conductor, silences the chatter with a softly sounded strain of a Chopin waltz, and the girls, fifty or more of them, balance lightly on toes, assume a statue like attitude, and wait for the curtains to part.

But there's delay. Something is wrong with the lights. They cannot, however, change their attitude. They are forced to stand, several minutes, and the strain makes itself apparent in their drawn faces. And then, at last, the curtains glide back. Comes transformation. The ballet girls seemingly revitalized by the sight of the sea of faces rolling back from the footlights, become new beings. They are back in their own element now. The very poetry of motion, they impress one with the belief they could dance on and on, never tiring, so long as the crowd out front was there.

And here comes Waslaw Nijinsky. It wasn't the publicity agent who whispered the secret that each noon this premier dramatic dancer is paid his $1,000 check. And who, watching him on stage and back stage, will say he doesn't earn it. Offstage he stands; an hour before the curtain is parted, going thru some strange sort of calisthenics, with endless genuflections that cause a play of muscles in his tights-incased legs that explain his endurance. Nijinsky, erratically temperamental, also rehearses many times daily. He is careful what he eats and drinks. He has no leisure for playing. His dancing art claims all his time.

Nijinsky has two valets always at his elbows offstage. They attend to his every want. They stand and wait while he is before his audience and catch him as he comes, still wearing his fixed smile, leaping behind the scenes, panting, exhausted. Lydia Lopokova, dainty, charming, coming up to all advance notices of unusual pulchritude, has two maids. But this rival of Pavlowa dances right out of the spotlights and on back to her dressing room without stopping, dances back to bow an encore, and dances back to the dressing room again, seemingly breathing with ease, not at all weary or tired.

But if dainty Lydia is beautiful, no less so are a good majority of the ballet girls. Russian types of femininity are many, and all are represented in this aggregation, gathered with infinite patience and much time and money. The ballet girls are young and fresh and

Nijinsky in America

exuberant with the sheer joy of living. Hard work it is, but it seems to be a work that is second nature to them. After the first set they are gay and inclined to pranks and playing. They cluster about the disconnected, dusty pieces of scenery, which soon are to be that breath-taking camp of barbaric splendor, and laugh and chatter in two tongues quite merrily.

And pretty soon now they are to be more merry than ever. At a shouted order they dart to dressing rooms and return in what seems no time at all, dressed in the, to us, outlandish costumes that give them wildly exotic appearance, and create an atmosphere that Gorky needs must describe. Now it appears they are carried out of Denver, out of this land of strange customs and sights, into HOME. And the ballet as well as the principals dance now with an exaltation that was not observed previously.

Now they are thru. There is a scramble to be first to the dressing rooms. Soon they emerge, clad for the street in chic little fur toques and natty American clothing. They are waiting now for Monsieur Herndon, chaperon, big boss, confidant, interpreter, with the title of manager, to take them out for their dinner. They have not eaten since 2 o'clock in the afternoon. They are hungry. And Mr. Herndon needs must go with them, to give their orders for them. After dinner it is hurry to bed, to sleep until 10 in the morning. And then its breakfast, a rehearsal, a light lunch at 2 and rehearsal again.

It's a hard, hard life.

(19 December 1916, *Denver Times*)

UTAH, Salt Lake City – 22 - 23 December 1916 – Salt Lake Theatre

Every age produces those noble-minded visionaries, who put personal gain aside for the good of the many. Such a farsighted man was Mr. Herndon; you may remember him from Denver, when we discovered that he played the role of "big daddy" for the ballet girls who worked so hard. Mr. Herndon was not alone of course, in this unsurpassed venture that brought the Ballet Russe to America; but his discourse on the matter explains the purpose behind this lofty undertaking.

BALLET RUSSE TRAVELS AT A LOSS

Famous Organization Reaches Salt Lake on Tour of America for Three Performances

CARRIED IN SPECIAL TRAIN

Stars Spend Day Sightseeing and Are Greatly Impressed With History of State

The ballet is becoming annually more and more an American institution and will eventually be as popular in this country as it is now in Europe, according to R. G. Herndon, business manager of the Ballet Russe, the largest organization of its kind to make a coast to coast tour in the United States, who is here with his company for three performances in the Salt Lake theatre tonight and tomorrow and Saturday matinee. At the Hotel Utah, where the principals of the company are registered, Mr. Herndon pronounced the present tour rather an educational one than an attempt by the Metropolitan opera company for financial gain.

"Now that the ballet has been coming here for some time we have learned to accept it, and we are growing immensely interested in it," said Mr. Herndon after telling of the immense organization and the principals in the different ballets. At first it seemed in this country like the wild west shows of America did at first in Europe. They did not know what they were looking at in Europe when a wild west show went through that country, and we treated the ballet much the same. America is adopting it now, however, and it seems to me not far off when this country will have such institutions of its own.

The organization brought here under the management of Mr. Herndon consists of 168 people. It is touring the country in an all steel train of 12 coaches and Pullmans and one dining car. With it

Nijinsky in America

are in addition to Waslaw Nijinsky, declared to be the world's greatest dancer, the following stars: Adolf Bolm, Alexandre Gavrilow, Nicolas Kremmeff, Mieczyslas Pianowski, Nicolas Sverew, Mrs. Janina Bonieckam Mrs. Margarita Frohman, Mrs. Lydia Lopokova, Mrs. Sophie Pflanz, Mrs. Flore Revalles, Mrs. Olga Spesiwitzewa, Mrs. Lydia Sokolova, and Mrs. Alexandra Wasilewska.

Lose Money on Tour

It was not the hope of the Metropolitan Opera company to make the trip a financial success, according to Mr. Herndon, but to make it rather an educational trip. He says the trip is being made at an expense of three-quarters of a million dollars, when the returns are not expected to be nearly that much. It costs between $33,000 and $35,000 a week to make the tour, including salaries and the cost of the special train, and Mr. Herndon explained that if the organization had capacity houses everywhere it would be impossible to clear expenses.

Nijinsky receives $1,000 a performance, and the other stars range in salaries from that figure down to $400 a performance, he says. In the orchestra are 52 musicians, many of them individual stars. It could travel alone, the manager said, with financial success, being one of the country's greatest orchestras.

Has Not Seen Child

Over in the city of Paris there is a small bit of humanity that is occupying more than its share of the thoughts of Monteux the famous orchestra director. For the big musician who has faced all sorts of danger in the trenches of the Allies and taken part in the gigantic struggle of Verdun, has not yet seen his child born while he was away at war. The soldier father was not allowed to leave the front at the time of its birth but has been forced to be content with the knowledge that the baby is safe with its mother, aunt and nurse in the French capitol. Monteux has been loaned by the French government for the present tour but is to return to the fighting line in February. He has announced his intention according to a member of the company, however, of getting his first glimpse of the wee youngster on his return trip and of sending it to American soil.

Like a troop of happy school children turned loose from their tasks the members of the company have been sightseeing this afternoon. [They arrived at 7:45 a.m. from Denver.] For in spite of the strenuous one and two night stands the dancers are never missing a

The American Tour of the Ballet Rouse

chance to see America during their trip. At the bureau of information they were busy obtaining every possible bit of romance and history connected with the old pioneer relics and was evincing more enthusiasm for the "country of the 'Mormons'" than the average tourist.

"We have nothing like it in our own country," they declared. Among the party in the relic hall beside the director Monteux were Lopokova, the premier danseuse and Flore Revalles, the famous character woman. The company after their appearance at the Metropolitan must return to their native country in March.

Nothing came of that final performance as the United States entered World War I. Utah's first newspaper, the Deseret Evening News, reported the above article. Established in 1850 in Salt Lake City, the paper is still in existence. The Salt Lake Tribune, another current paper, also wrote about the ballet. Utah's populace, although few in numbers, had always been very supportive of the arts. It is no wonder then, that Pavlowa had been there, as well as other artists, managed and accompanied by Mr. Herndon. Salt Lake City residents' appreciation of the orchestral music alone illustrated the level of cultural sophistication. They were understandably disappointed then that the turnout for the ballet was so poor. Nevertheless, those that did attend were aware of the unrivaled event of which they were a part. The Tribune informed its readers and consequently posterity, of an interesting detail about the tour's logistics: from Seattle, they went to Vancouver "because of expiration of its American rights for this tour necessitating re-entry into the United States to resume its trip east." Talk about red tape and bureaucracy!

California

What images come to mind when you hear that name: the endless seashore of golden sand and rugged coastline of a turbulent sea, palm trees and giant redwoods, snow covered peaks and an unforgiving desert; or do you think of earthquakes, gold rush, San Francisco, and the City of Angels; do you picture Chinatown, twisting-turning freeways, orange groves and Disneyland; or perhaps your mind wonders about the history of the Missions; perhaps I caught you day-dreaming about Hollywood? Whatever your association with California, all of it is true, and then some. You may have been there once or many times, perhaps only in your dreams, maybe you live there; whatever the case may be, I'm certain, it has had an impact on you. California is an entity all to itself - a state of mind. It was ever so, even back when the Ballet Russe arrived there for a two and a half weeks stay.

The Russians were slated to visit three cities in *The Golden State*, Los Angeles, San Francisco, and Oakland, a week each in the first two and two days in the last. But before we get comfortable in sunny California, I'd like you to look at the calendar. It was 24 December, Christmas Eve, when that special train began its journey from Salt Lake City. Now, take a look at a map and trace if you will, the route they took, down through southwest Utah, southeast tip of Nevada, and then through San Bernardino to Los Angeles. For touring artists, traveling during holidays was (and still is today) part and parcel of their calling. But once again, there were those noble-minded souls who were concerned with the welfare of others, and so on Christmas morning the good people of Los Angeles could read the following charming story in the *Times*:

Unique Celebration,

DANCING STARS FROLIC GAILY IN BAGGAGE CAR.

Perhaps for the first time in history, denizens of the Southwestern deserts last night saw world-famous dancers perform their steps. That is, if the denizens were very alert. For the dancers were trod on the reeling floor of a baggage car, gay with Yuletide decorations, while a special train de luxe hurtled toward Los Angeles with the Diaghileff Russian ballet company aboard. The troupe will arrive early this morning from Salt Lake.

The American Tour of the Ballet Rouse

When the engagement at the Utah city was ended, the president of the Salt Lake Railroad turned over to the company, for the trip to Los Angeles, his private car and the extra baggage car, that was made bright and ready for a Christmas Eve party. Members of the Metropolitan Orchestra of fifty pieces, that accompanies the Russians, provided the music and during the evening, every member of the ballet, including the principals, merrily danced the modern ballroom steps...

In the company are 150 people, and in addition to dancers, musicians and stage crew, there is a large contingent of wives, babies and pets, making altogether an army that presents a continual problem in mobilization.

CALIFORNIA, Los Angeles – 25 - 30 December 1916 – Auditorium

In an upscale "watering hole" I sit, in the heart of downtown LA, sipping a cappuccino. It is 1996. I had just maneuvered three different freeways in the rain, parked my car in a garage that will cost me $22 for about three hours! I am trying to calm my nerves before I enter the newly refurbished Los Angeles Public Library. My surroundings remind me of the twenties, or at least as I think it might have been. The exquisitely appointed bar and restaurant has a touch of art deco. The bar tender is friendly; I inquire about Fifth and Olive. "It's just around the corner," she tells me. The high rise office building has three entrances, for which I'm grateful as it begins to rain harder. I exit on Olive, a few steps more and I'm on the corner of Fifth and Olive. This is where the Auditorium once stood! I stroll on Fifth for a feel of the place. What did members of the tour see? Certainly none of the skyscrapers reaching to the heavens, nor the six lanes of cars, bumper to bumper. I arrive to the entrance of a magnificent building; it is the Library, standing there proudly in its entire renewed splendor. It was not completed in 1916, but photographs illustrate its beginnings, the wide streets of Los Angeles, with streetcar tracks and numerous Model T Fords. Buildings were only six-seven stories high, but the palm trees swaying in the ocean breezes and the sun, warming pedestrians was the same. And how the Russians must have appreciated the warmth after Utah and Colorado! Why am I digressing again? And what am I doing in Los Angeles eighty years after the Russians were there? This metropolitan city of seven and a half million people is not my home. But I am visiting someone, someone who at twenty has a striking resemblance to Nijinsky. It is here that Waslaw's great-grandson, the young man to whom this book is dedicated, attends a university that traces its roots back to 1865. As we make our way across California, we'll discover other such curious twists of fate. But now, let us go back to the turn of the century.

Los Angeles' population in 1900 was 100,000 plus. The Southern Pacific Railroad finished in 1876, connected it to San Francisco and the Santa Fe completed in 1885, and gave a direct link to the Midwest. Having two railroads gave way to competition. For as

The American Tour of the Ballet Rouse

little as a $1, one could travel from the Midwest to Los Angeles. Many did, permanently. The Port of Los Angeles was begun as an artificial harbor in 1899, completed in the same year; 1914, the Panama Canal opened. By 1916, Los Angeles was a major seaport, important tourist destination and Hollywood was booming. So the arrival of the Ballet Russe, although exciting, was only one of many attractions. The Russians stayed a week and performed every work in the tour's repertoire.

As early as 10 December, there were ads in the *LA Times* encouraging prospective audiences to see the "Sensation of the Century." The ballet performed Monday through Friday evenings and a matinee on Saturday. Tickets, once again, ranged from $1 to $4 and could be bought through the mail, accompanied by a check. A certain L. E. Behymer backed the Los Angeles stay. The *Los Angeles Sunday Times* had a special feature called "The Cream Sheet-Life's Finer Side." The 17 December issue ran a picture of four girls from the "Diaghileff Ballet Russe coming to Clune's Auditorium," in an alluring pose. Surrounding this photograph was the promotion of "The Dancing Girl of Delhi," at the Orpheum and Dorothy May appearing at the Hippodrome. A week later, "The Cream Sheet" was covered with larger than life photos of Waslaw, one as the "Spectre de la Rose" and the other in "Les Sylphides." The several pages long article informed the reader about everything they might have wanted to know about the Ballet Russe, interspersed with bits of information about other artistic events. Here is a sampling:

> Have you a matinee idol?
>
> Now is the time to raise your lorgnette to your eyes and take a good look at him. There are some real mannish attractions at the theaters this week.
>
> Nijinsky for instance.
>
> It's not every day a troupe comes to town in which male dancers are featured, and they are real terpsichorean these. Incidentally, however, feminine beauty is to be strikingly visible in the ballet productions...

Nijinsky in America

Some years ago the rattling bones of a dead art form were stood upon stage. They were cajoled with the music of masters. They were clothed with the dreams of inspired painters. And they were made a beautiful, living thing of flesh and blood - the new ballet, revived by the genius of the Russians.

In the present remarkable renaissance of the dance, there are two concurrent forces. One is the "natural" dancing that came out of the West; the other the glorified ballet, from the Muscovite East. Isadora Duncan captivated Europe with her pioneering in the "natural" field; then came the Serge Diaghileff ballet and revealed to an astonished Western Europe that ballet, long consigned to the limbo, or near oblivion, was a vital, astonishing, inspiring thing, of an appeal that gripped the world. And some of the best of what the Diaghileff artists did for the enlightening of Europe and some of the most eminent of those artists, will be presented in Los Angeles tomorrow.

Waslaw Nijinsky, perhaps the greatest living danseur, though peerless in his native land, was…given his release from the Imperial service (in Petrograd) because of advanced ideas.

These revolutionary thinkers (Fokine, Nijinsky) brought forth a ballet that was new. The excellence of the Imperial school was one of method and technique. They built upon that foundation the superstructure that the Western world now knows as the Russian ballet.

First and foremost, the importance of the male dancer had been maintained in Russia alone. The "principal boy" in England was, until six years ago, always a girl; elsewhere the male dancer had become largely a tolerated "prop" for the danseuse. But in Russia the danseur was developed as highly as the ballerina, and his function was fully as important.

The virile element thus retained in the Russian ballet has had a huge effect…

The sources of their choreography are three…steps and movements that have been universally know…native dances of their steppes…and…the oriental and classical.

Furthermore they recognized the necessity of the strict co-ordination of the four elements of ballet, as represented by composer, choreographer, painter and musician…

Thus the ballet has been made an artistic whole, every factor conducting to the one effect with singular unity…

The American Tour of the Ballet Rouse

It has been questioned if the Diaghileff Ballet would be possible without Waslaw Nijinsky. This youth, who began his study in 1898 and graduated from the Imperial School of Ballet in 1907, has danced all his life. His father and mother and grandfather and grandmother were Imperial Theatre dancers. If any name is more conspicuously intertwined than any other with the western revival of the dance, through Russian influence, it is his. Critics have passed over his wonderful technique to dwell on his art, by which is said he is masculine or effeminate, a courtier or a negro of abrupt gesture as his role requires...(Frederick B. Moore)

Having been invested with this profusion of background information, are you curious as to the reception of the ballet in Los Angeles? I will keep you waiting no longer. All of the ensuing reviews were from the Los Angeles Times, starting with critic Edwin Schallert, on 26 December:

> Daring to the last degree in its big conceptions, startling throughout in its massing of color, and breathtaking in the swiftness of its supreme moments, the first performance of the Diaghileff Ballet Russe last night at Clune's Auditorium, made all other dancing we have seen here like child's play. The troupe reveals itself as capable of doing all the things others have accomplished, and many things we never dreamt existed. Their work in some respects is as far ahead of any previous ballet that has visited here, as those troupes are to the stilted old French ballet of fifty years ago. For all that I do not believe they were seen at their best last night. Lack of familiarity with the Auditorium stage, delays in the shifting of scenery [a complaint in many other cities throughout the tour] and one or two other deterring circumstances prevented the impression from reaching its full vividness. The entire performance was a little too much like an elegant banquet, wherein the waits between courses are too long, and the courses too short. By tonight the smoothness of the whole will be greater. The impression on the audience, which was a brilliant and artistic one, was nevertheless a decisively splendid one.
>
> It is when the whole strength of the troupe begins to appear before you that you realize the power of the Diaghileff Ballet. There is something of the velocity of light about the big productions of this company. They have an all-consuming energy that leaves you dazed, captivated and inspired at once...
>
> The Diaghileff is the first troupe to do a number of things. It is the first troupe to attempt disorder, to my knowledge, in any art which

has ever been devoted to order. The "Till Eulenspiegel" was as fine an example of this as one can give...This ballet was the most revolutionary...but the fullness of it cannot be grasped...in one sitting...

The Diaghileff troupe also does another significant thing. They give the male...dancer his proper importance, and with Nijinsky as the stellar performer...they have shown their right to do so. Nijinsky made plain the marvelous rapidity and beauty of his art, in his lyrical "Princess Enchantee," as well as in "Eulenspiegel." His technique is wizardry in the power it gives him to do what others cannot...

Edwin Schallert, 27 December:

...

Strange realms does the genius of Waslaw Nijinsky invade. Amid the floating clouds of his imagination's horizon arise unreal colors and mysterious shapes of things wherewith to create the background for realities that venture into untried provinces in the world of art. He opens by turn the portals of charm, of fire, of magnificence; he treads the corridors of symbolism and drama and the plastic arts, and he and his assistants lead their audiences through the ever-varying suggestions of these things.

...Nijinsky and his people come as near defying the axiom that there is nothing new under the sun [one I have quoted often] as a man could. They at least say nothing twice the same and I have never heard them repeat anything anyone else said before them in their art.

...

"The Afternoon of the Faun" is withal the strangest of the many strange things Nijinsky has done. He makes it more peculiar than you might anticipate by conceiving the dance on a plastic scale. It is like painting or sculpture in its outlines, instead of being like music, as dancing ordinarily is. The faun in the Nijinsky version is as strange as the creature of Mallarme's poem that Debussy sought to recreate in music that is far away from trodden pathways.

...There is an unforgettable trick that Nijinsky does in the "Carnaval." He gives an effect in his dance with Papillion that is positively like nothing else but the revolution of a wheel.

Frederick B. Moore, 28 December:

...

The American Tour of the Ballet Rouse

When one thinks of Nijinsky one thinks of ballet. As a ballet dancer he rose to eminence. Yet in his work this week there is unmistakably something else that isdifficult to define, that seems to be to dancing what the product of the futurist is to painting.

In the "Apres-midi d'un Faune" this strange element is dominant. The Diaghileff management has been frank enough to announce that this particular ballet, designed by Nijinsky himself, "discards conventions," even to the place where "the line of beauty" is lost. That is true. There isn't anything beautiful about "Faune." Nijinsky's art appears in that he ceases to be human and is a mawkish beast - and it is all very effective.

...There is another side to Nijinsky's work, well exemplified in "Princess Enchantee." That is ballet of the kind known throughout Western Europe for these many years. There Nijinsky is a ballet dancer, and nothing more, doing the sort of work with which he electrified Europe some years since. And when Nijinsky dances in "Princess Enchentee" one is tempted to believe there has possibly been something sacrificed to the futuristic - if that is the best word.

Grace Kingsley, 29 December:

A sumptuous variety of form, color and movement characterized the offering of the Ballet Russe at Clune's Auditorium last night. The program was balanced with artistic nicety, offering the richest variety of entertainment yet produced by the Nijinsky aggregation.

...

In this ballet ("Les Sylphides,") Nijinsky revealed a new phase of his many-sided genius. The motif called for that height of rhythmic perfection, delicate, yet virile suppleness and swiftly changing poise, of which he is so completely master...

Trivia from the same column:

Nijinsky...is no particular believer in inspiration. He thinks with Edison "inspiration is 99 per cent perspiration." Nijinsky composes his own ballets, works fourteen hours a day, seldom attends parties, but loves the theater. He claims it is nearly impossible to tell how one gets his ideas.

"It is nonsense," he said last night, with a fascinating little accent quite impossible to convey, "to see when one gets his ideas or how. When I comb my hair maybe I get a beautiful idea for a dance; and maybe in church I think about a clown dance. Inspiration is what you call one rare bird."

You may have noticed that during our journey there have been considerable discrepancies in the number of train cars, troupe members, and whether Waslaw understood any English at all. Back in Wichita, Kansas, Waslaw had expressed his opinion about American football through Romola, who acted as interpreter. Well, those reading the 30 December issue of the *LA Times* got a different story altogether.

> Nijinsky...is an accomplished swimmer, but cares little for games. He thinks football brutal and not at all amusing. The dancer attended the Yale-Harvard game on Thanksgiving Day with his American manager, R. J. Herndon. "And he didn't watch the game at all," said Mr. Herndon. "He was simply fascinated by the university rooters, though, and the field maneuvers of the yell leaders, which later he seemed to think, were some new sort of dance step."

Let us take a brief respite from ballet and go to the movies. The "flickers," a term of endearment, were "silent," until some time later having found their voice, became the "talkies." As early as 1914, a little town outside of Los Angeles had fifty-two companies spending $5,720,000 a year to make "movies," something a lot of people wished and were certain, would go away. Naturalist, John Burroughs, claimed that moving pictures deprived viewers of brain power. What would he have said about Television?! In any case, Hollywood was the little country town outside of LA. Moving pictures were an entity to contend with, "occupying\ fifth place among the industries of the United States, being surpassed by railroads, the clothing industry, iron and steel and oil. The automobile - manufacturer is minor in importance." (*The Picture - Play Magazine*, 1916)

Names synonymous with the early movie industry were of such weight as Cecil B. De Mille, Selznick, Sam Goldfish, better known as Samuel Goldwyn. They were rich and powerful and they knew it. The following little story is proof:

> Glowing in the new light of prosperity and respectability...[they] gained an air of cocksure self-importance. After the overthrow of Czar Nicholas II in the revolution of 1917, Lewis J. Selznick, a Jewish immigrant...sent the cable below.

The American Tour of the Ballet Rouse

Nicholas Romanoff, Petrograd, Russia
WHEN I WAS POOR BOY IN KIEV SOME OF YOUR POLICEMEN WERE NOT KIND TO ME AND MY PEOPLE STOP
I CAME TO AMERICA AND PROSPERED STOP
NOW HEAR WITH REGRET YOU ARE OUT OF A JOB OVER THERE STOP
FEEL NO ILL WILL WHAT YOUR POLICEMEN DID SO IF YOU WILL COME TO NEW YORK CAN GIVE YOU FINE POSITION ACTING IN PICTURES STOP
SALARY NO OBJECT STOP
REPLY MY EXPENSES STOP
REGARDS YOU AND FAMILY
Selznick
(*This Fabulous Century*)

And then there were the stars! Who has not heard of Lillian and Dorothy Gish, Mary Pickford, Fatty Arbuckle, and of course, the unrivaled Charlie Chaplin. Which bring us to a fascinating vignette about Waslaw and Charlie. They mutually admired each other's art and talent. Chaplin invited Waslaw to watch him film; an invitation Waslaw happily accepted. This much we know for sure. From here on, the story gets a bit muddy, being that much time passed and people who wrote about this celebrated meeting, had either a lapse of memory or inaccurate sources. The essence of the tale is that Waslaw watched Charlie at work a number of times, but never even cracked a smile. This unnerved Charlie so that he instructed his cameraman to remove the film, fearing loss of wit in the presence of such woefulness. Allegedly, that fateful day, at the end of the shooting, Waslaw and Charlie improvised a bit of a "soft shoe" number, forever to be lost. The dates and cities of this tour are fact. The reviews and reports are of course, personal opinions; nevertheless, they are an assurance of the Ballet Russe's presence in a specific city at a precise date. And then we have three books, brought out by world renowned publishing houses, stating some very contradictory information; specifically, my grandmother, Romola Nijinsky's book, *Nijinsky*, published in 1937, Chaplin's *Autobiography* in 1964, and Richard Buckle's *Nijinsky* in 1971. Each of them discuss the tour and the famous meeting, and each one is different. Therefore, I chose not to

Nijinsky in America

reprint these stories, but let you decide if you wish to investigate further.

CALIFORNIA, San Francisco – 2 - 8 January 1917 – Valencia Theatre

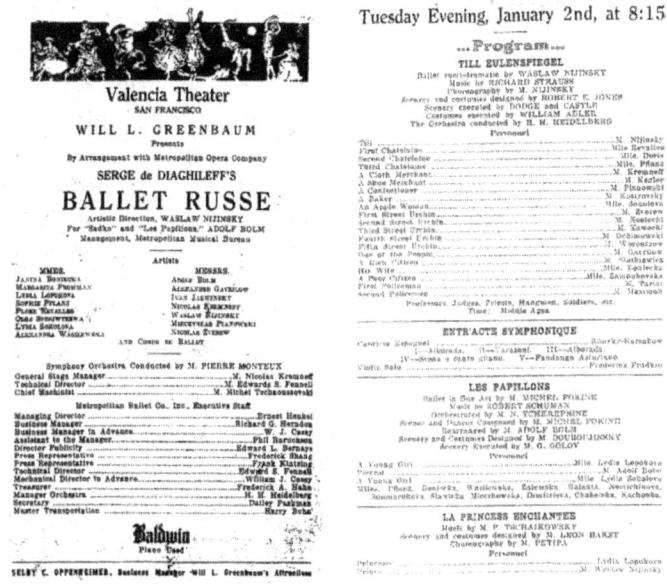

Figure 2.

"I left my heart in San Francisco," so goes the song. But in the case of the Ballet Russes' visit, it was San Franciscans who gave their heart away. The Russians' triumph was so overwhelming that they gave an extra performance as a farewell to San Francisco. What a ride it must have been, traveling north on the Pacific Coast, safely ensconced on the Southern Pacific Railway Lines! If the Russians were pleased with their reception in Los Angeles, they were going to be overjoyed with what San Francisco offered. A city which not only has a Chinatown, but a Russian Hill. Little wonder then, that a number of the troupe would later return to make their home there. You will recall that Monteux, the soldier conductor, was slated to go back to the front, but here is what really happened: at the end of the tour, he was appointed conductor of the Metropolitan Opera in New York. Two years later he took the helm of the Boston Symphony, followed by a return to Europe from 1924 to 1936. In 1936, he came back to the

Nijinsky in America

United States and was named principal conductor of the San Francisco Symphony, a position Monteux held for sixteen years.

"Please fasten your seat belts as we prepare for landing." The voice over the speaker woke the elderly woman from her slumber. She was coming home from a long journey, lecturing about the magic and wonder of the man she was married to for thirty-seven years. Although he had died a long time ago, his spirit and memory was alive; she would make sure of that. She crossed the globe a number of times, talking about him, regaling her audience about the phenomenon of his being. She was grateful for the modern ingenuity of jet travel, which made it so fast and easy to get from one place to the next. San Francisco's breath taking skyline came into view and she chuckled to herself as the memory of another airplane ride popped into her mind:

> In San Francisco, Waslaw discovered a second-hand flying-machine which looked more like an abandoned sewing-machine than anything else. For $2.50 a ride was promised. Waslaw was at once all for the trip. We tried to keep him back, but he had set his heart on it, and, before we had time to realize it, was circling above us. Even with an expert pilot and in a first-class machine, at that time flying was a great risk, but there in these conditions it was tempting the gods...He was enthusiastic and pleased, and explained that it was one of the most glorious, exhilarating feelings one could imagine, and that from the air the world was extremely beautiful. (Romola Nijinsky. *Nijinsky*)

On Valencia and Fourteenth streets stands a building from the last century. It is a museum, dedicated to a German immigrant, clothing manufacturer, who is known for something that is as American as apple pie, the denim jean. In 1853 Levi Strauss opened a business in San Francisco. Across the street is another structure that has been rebuilt and remodeled many times, and which was for decades, and even today, is a church. How appropriate, it used to be a theatre, the Valencia Theatre, where the "god of dance" performed.

> William Greenbaum has to pay a round $25,000 for the services of the Russian ballet before he can pocket a single penny profit. But he has small reason for anxiety. There was not a single vacant seat in the Valencia Theatre last night, and the artistic success of the

The American Tour of the Ballet Rouse

enterprise was so signal that I regard its financial success as a thing assured.

In the first place, Waslaw Nijinsky is as great as his reputation, and that is a rare thing to be able to say of any artist who has been the theme of what afar off, might seem to be an inflated and hyperbolical press agent. We have been told that New York went wild over him and that, until the war broke out, art-loving Europe could talk of nothing else. Having heard these things of other artists and having been disappointed, people preserved an attitude of benevolent skepticism. They were willing to be convinced, even anxious, but one and all of last night's audience were like the man from Missouri - they wanted to be "shown."

It was as Till Eulenspiegel that we had our first glimpse of him. But I think people were more moved by the wonderful music of Strauss and the phantasmagoric perspective of Bakst's [Robert Edmund Jones', not Bakst] mediaeval German city than by the grotesque miming of the Russian artist.

FIDELITY TO ART.

The fact is that we wanted a superb specimen of physical manhood, and, as Till, Mr. Nijinsky masked his muscular endowment. He was the perverse and irresponsible jongleur of the Teutonic middle ages, fantastic, mischievous, and impish. Those who best knew the score and the legend rejoiced; for they saw in the Russian a man who put fidelity to an artistic ideal above vulgar self-exploitation.

We rejoiced in the roguishness of the man; we were touched by hints of pathos; we shuddered at the gallows-like realism of the music and the almost ghoulish verisimilitude of the last grim scene.

But it was in the "Princesse Enchantee," a ballet of which music was written by Tchaikovsky, that Nijinsky revealed himself the man and the artist that people had hoped against hope he would prove himself to be. So complete was his triumph that he might say with the old Roman who bored us so effectually at school: "I came; I saw; I conquered."

Picture to yourself a denizen of the woodland, a sort of glorious savage, with thighs of steel, muscles of grayish ivory, and the natural dignity of a Dionysus, and you have Waslaw Nijinsky as he appeared to us in that forest of living flame painted by Leon Bakst. The man's movements are those of a panther. I thought as I looked at him of

Kipling's Mowgli, and imagined a wolf might have mothered him with her cubs and taught him the lore of the wild beasts.

GENTLE YOUNG SAMPSON.

Yet he was gentle withal and Lydia Lopokova was the enchanting reason why. We seemed to have harked back to the days when brides were won by capture and the loveliest was the prize of the bravest. Here was no dancing faun, half shorn of his manhood by an emasculating art, but a young Samson who might have thrust his arm down the throat of a lion and torn out his heart.

To-night we shall hear Debussy's "Apres Midi d'un Faune," Schumann's "Carnavale," Borodine's "Prince Igor." Not to be there would be a crime against the gods of good taste.

(Mason Redfern, 3 January 1917, *San Francisco Examiner*)

Among critics, the opinion was unanimous, "Nijinsky's success was tremendous. The audience cheered him spontaneously. The perfection of technical skill is reached in his art, and though a tangible person of flesh and bones, he suggests flying even when he is standing still." Walter Anthony had the following recommendation: "I am bold enough to advise you to permit yourself one orgy at the Valencia at least. Go and hear these splashing settings and see the gorgeous music." (3 January 1917, *San Francisco Chronicle*)

CALIFORNIA, Oakland – 9 - 10 January 1917 – Auditorium Opera House

In 1906, Oakland's population nearly doubled the year of the horrific earthquake and consequent fires across the bay in San Francisco. Of about 400,000 residents over 3000 died, and an astounding number, 225,000 lost their homes. Although the city was rebuilt with relative speed, many opted for not tempting fate and moving to Oakland. Mr. Greenbaum was generous enough to underwrite the Ballet Russe in this city too. The *Oakland Tribune* guaranteed that Nijinsky, the "greatest of all terpsichorean stars," along with Lopokova, Revalles, Pflanz, Sokolova, Gavrilow, Bolm and others would appear in both performances. Tickets were on sale "ONLY" at Sherman, Clay & Company. They were priced as usual: orchestra, $5 and $3; balcony (3 rows), $3; balcony (balance), $2; gallery, $, 2 and $1. Above an article by Harry L. Sully, a full figure picture of Waslaw was portrayed in the ballet, "Carneval." Mr. Sully was a man with tremendous artistic insight, providing posterity with a keenly perceived review.

Nijinsky and Lopokova Weave Magic at Civic Auditorium

To one sitting, listening to music, there comes a moment when the outlines of the theater, the faces of people and the leader with his moving baton fade, are gone. Visions called into being by music shape a real, unreal world. Fantastic colors and lights are there, moving and changing. Sculptured forms endowed with rhythmic life drift with ever-flowing current of sound. Music builds dream architecture - sweeping Gothic curves and arches rising and growing with a pulse and moving symmetry of their own.

The music stops. The visions fade. Forms resume their normal aspect. It is of this dream magic that the dance poems of the Russian Ballet are created. Music is the soul of the vision. The spectacle presented by the Russian artists is its vesture of flesh and blood.

...[the] Ballet Russe...is an evolution of the dance away from the artificial posturing of the Old Italian and French schools toward an imaginative and creative miming, in which painting, drama in motion and dancing image forth the inner meaning of the music.

SENSES MESMERIZED

Nijinsky in America

This union of the arts has an almost hypnotic effect upon the senses. Splash raw color, vivified by light, across the great canvas framed by the proscenium arch - using hot reds, cold, vibrant blues and shrill green - and you get an effect which takes the senses by storm. Such combination in so intense a tone must either send you fleeing from the theater or, as they are handled by Leon Bakst, mesmerize you into helpless wonder and admiration.

The glowing figures which move against his vivid background, clad in garments which are colorfully at one with their surroundings, hold us at will under their spell. The extraordinary triumph of these artists in the capitals of Europe is no longer a matter of surprise. The wonder is that there are many who have withstood the spell.

I sing the glory of Nijinsky, a glory that has been well sung before. He appeared unto us last night first as the prankish spirit of fanciful irony, Till Eulenspiegel, Till Owl glass, the German folk Puck.

COLOR MEDIEVAL

In this setting of the free symphonic tone poem of Richard Strauss, greatest of the moderns in Germany, Nijinsky was a thing of flame and fancy, a dizzy personality, blazing and audacious - a whimsical creature, half human, half devil, almost at moments touched with the humor of the Osgard of Olympian gods. What a wonder world of medieval color and costume Robert E. Jones, the young American artist, who designed the scenery and garments for this ballet, has placed upon the stage. It is an evocation of all that was fantastic and gorgeous about this extraordinary period of the middle ages, when a race, still in its unruly childhood, was going through the experience of readjustment to a rebirth.

The towering headgear of the women, the great flounces and stunning colors, the tortuously long trains - all the grotesquerie of the period has been crammed into this German folk tale setting, with Till's gargoyle face leering and leaping in its midst.

It is the Strauss conceptions to the last speak of poor Till, gibbeted and apotheosized to make Ballet Russe. Nijinsky is its center and spirit, giving life and unity to the whole.

WILD RHYTHMIC GRACE

But it is in La Princess Enchantee that the opportunity is given for a full appreciation of Nijinsky's art. Jean Cocteau said of Nijinsky, speaking of the aerial quality of his dancing, "Apollo holds the string by which he is suspended."

The American Tour of the Ballet Rouse

To me not Apollo, but the wild Dionysus, comes as the fitting symbol of this creature genius in moving sculpture. Not the Latinized and civilized Bacchus, worshiped of women and with vine leaves in his hair, but the primitive Thracian deity, born of fire and dew, whose life was filled with a wild music and a wild rhythm, is the archetype I seek for the dancer. He is a barbaric Dionysus of the steppes…"There is all through Greek history…a struggle between the palpable and limited human form, and the floating essence it contains."

Nijinsky is the very vortex of such a struggle. He is a thing of disciplined and suppressed violence. The essence within him is always at boiling point, and he walks with a certain violent grace, as though at any moment he might tear himself from the earth and go swinging in great electric, darting curves, through the air.

Not even the beloved Lydia Lopokova won so furious applause as her partner in this dithyrambic dance.

OREGON, Portland – 12 - 13 January 1917 – Heilig Theatre

Portland, named after Portland, Maine because of a coin toss won by Francis W. Pettygrove, had a population of 90,000 at the turn of the century, and in ten years grew to an incredible 207,000. Had Asa L. Lovejoy, the other land developer won the toss, today we would call this Oregon city by the name of Lovejoy's home town of Boston!

For the relatively cool preview given about the Ballet Russe, the review was astounding. Having arrived to our 31st city on the tour, it is truly amazing how critics found new words to describe what they saw. They spoke of being "enthralled," "wrapped in wonder spell," an "acme of colorful beauty," and of "music of motion perfect."

> Music of faces and music of wonderful bodies, music of muscle and music of brain stirred and pulsated deep in our consciousness and sung or sobbed in our hearts like wind in the trees, under the spell of the Russian magicians...Joy of life and glory of existence, mystery of love and beauty of the human body they expressed for us in dances that men and women danced thousands of years ago. Wide open they flung for us the door closed years ago on youthful dream fancies and ideals. They gave us food to think on. They gave us of substance, not shadow. Watching these Russian magicians we forget for three golden, glory hours our more or less undressed male and female physical selves.
>
> We ceased wondering how on earth the so-and-sos could afford to be among those present, and we nailed our grosser selves and our neighbors' grosser selves upon a cross and the theater walls faded into nothingness, and our spirits, which someone has said Thank-God-can-brake-all-natural-laws, crept through sweet spaces into the presences on the stage and danced with them and youth incarnate in the lovely forest of imagination. We caught the smell of green woods, of deep, drooping cypress trees, of swaying flowers, the bird song, and we laughed and danced and sung and loved and lived with these Blessed Barbarians from the land where the East and West touch, hand and brow.
>
> As an expression of life's harmony and its splendor the artistry of these dancers from the land of the Czar is perfect. There is no emotion they did not express for us in the music of their feet, and hands and limbs and eyes and lips. Laughter echoed in our hearts,

and terror flooded our souls at the bidding of their mood. Into the depths, with tear-shrouded eyes, or soaring joyous into such height as we never dreamed, they flung us. (Leone Cass Baer, *Morning Oregonian*, 13 January 1917)

What more can be said?

BRITISH COLUMBIA, Vancouver – 15 January 1917 – Vancouver Opera House

Due to the political red tape mentioned earlier, the Ballet Russe had to leave American soil, only to turn around and enter the country legally once again. And so, the opportunity was afforded

The American Tour of the Ballet Rouse

them to have a one night stand in Vancouver, Canada. The scenery along the way was certainly splendid and their reception by Vancouverites no less so.

Like so many of the Western States in the United States., the Canadian Pacific Railroad's opening helped Vancouver to become a boom town. Its location on the Pacific Coast was the other important factor, making it the fastest growing city in Canada at the turn of the century. The opening of the Panama Canal in 1914 proved to be an added bonus. Population, then about 86,000, doubled in five short years.

The Sunday edition of the *Vancouver Daily Sun* featured a large add for the evening's performance, with an 8:30 curtain time; along side of it, two photographs of Flore Revalles and an entertaining article with a different approach. The journalist described Revalles' costume for "Cleopatra," which consisted of about 200 yards of material wound around her. As the ballet progressed, two dancers dressed as Negro slaves, marching in opposite directions, unwound most of the material. Revalles' body was painted and covered with gold and bronze powder, making it difficult to tell how much of the costume left on her was fabric and what was flesh. No wonder throughout the tour, critics found this one of the most sensuous ballet in the program. An interview followed and the newspaperman discovered that Revalles, born in Geneva, Switzerland, felt very much at home among Vancouver's stately mountains... She also permitted the "lucky" journalist to touch her pet alligator, replacing a snake, which, after attacking its mistress was banished to a Boston zoo.

Waslaw was also presented in a favorable light.

The greater the artist - the more approachable. How many times have I wondered what I should say to Nijinsky when he came to Vancouver? Imagine the feelings of a newspaperman up against a dancer who has learned what it means to have kings and queens and emperors offer their congratulations and fire at him a few every day questions. I didn't attempt it. In the first place, I didn't speak Russian and Nijinsky knows little or no English, so I sought the good offices of his manager and found out by his interpretation that Nijinsky had danced since he was four years old...

Nijinsky in America

> When shown the stage he was to dance on, Nijinsky immediately demanded to know why he had not been advised as to the size of the stage and at once ordered that Cleopatra should be staged in place of Les Sylphides as this was the largest stage they had played on since leaving Philadelphia. Cleopatra is the largest ballet produced on their tour and word was at once given out to the whole company for a rehearsal at 12 o'clock today...
>
> ---------------------
>
> ...Cleopatra is considered the most important work in the repertoire. (H. C., *The Vancouver Daily Sun*, 15 January 1917)

Earlier in the month, 1 January as a matter of fact, another "clothing" article appeared along side a picture of Waslaw and Lopokova in "Le Spectre de la Rose." Today's emancipated woman would not likely to find this clever article, humorous.

> The Master of the House and the Boudoir Robe
>
> For the man who is particular about appearance of the nymph who pours his coffee.
>
> ...a nymph will appear in "L'Apres Midi D'un Faune," in a Grecian garment that bids fair to put the kimono out of business...It is of white silk, with designs quite unique...
>
> Now there has been for some time deep discontent on the part of the Man of the House towards the kimono. This garment came in along with Japanese prints and...other Oriental treasures. It was such a time saver that the mistress of the house was always tempted to slide into it, instead of a more complicated garb. Consequently her husband has been served with kimono three times a day. Instead of getting a housekeeper in the trim and dainty little morning frocks he used to glimpse in his courting days, ha had a companion whose daily garb is a cross between a nightgown and a chorister's robes. The last thing he saw in the morning was his wife's kimono sleeve perilously near dangling in her coffee. The last thing he saw at night was his wife getting out of her street garb and into something loose which invariably was a kimono.
>
> Wouldn't it be a relief to him if he should sit across the table from a Grecian nymph? Wouldn't it be a pleasant chance? And since he is the one who has to suffer, shouldn't he be allowed a vote in at least one portion of his wife's wardrobe? Moreover, when he attends "L'Apres Midi D'un Faune," . . . he will have opportunity to make a

The American Tour of the Ballet Rouse

choice of the nymph he would like to have pour his coffee of a morning. For there are a number of nymphs in any number of robes. (1 January 1917, *The Vancouver Sun*)

WASHINGTON, Seattle – 16 - 17 January 1917 – Moore Theatre

Figure 3.

Stay in the heart of downtown Seattle next to Pike Place Market in the Moore Hotel's newly renovated large rooms, where you will find comfort and security at economical rates. You may choose from suites, kitchenettes, senior citizen, and group, corporate and special weekly rates. Available also are meeting accommodations for up to 1,200, with lounge, catering, and 24 hour dining, dancing music, nearby. It is an inviting offer in a part of town that after years of a transient population and seedy bars is now experiencing an upswing and redevelopment, with trendy shops and good restaurants moving in.

Also, don't forget the supper dances at the Washington Hotel; music every evening under the direction of Misha Guterson, leader of the famous Russian Orchestra. You may easily get there by calling the Blue Taxi Company. Can't dance? Guaranteed dancing in 1 or 2 lessons, taught all day and evening the year around, including the newest walk dances. If you can walk, Mr. Stevens will guarantee to teach you to dance. Or perhaps you'd rather be an observer, well then; Seattle's leading playhouse, thoroughly fireproof, owned by the Washington Hotel & Improvement Company is the place for you.

The American Tour of the Ballet Rouse

For three performances only, arranged by J. W. Sayre, you may revel in the incomparable dancing of the Russians.

The first paragraph above deals with Seattle of the 1990's; it is separated by some eighty years from the passage that follows it. The building and the Moore Theatre, where the Russians triumphed so long ago, are still standing. In those days, the corner of 2nd Avenue and Virginia was the place where high society mingled with high and low brows, with only one thing in mind, to see the Russians in person. Not everyone had $5 to get a seat in the "Soup and Fish" downstairs, but perhaps that was their good fortune.

The people who wore the "soup and fish" costumes downstairs at the Ballet Russe may think that they had the best of it; but they didn't. That was for the "high-in-heaven-thundering gods."

In the first place, it was a very select audience up there in the gallery. Not to mention names - there was the head of the fine arts department at the university and a psychologist who could give the mathematical formulae for harmony of lights and movements, which made so pleasing a stimulus to the nerves of sight and hearing.

There was an etcher whom Seattle recognizes as one of her most accomplished sons, and a young writer who can use more "amber words" per sentence than anyone else in Seattle; not to mention a few recognized from seeing their names in the "society" columns and who were admitted to the circle of the gallery's elect only because they could not get seats downstairs.

In the second place, there is the authority of Lydia Lopokova herself that the gallery is the place from which to see a ballet, because "the performers in front do not mask those behind so you cannot see them," said the famous dancer. "You get a much better impression of the ensemble."

Of course, this may merely be Miss Lopokova's courtesy trying to console the "gallery gods" because they have to sit so far from her twinkling toes, but anyhow, she said it at the New Washington Hotel last night while dining after the play.

Lessons in Russian

Between the acts, many of the "gods" left their Olympian seats and gathered in the little hallway. There were a number of Russians in the gathering - men who had come over from Vladi-Vostok in the steerage perhaps, but who had seen the ballet at Petrograd and Moscow since their kindergarten days. Some of them confessed to be exiles.

The Germans, these compatriots of Lopokova and Nijinsky explained, had not been content with trying to tear province after province away from Holy Russia; but they had so misspelled Russian names that no Englishman could pronounce them. The pronunciation is really very easy, according to them, when the names are spelled correctly.

For instance, under German influence, all the "vs." in the names have been changed to "w" in American programs. The double "f" at the end of a number of names should also be pronounced as an English "v,"...the "ie"...should be pronounced simply as a long "e" as should the letter "i"...

The spirit of Russian art, the effect of the war on the ballet - these and many other things were discussed in the "varsity box" last night; but of course there may be un-aspiring souls who prefer remaining in blissful ignorance to climbing the unending flights of steps which lead to "heaven."

There was one advantage the "soup and fish" costumed folk had over the gallery gods. Some few of them were at the Hotel New

The American Tour of the Ballet Rouse

Washington when the little butterfly that flitted like incarnate music . . . had become again simply Lydia Lopokova, the little "lass with the delicate air," dining daintily before tumbling into bed to rest for her next performance.

Misses Her Mother

You would have thought her very like your own daughter or sister, if you could have heard her say wistfully, "I am not exactly homesick, but very often I wish to see my mother." [Waslaw suffered from the same malaise.] A letter had come from that mother in far-off Petrograd just before the performance. It had been three months on the way, owing to war-time delays...

The same wistfulness appeared again when she was telling of the splendid and broad cultural training in the Imperial ballet school..."It is a long way from here." She has been in America now five years.

At one time she pointed to the name of a popular beverage of this state, and asked what it was. When one of her dinner companions explained that it was a "near beer," she replied, "I do not like anything 'near.'"...(Perhaps that explains why she is)...not content to be "nearly" a dancer. (18 January 1917, *The Seattle Daily Times*)

Seattle Post-Intelligencer's Cyril Arthur Player was completely enthralled by the "transcendent art" of the Russians.

Faded away the wrangling street; faded away the clattering footsteps of the throng; faded away the theatre trappings and familiar faces, which terraced the Moore last night from orchestra to gallery door; reigned only there the dream music of that throbbing orchestra, swelling up in glorious ecstasy of echoing appeal; clanging in magnificent spectacle, sinking into delicate whisperings which trembled like leaves at the gentle waiving of a tree, floated through away to the stars and became a memory.

Not a word was spoken; not a note was sung; yet the spirit was filled with sweet pictures, ardent outreaching, soul-swaying passions, dainty, fragile, pastorals and wondrous mosaics...oh that a critic should live to admit it - is even what has been said of it (the Ballet Russe.)

Its story is in the imagination, for words fail and pencil falters.

Art supreme; wonderful, lithe, graceful beings; sprites of the air; melting into colors and then mounting on the wings of music; sinking into dulcet reverie; roaring on the wings riotous bacchanalias. What an evening to describe!

...

Nijinsky, as the spirit of the rose, selected this fragile bit with consummate taste. The final leap, following his abundant grace, his matchless technique and poetic expressiveness, held the house spellbound for a matter of seconds, until the audience came to itself and made the big theatre resound with applause...

The following day, Mr. Player continued to pay homage:

Nijinsky Is Star of Evening in Splendid Show of Genius

To all of those who had eyes to see and ears to hear...the Ballet Russe...opened new doors into the infinite, new vistas through the Garden of the Spirit. It is as if we have entered into another chamber whose walls await great masterpieces of the future.

Last night saw Waslaw Nijinsky at his best and greatest. It was the pinnacle of the engagement...

Nijinsky clothed remarkable feats of skill in as remarkable a beauty. Without a mask, and suitably costumed, his distinguished manly beauty and strength, exceeding grace and agility of motions, rare artistic sense of poise between music and the dance, himself and the atmosphere, was easily apparent and Nijinsky proved in a short ten minutes that he is the great male dancer of his age. In truth, he danced as though inspired, with a positive genius for rhythm and a heart-whole abandonment to his part which went right home to the audience. Little wonder that again and again and again, a full dozen times in all, they brought him to the footlights. Not mere up-and-down curtain calls, but demands that rang from gallery to orchestra. And then whenever Lopokova, who shared equally, it seems, the affection of the audience, he consented to repeat the beautiful number, the audience broke into an ovation which carried the wonderful pair clean through the dance and off again.

A critic from the *Seattle Daily Times* agreed wholeheartedly, even if his numbers were a bit different.

Last night's Ballet Russe concluding program before a very large audience at The Moore was incomparably better than either of the other two bills. The Tuesday bill proved the extraordinary merit of the . . . organization, but had the Wednesday ballets been danced the

The American Tour of the Ballet Rouse

first night, it may readily be believed that hundreds would have been turned away from the Moore Theatre last night.

An instance of the popularity of the final offerings was the reception accorded "La Princess Enchantee." Danced without the corps de ballet by Nijinsky and Lopokova, it proved the best-liked of the whole series of nine ballets accorded Seattle, and was given nine curtain calls. After the ninth curtain the two stars succumbed and repeated much of the dance...

Nijinsky's Great Work

Compared with what he did last night, Nijinsky really did not show himself in the full degree of his powers the opening evening. Last night after his wonderful contributions to "La Princess Enchantee" and "Carnaval," not a soul in the house would have disputed the claim made for him that he is the world's greatest male dancer. The Mikhail Mordkin of six seasons ago in no sense surpassed the Nijinsky of last night.

It was Nijinsky who made the evening memorable...

So far you have read what Seattle's two leading papers had to say immediately following the performances. Now let us hear from an opposing view, keeping in mind that the article appeared on the 27th, by which time the Russians were enjoying a well earned respite in Chicago. Furthermore, the feature you are about to peruse was in a paper which no longer exists; the other two however, even today, are the leading papers of Seattle.

Russian Dancing

By I. Newton Greene

I probably shall be taken for a barbarian by those who read this. They will, no doubt, consider me as one who lacks artistic temperament; as one possessing imagination densely surrounded by coma, incapable of being awakened until friend Gabriel honks his horn. Nevertheless, the fact remains that I did not appreciate, to a point of enjoyment, the Russian ballet given at the Moore.

I gathered information from my program that I had the honor of witnessing classic dancing, and possibly the proper programs were circulated, though mistakes will happen. In the first place I could not restrain a feeling of compassion for those movies in the filmy fabrics; for, dressed to withstand the rigors of winter as I was, I felt none too

Nijinsky in America

warm, even though I found myself somewhat heated about the five pieces of silver extracted from me by curiosity and alluring publicity notices.

That battery of Russian dancers, I thought, viewing them with alarm, placed before the advancing Prussian column, would terminate the present engagement in one theatre of European war, or I am a poor military observer; and personally I am neutral. The art of armed conflict largely lies in keeping the other side guessing, which latter position I occupied while vainly endeavoring to decipher the cubist movements of the oversea prancers. One moment I thought someone on the stage had a friend in the scene loft toward which she occasionally unwound a powdered arm. Again the thought came that a company member discovered one of those new ten-cent pieces on the floor, toward which she yearningly swooped, stopping slightly short of the mark, as though fearing to fracture her gossamer draperies. Of course all this sounds foolish, which is exactly the way it appeared to me.

Why anyone should divorce himself or herself from five perfectly good dollars to watch grown-up women blow soap bubbles is beyond my comprehension, when one may buy a clay pipe and a bar of soap and personally settle down to the frothy occupation in one's own domicile.

As the Russian ballet impotently reached out for something they could not attain, a feeling of fellowship swept over me, because I, too, have reached - in a different manner - nor did I charge people five portraits of the Goddess of Liberty to view my futile efforts.

Willingly would I have exchanged places with Cleopatra, for I was tired by that time and her couch looked more comfortable than my opera chair felt. Cleopatra, by the way, seemed to suffer with her neck - Charley-horse, perhaps - and I noted how she frequently wiggled her head foundation as though to make sure it was in gear. I heard an uncouth man sitting near me ask his neighbor who the reclining dame might be, and when told she was the Lady of the Nile, the questioner remarked how glad he was to meet her, because she happened to be the first Nihilist he ever saw, although he'd read of them. This man's five plunks were not entirely wasted, as he had learned something.

After all is said and done, it is a human trait to attempt covering up when we are a trifle shy on a subject. I believe there were many like myself in the Moore. I base this belief on observations made during

The American Tour of the Ballet Rouse

two twenty-minute intermissions, when the orchestra appeared to be on strike, told another and equally interesting story. "What's the idea?" was a simple translation of many facial expressions during the dancing.

Do you suppose if the dance had been English instead of Russian that the solution would have been easier? A majority recognized class when the gentleman kicked high "C"; but I doubt if many would admit that all save the high kicking went over their heads. (27 Jan. 1917, *The Town Crier*)

WASHINGTON, Tacoma – 18 January 1917 – Tacoma Theater

Now given Mr. Greene's views, let us see what Tacomans had to say. Located a mere twenty-eight miles south of Seattle, one might think that those interested in the Ballet Russe would have simply traveled the distance, perhaps some did, we shall soon find out. Tacoma however, had a beautiful theatre, more splendid than that of Seattle, and her citizens brought about their very own performance by the Russians. Tacoma Theater opened on 13 January 1890. It had a capacity to seat 1,300, which was later increased to 1,800. The stage measured 55' x 42', 55' to the loft. It was known as the Broadway Theater in the 1920s (being located at 902-14 Broadway), and from 1933, the name was changed to Music Box Theater. Unfortunately, fire destroyed the building on 30 April, 1963. [Information received from Jean Gillmer, Tacoma Library.]

About a week before the single performance Tacomans were to see, an interesting bit of trivia appeared about Flore Revalles, along with her photograph, in the *Tacoma Sunday News-Ledger*. Revalles declared that she was "fond of the United States," and had a desire to become a naturalized citizen. The entertaining part of the article was how Leon Bakst had discovered her.

> About three years ago, Leon Bakst, artist extraordinary of the Serge de Diaghileff Ballet Russe, happened to attend a performance of "La Tosca" at l'Opera de Geneve. As M. Bakst is a Russian artist and not an American social constellation, he was in his seat before the curtain rose. And so he saw the first entrance of La Tosca.

Must have been an American trait to be late for curtain time. Fortunately for artists, most halls these days do not seat after the curtain rises. The article continues:

> Perhaps it is well to recall at this point that three years ago Bakst was already recognized in Europe as the ultimate genius of modern stage decoration. An entire continent was still discussing with wonder his exotic backgrounds for the shifting figures of the Diaghileff mimes and dancers. In short, at that moment Bakst was not an artist with vague notions and vaguer hopes. He was recognized master of a new art. Therefore, there was more than a passing significance in the remark he made as he sat with his eyes fastened on the Prima Donna who stepped on the stage as La Tosca. "Ah," he cried to the dancer

The American Tour of the Ballet Rouse

who was with him, "now I can design costumes." Then he looked at his program and found this: "La Tosca, Mlle. Flore Revalles." And that is how Mlle. Revalles became the leading feminine pantomime artist of the Serge de Diaghileff Ballet Russe, which comes to the Tacoma Theater January 18 with the symphony orchestra...

Revalles was a French opera singer, tall and with an imposing figure, that was enough to hire her as a mime for the Ballet Russe. This explains why in some cities, the Russians were advertised not only as a ballet company, but mime too.

Five days before the engagement, a free recital was given in the Temple of Music, by the Hopper-Kelly Talking Machine Company. Talk about an advertising coup! One could hear Rimsky-Korsakow's "Scheherazade," recorded by the Ballet Russe Orchestra, as a "teaser," for the actually performance. Some other offerings that evening were a banjo and an accordion solo, a solo by a soprano, a tenor and a bass, a French duet, an American march played by the New York Military Band and a highly racist titled piece: "2. Colored Specialty, 'It's Too Late Now' ... Von Bilzer, Arthur Collins and Byron G. Harlan." The Tacoma Sunday News-Ledger dedicated a large portion of its entertainment page to show photographs of a number of artists, including Waslaw in "Le Spectre de la Rose," along with the synopsis of the ballets to bee seen. The critic had obviously been to either the Seattle or Portland performance and stated that Waslaw, in the role of the

> ...Spectre clad in rose petals with the smile of the night on his face, with eyes shining like stars. It seemed a full moment before this figure alighted at the front of the stage, resting as thistledown might after being blown about by soft winds. It was the most extraordinary expression of ballet dancing I believe I ever witnessed. After a moment's hush the entire audience, thousands of people, broke into wild applause. This man, Nijinsky, had stirred the emotions. He had brought us, in this one great gesture across the stage, memories of rose gardens, tender recollections of subtle perfume, moonlight; he had brought the atmosphere of fairyland into the Bakst room. (14 Jan. 1917).

Tacomans, it seems, were a discerning audience with a mature artistic taste, demonstrated not only by their theater building, but by their response to the Ballet Russe, many of whom did attend the Seattle performances.

> Art---the graceful, delicate, refined art of Waslaw Nijinsky and of Mlle. Lydia Lopokova-and not the blare of Bakst's exotic coloring, made memorable the first appearance in Tacoma last night of the...Ballet Russe. Aside from the expressions of adoration that were heard on every hand for the master of all male dancers and his sweet-faced, sparkling-eyed companion of "Le Spectre de la Rose," which undoubtedly was the triumph of the evening, it was the orchestra, not the much discussed color riot of scenic designer, that was the cause of happy comment as the big audience left the theater. In passing, it should be said that the audience was undoubtedly the most brilliant, socially, of the year. That it was a delighted audience, there can be no doubt, but it was not one stunned or overwhelmed as it had prepared to be...Half dozen curtain calls for Nijinsky and Lopokova told the story of where the enthusiasm of the evening was bestowed...[Le Spectre] brought out clearly the superlative qualities of his [Nijinsky's] dancing-a lightness that never loses masculinity, a grace that seems in conformity rather than in contrast to his sturdy physique and a refinement of characterization as notable as his poise. And with what sheer abandon he leaps! It is to be taken for granted that it is a very different Nijinsky that is seen in the more purely Russian numbers, but one who has seen him once will believe readily that Nijinsky's art will be refined in whatever he seeks to characterize.
>
> ...
>
> Flora Revalles, as has been said repeatedly before, was "grace in angles." She did not really dance at all, but her postures and her expressive though immobile countenance were eloquent with the spirit of what the drama portrayed.

This certainly is a different perspective from that of Mr. Greene in Seattle.

The Tacoma Daily News' review, though brief, was also generous with its praises:

> SLAV DANCERS WIN HEARTY APPLAUSE
>
> Orchestra a Delight under the Baton of Monteux...
>
> Waslaw Nijinsky appeared for a few short moments, and his memory remains as a breath of the rose he personified. His one

The American Tour of the Ballet Rouse

appearance...was the triumph of the evening, and the two dancers [Lopokova] bowed to a storm of curtain calls...

WASHINGTON, Spokane – 19 - 20 January 1917 – Auditorium

The second largest city in Washington State, Spokane was important and grew as rapidly in population as all the other Northwestern cities of the time. Located on the Eastern border of Washington and just 15 miles west of the Idaho border, this was the final stop before the Russians returned to the Midwest and then the East Coast.

The critiques and reviews about the Ballet Russe had so far ranged from formal examination, to social commentary, to theorizing, to rumination, summation and speculation. The following essay does all that and more. It gives the reader a clearer description of what the audience actually saw on stage and an insight into what they might have felt. It is so ingeniously written that one is virtually transported to that performance on the 19th of January, infused with the excitement of the occasion.

> The advance notices of the Ballet Russe have given the theatergoer an idea of artistic and bizarre arrangements of ballets designed by a fellow named Bakst, and danced by a press agented person called Nijinsky. Exotic and erratic are other mental associations with the term. After seeing last evening's performance at the Auditorium the Ballet Russe will signify beauty to those who were fortunate enough to see it; beauty in every varied meaning of the word, beauty of sound, motion and color.
>
> The lobby benches were filled with people waiting for gallery seats and the program sellers were calling out loudly: "Illustrated program! Must have one if you are to understand the performance." Fully to understand the performance the scores of several operas and membership in an archeological society are needed, also a wide acquaintance with the novels of the Russian authors and a thorough knowledge of the tints of the color cards of the last three seasons.
>
> The theater was filled with scent of sandalwood. The orchestra, which occupied the orchestra's reserved space and the boxes and the first few rows of seats, was a sleek foreign looking aggregation of musicians who looked over the audience critically as if they were trying to see some faint family likeness between the Spokane audience and the Diamond horseshoe of the Metropolitan.
>
> Most of the groups were family parties, father and mother and the girls. The debutantes were there in their light party cloaks and the

The American Tour of the Ballet Rouse

older women in furs. The eagerness of anticipation was interfered with occasionally by the request of the usher to "let the lady in, please," and the whispered warnings of the people behind who were always announcing - "hush, they are beginning." The husbands whose wives were out of town enjoyed their freedom by appearing in business clothes. There were coos of the lady who "just loves Chopin," and who was so glad they were going to dance "Les Sylpilides," who wrestled bravely with the Russian names on the program; thought it was "Nijinsky," and was glad she was going to see "Coco Kola" again. "Chowsoakski" was a favorite composer of hers also.

The people in the audience are always interesting, and last night there was a beautiful brunette with pearls and a hat. A man said it was her beauty, but a woman declared it was her hat that was so attractive to look upon. There was a lady whom one romantic soul thought had lived much, judging by the tint of her hair and again another lady suggested the color of the tresses was due to a wrong wash.

Pale words came from behind the panorama of Yellowstone National Park on the curtain and the man at the left of the orchestra, who played bass viol, rapped for silence on the stage apron. The curtain rose.

It was the same Auditorium stage whereon often Spokane folk have gazed, but it did not seem the same place, for a Fragonard wood, a Watteau scene, was there with a little domed and pillared temple of love in the back, and arching skyward the leaves of a wooded park. They were Bakst leaves and almost a peacock blue.

In the park were a pair of lovers and around them and on each side were rows of girls. Ballet girls of the time of Fannie Ellsler or Taglioni with white tulle skirts well below the knee and tight fitting bodices of the style of the late 50s. Their coiffures were like those of the Victorian epoch, smooth and parted, with wreaths of forget-me-nots banding them.

The lovers were Mlle. Lydia Lopokova and Waslaw Nijinsky. She was in white, was wreathed with rosebuds, and he was a poet in white silk hose and tunic of black velvet. His curls were the looks of the poet of romance and in every moment he was the dreamy creature of dreams and sighs. The whole number was the acme of ballet dancing, as if the company would first show the audience that in the technique of the formal ballet they were without peer. The girls danced as primly and as archly as boarding school misses, dead and become tarleton clad angels pirouetting among the glades of paradise. They twittered on their toes and swung around with skirts stiffly outstanding.

Nijinsky's balloon style is marvelous. In every movement he had the right note of affectation the fantasy demanded and he was as artistically artificial as he should have been.

Lydia Lopokova was as artless and easy in all her difficult steps as if she were a little girl romping with sunbeams in an old garden.

Sokolova danced the prelude and Mlle. Alexandra Wasilewska the valse in that number. The curtain fell after the finale, with much applause.

Les Sylphides was the primer of the evening's course of entertainment. Simple, child-like and easily understood. It was charming but not intricate and while it engaged the admiration of the audience it was not a thrill-full portion of the program.

"Cleopatre" is more than a "Choreographic Drama," it is a dance; it is a sermon, a symbol and a tragedy. Also it is of a beauty and intricacy not to be told. The curtain rises on the columns of an Egyptian temple, the temple of Karnak of the old school geographies, but instead of grey stone the pillars are a deep scarlet and between the pillars is the glimpse of a turquoise and tan desert. Whatever color combinations Bakst achieves, the memory of his scenes always brings that thought of gold. In the set for Cleopatre, in the costumes and the back ground, despite the flaming pillars, gold was the light and gold the loudest note in the color symphony he composed.

There is the scene first between Tahor, Mlle. Lydia Lopokova, and her lover, the archer of the desert, Amoun. Her postures are those of the ladies in the hieroglyphics, yet instead of seeming stiff, it is as if the ancient Egyptian manner was the most modern, and so real is the whole drama that the centuries fall away, and all the glory and lure of ancient Egypt is revived. The lovers' dance, a most marvelous example of the suppleness and grace of their art. The costume of Amoun is of black and orange stripes, with barbaric jewels on his breast, and his humble love is in black and gold.

There is the savage pomp of the entry of Cleopatre and the audience is breathless as, after the high priest, come the bacchantes in their soft tinted robes. The Grecian men, the Egyptian men in the capes designed after the old drawings, and the women in colors richly dull beyond all description; after the whole procession finally arrives

The American Tour of the Ballet Rouse

Cleopatre wrapped like a mummy. She is in a palanquin of black and gold and her feet in high gold lacquered clogs. She is lifted out and set upright. She is unwrapped, veil after veil being removed and revealing Revalles in a clinging gold and black robe with a wig powdered with gold on her head and on her face the inscrutable lure of the sphinx. She crouches on the tiger skin of her couch and Amoun, who all the time has been watching her, struggles with his better self, his love for Thor. He asks of the enchantress love, even if it means his death. It is the old allegory, the story that movie fans know by heart, the age old plot of the wages of sin, etc. Circe and the Vampire.

It is decked and garlanded with dances of the bacchantes and a dance of veils. It is strewn with rose leaves and woven into a tapestry of loveliness that bewilders; it is so intricate in color and design.

When the revel is at its height the high priest approaches, the poisoned cup in his hand.

Cleopatre gives it to her lover, who falls dead. Exeunt the queen and her train. Little true love in the form of Tamor comes questing, after the Sin has left Amoun. Among the roses in the courts of death she finds her beloved. She dies too.

La Princesse Enchantee is portrayed by Lopokova. A dream tropic island of red palm trees, with wide leaves spreading over a bay of midnight blue, is the setting and the scene was so beautiful that the audience applauded it before the fairy inhabitants appeared. Nijinsky was gorgeous in a tari costume studded with turquoise and gold. Lopokova looked like a tropic bird in her mauve dress, with green and gold brocade and a head dress of seed pearls on her hair. It was an enchanted island and only folk like Nijinsky and she could have danced there, so magical were their pirouetting, their leaps and their swaying. They seemed as unreal as the scene.

And finally, so that you may get the "feel" for the ballets truly Russian number, a description of Prince Igor:

> The last number was Prince Igor, "Polovetsien Dances," as the program called them, were the feature. The number was the spirit of the steppes done into color and dancing. The scene showed wide flat hills in the background and the squat Tartar tents. The curling smoke from the campfire was in dim tans and blues. In contrast to the semi-nudity of the other dances the girls were covered to their wrists in soft silk peasant frocks of Bakst's own imaginings. The men were in

barbaric reds and browns, and carried bows. The dancing was wild beyond words. It was as if all the spirits of all the tribes that had wandered since the dawn of history, from that vast northern country, were holding high carnival in some dream world. When the curtain fell at the last the audience came to with an audible effort.

And all the way out might heard people scheming to rob the butcher or the baker in order to find money to see the dancers again tonight. (20 January 1917, *The Spokesman-Review*)

MINNESOTA, Saint Paul – 23 January 1917 – Auditorium

This book was based on my grandmother Romola's handwritten itinerary, as she accompanied Waslaw on the tour. According to her notes, 21 - 22 January was a lay-off period for the ballet in St. Paul. Lord knows they needed a rest! But in reality, they had to make their way from Spokane, Washington to St. Paul, Minnesota, crossing Idaho, Montana, and North Dakota and then to the eastern border of Minnesota, in the dead of winter; at a time when the weather is not at its optimum in that part of America; actually, it can be down right nasty! Not surprisingly, they were delayed and barely arrived for the performance, due to a number of complications, the least of which was the weather, or was it? As a matter of fact, the St. Paul engagement seemed to be riddled with problems. Let's look at them one at a time.

The *St. Paul Dispatch* reported that the Russians "rumbled in" at 2 P.M. on the day of the performance, 23 Janurary. They left Spokane 20 Janurary, at midnight, presumably right after the performance, traveling on the Northern Pacific railroad. At Mandan, North Dakota a "truck on one of the baggage cars broke," delaying the troupe. Allegedly, some of the baggage was sent ahead and was being unloaded by the time the troupe arrived. According to the review the day after the performance however, the train was late because of a snowstorm, causing a poor performance, but we'll get back to that later.

Other mishaps were more of a personal nature. On 21 January, The *Saint Paul Pioneer Press* reported the following juicy news:

> R. Barrocchi, husband of Lydia Lopokova and one of the managers of the Russian ballet...has retained H. D. Frankel, St. Paul attorney, as his mouthpiece in discussions of his reported matrimonial troubles.
>
> The ballet manager is accused of bigamy by Mrs. R. Barrocchi, a London woman. Barrochi has denied being married to her.
>
> Mr. Frankel will meet his client in Grand Forks, North Dakota, today and will return with him to St. Paul tomorrow.

Nijinsky in America

Does that mean that on 21 January the troupe was already in Grand Forks? The following day, the *St. Paul Dispatch* mentions Frankel in an unrelated matter:

> St. Paul citizens not fortunate enough to have reservations for the Auditorium performance tomorrow will have an opportunity to see what a real Russian ballet dancer looks like, if they happen to go shopping tomorrow afternoon.
>
> Serge Diaghileff's payroll, aggregating approximately $70,000, in certified checks, arrived from New York today and is now in the safety deposit vault of a St. Paul bank, awaiting the belated troupe of nearly 300 performers.
>
> H. D. Frankel, local manager of the production, who returned at noon today from Grand Forks, North Dakota, after being delayed four hours by the storm, predicted that the big company will not reach the city before noon tomorrow.

And then, there was this baffling advertisement in the 23 January issue of the *St. Paul Pioneer Press*:

> Advance men for the Russian Ballet, which will arrive in this city this morning, are combing St. Paul for twenty-five handsome Apollos and fifty beautiful young women to appear as supers in various productions in addition to 300 performers...
>
> H. D. Frankel, local manager, has received a message from Nijinsky, the Russian dancer, denying rumors that he would not appear with the company. "La Spectre de la Rose" has been substituted on the program for "Princess Enchantress."

We must pause for a moment and recall that the Ballet Russe had been in the *Twin Cities* of Minneapolis and St. Paul before, but without Waslaw. Those living in St. Paul could chose to see the Russians perform in both cities; many of them did. And before I present the St. Paul review, I'd like to bring to mind the arduous trip the group had to endure since leaving Washington state. One would imagine that it would certainly be a factor in critiquing the performance. It seems to me however, that C. M. Flandrau of the St. Paul Pioneer Press had either an axe to grind or was very sure of himself and his expertise in the arts.

The American Tour of the Ballet Rouse

Some of the disadvantages under which the Russian Ballet performed last evening were unavoidable; owing to the snowstorm its train was late, and owing to the consequent necessity for haste, the scenery became rather hopelessly mixed for a time, and when the curtain finally went up it was long past 8:15. But making every allowance for the unavoidable, it cannot be said that the performance last evening was an especially brilliant one.

It had moments of interest and picturesque ness, of course, but - I am under no obligation whatever to dissemble the fact - the company has obviously deteriorated during its sojourn in this country.

Except for the principals whose roles were not arduous, the dancers were by no means the best of their kind, the stage management was exceedingly slipshod, and the local supers disastrously out of place in a form of art whose only excuse for existence is a harmonious alliance of the pictorial, the musical and the choreographic.

"Till Eulenspiegel" (with which the evening began) is furthermore not a very successful ballet. Richard Strauss' music in itself is a decided tax on one's attention, and to add to it a not particularly coherent pantomime is demanding of one's audience a good deal. As the mischievous, prank-playing Till, M. Nijinsky is given no opportunities for dancing and failed to make much impression. The scenery and costumes designed by Robert E. Jones for this offering were effective.

"Thamar"...was, perhaps, the most interesting and best given of the four numbers.

The Leon Bakst set...the cruel, heartless character of Thamar, as portrayed by that talented actress, Mlle. Flore Revalles, were all impressive.

"Le Spectre de la Rose"...by Mlle. Lopokova and M. Nijinsky...Is a dainty and pleasing little fantasy, which while not displaying Nijinsky at his best, possesses considerable charm.

It was a small wonder Lopokova would dance with all that was brewing about her husband. And if Flandrau did not enjoy Waslaw in the Till or the Spectre, in what role did he like him? We shall never know, because he did not say. In closing, he managed to criticize their signature piece as well, and to add insult to injury, he had words even for the orchestra!

Nijinsky in America

"Prince Igor," a series of Slavonic dances without a plot, was not presented with anything like the fire and skill with which it was invested last year. Borodine's music for it, however, was admirably played by a large but not exactly over careful orchestra.

Always making due allowances for the unavoidable, it is my opinion that the Diaghileff Ballet Russe is at present existing chiefly on its past reputation and the name of Waslaw Nijinsky.

MINNESOTA, Minneapolis – 24 - 25 January 1917 – Auditorium

AUDITORIUM
MINNEAPOLIS

Two Performances Only

Thursday Night, March 2 ——1916—— Friday Matinee, March 3

Engagement Extraordinary
Under the Direction of the Metropolitan Opera House Company, New York City.

of

SERGE DE DIAGHILEFF'S BALLET RUSSE

In A
BRILLIANT REPERTORY
of

BALLETS and MIMED SCENES

Which for six years has been
the sensation of London, Berlin,
Paris, Vienna and Petrograd.

Scenery and Costumes by
LEON BAKST
THE FOREMOST DECORATIVE ARTIST OF OUR TIMES

Ticket Information

Applications for seats for both performances are now being received and will be filled in the order of their receipt

All orders for seats should be addressed to
L. N. SCOTT
Metropolitan Opera House, Minneapolis, Minn.

Boxes (seating 6)	$40.00
Orchestra and 1st 10 rows Orchestra Circle	5.00
Last 10 rows Orchestra Circle	4.00
First Balcony (first 2 rows)	5.00
First Balcony (next 2 rows)	3.00
First Balcony (last 5 rows)	2.50
Second Balcony (1st row on side and 5 rows center)	2.00
Second Balcony (last 3 rows center)	1.50
Second Balcony (2d and 3d rows on side)	1.00

Regular Seat Sale opens at the Cable Piano Ticket Office, Monday, Feb. 21st.

Figure 5.

While Mr. Flandrau's views are still fresh in you mind, let me offer a different perspective from Minneapolis, keeping in mind that the members of the ballet did have a chance to "warm up" in St. Paul. We also need to remember that Minneapolis was and still is, the larger of the two cities, with a cosmopolitan, sophisticated population that had a lot of entertainment choices, the Russians

Nijinsky in America

were not the only game in town! The journalists writing for the Minneapolis papers had also seen the Russians a year earlier, as well as the current St. Paul performance.

A new force was to be felt in the Russian Ballet which last night reappeared at the Auditorium. That was the force of a new and driving individuality, Waslaw Nijinsky is now the captain of the band, which a year ago invaded Minneapolis...The presence of the youthful Russian is unmistakably felt even when he is not visible in person at all. If last night's performance mirrors accurately the present state of the troupe, the company has gained alike from his virtuosity and his generalship. The performance in St. Paul on Tuesday night gave rather a different impression. He was thus simultaneously lauded for its improvement and censured for its deterioration. But last night found the band inspirited and revitalized, excellently drilled, and superbly equipped for its task...

"Till Eulenspiegel" tells the story of Till, a prankish knave who mimics and mocks dignitaries of a medieval city. It represents Nijinsky's interpretation, or translation, of the Strauss tone-poem of similar title. The translation is so free as to be audacious, and yet it is indisputably clever. I was quite decidedly disappointed in it when I first heard it in St. Paul; last night it grew upon me immeasurably. The setting by Jones are nothing short of brilliant; the jumbled pinnacles, the gabled roofs, the topsy-turvy turrets, the peaked head-dresses, the steeple-like crowns are at once grotesque and delightful. Nijinsky showed himself the rare artist that he is by burying the virtuoso in the actor, the dancer in the character.

Mr. William McNally of the *Morning Tribune* continued this review at length, in much the same vein. His colleague, Carlton W. Miles, of the Minneapolis Journal had very much the same opinion, which he developed in three consecutive articles. But rather than reading another review, let's look at a bit of what life was like in Minneapolis, Minnesota in early 1917. In the Amusement Section of the Minneapolis Journal of 21 January, an absorbing biography of Robert Edmond Jones was presented. A Miss Harriet S. Flagg provided the insights as well as an in-depth interview with Mr. Jones about his philosophy of scene design. It is a riveting article, well worth looking up.

We have talked much about the dancing and artistry of the Russians and of Waslaw, but in very few instances, did journalist

The American Tour of the Ballet Rouse

probe deeper, behind the scenes. One *Minneapolis Journal* writer did just that. The result was two charming articles that not only entertain, but once again gave posterity something a little "extra."

He stood, tall, stately, long armed and commanding, in the center of the Auditorium stage last night, two hours before the curtain rose on the performance of the Ballet Russe. He had an authoritative manner and he looked as if he might be Nijinsky, or Diaghileff or somebody like that.

Nikolov Kremnieff, stage manager, straight from Russia, and his assistant, Louis Hehrmann, a Belgian, conferred at one side of the stage and signaled orders to the tall one whose booming voice always thereafter rolled out in heavy bass, while stage hands jumped about right lively.

A scene that looked like a giant fried egg was to be a background for the ballet, buckled for a time but finally went into place. It was an hour before the time for the evening show and the ante-performance rehearsal was on.

Maurice Roeg, a Hollander, near the stage entrance where the mail box hangs, was calling out in monotone the names of company members who had letters waiting.

"Rop-ski-op-skop-o-loff-a-loff-ski-in-ski-opskoff" was what it sounded like as the scattering syllables came in upon the stage through a confusion of sound caused by the dropping of stage properties, the flapping of canvas, swirling of ropes, stamping of feet and clash of voices. The Russian ballet, bag and baggage, was on the stage, in dressing rooms, and everything was getting set for the "real" curtain 60 minutes away.

"Kavortski - Bessrodnay - Shakkovski - Chamberlin" droned out the voice at the door, the last name fitting incongruously into the drone. Chester Chamberlin, dancer, the only Simon pure American in the cast came up and got two letters from New York.

Alois Fromberg, who is French, notwithstanding the last syllable of his name; Antonia Marin, an Italian; Frederick Fredken, orchestra concertmaster, whose name comes from that country where the great battle of Tannenberg was fought and is half German half Russian; Ernest Shlenker of Bavaria; Stephen Ragooz, whose forbears fought for Hungarian independence; Frank Gurovitch, with a name suggestive of the Balkans, and Louis Del Negro, courteous of manner and either French, Italian or Spanish, N. Sumourakov of Moscow,

149

and Jan Kavortski, who hopes, he said, that one day Poland will be free, had letters waiting. So had Lydia Lopokova and Waslaw Nijinsky, also Mme. Romola Nijinsky.

Some of the epistles had traveled far and had strange marks and far back dates on them.

Riga, Petrograd, Odessa, London, Paris and Rome, Rio de Janeiro and Buenos Aires and other Latin American cities were represented in the letters, most of which came in bunches of two or three, enclosed in a large envelope, re-mailed at New York.

Two French dancers, jumping up and down and testing their biceps, came on the stage and flitted off again. The girls of the chorus lined up in the flies. Saxony and Austria and Switzerland and Spain were here, but mostly it looked like Russia. Then the dark, sad eyed, soulful looking men dancers came in and gave their poignant looks, and girls of the orient moved in and someone shoved out the front of a Russian house and everything became orientalized, and foreignized and etherialized and sentimentalized and romanticized.

But more romantic than them all, still stood the dark, long armed, commanding, foreign figure in the center of the stage.

Then one of inquiring mind approached him, wondering the while if the tall one knew any English, and if he should be spoken to in Russian, Spanish, Portuguese, Italian or any of the other romance languages or whether one ought to have an interpreter. And the tall one was asked his name.

"O'Fallon" came the quick, sharp reply. "I'm supe captain. Just now I'm back plastering with the big drops but my regular job is telling the supes to do something and believe me when I tell them they do it."

"Then you are not Russian, Mr. O'Fallon?"

"Say," he said, "are you kidding me. Do I look like a Russian? I'm the boy that fits the thing together so that these fellows with the 'skis' and 'skoffs' can dance. Without me there wouldn't be any show."

Then B. Kohon, who is a cosmopolite, but primarily a Russian, and Flore Revalles, whose name reminds of the Parisian boulevards, came in and the rehearsal went on. (25 January 1917, *The Minneapolis Journal*)

The American Tour of the Ballet Rouse

And now, a word of advice from our illustrious director: Minneapolis men are overfed and over fat and lazy.

This is the diagnosis of Waslaw Nijinsky, star of the Russian ballet, after looking at some thousands of men on the downtown streets and in the Radisson hotel lobby.

Minneapolis men think too much about their stomachs and too little about their feet, he says. Not one Minneapolis man in many has the slightest conception, apparently, or grace of motion as an accomplishment, in the Russian view.

Some Minneapolis men waddle, some shuffle along, some plunge along, puffing loudly. Few of them breathe properly and most of them appear to be in a condition of discomfort because the weather is cold. They are living, in fact, when winter is over Minneapolis in a climate and under conditions conducive to vigorous health. They seem not to have been taught how to live.

Mr. Nijinsky was out twice yesterday, about the Minneapolis streets, and he walked perhaps three miles altogether during the day, just to limber up. When he came in about 5:30 P.M. yesterday from a short, brisk walk up toward Loring Park. He sank into a chair in the Radisson lobby and rested 10 minutes before going to his room.

"Too fat," said the lithe, graceful Russian, waving a slender hand toward two men, each apparently 35 or 40 years of age, each portly, who were passing. A companion helped him a little with his English. "They do not exert enough. They do not sufficiently exercise. They should walk."

He lighted a cigarette and grew meditative as the blue smoke curled up.

"It is not good health to be fat," he said. "How many Minneapolis men that you see on the streets could walk far, or jump, or run? Not many. No sir, not many.

"Walking is the best of all exercises. A man may," - he hesitated for the word, "a man may, systematic, no gymnasium, I mean, he may exercise in a gymnasium, which is splendid. But if he has no other means, at least he can walk. Too many men are in streetcars and automobiles."

Mr. Nijinsky threw one muscular limb across the other and teetered his toe up and down. He watched a large, fleshy man, making his way towards the dining room.

"He should not eat," he said. "Even if he feels hungry. He does not need it. Already he is over nourished. If he would exercise, ah, then he might eat, but he is lazy, you can see that."

Mr. Nijinsky says he likes Minneapolis.

"Splendid," he said. "I like the weather. And the city is interesting and a good city to walk in. You do not get lost. I have been walking" - waved his hand, to indicate a wide sweep - "I do not know where. But I enjoyed it. And I dance better when I have been able to have a good walk in the cold air." (25 January 1917, *The Minneapolis Journal*)

This may have been the key to the St. Paul performance. They had arrived in the afternoon and Waslaw had no time to really limber up. My grandmother often spoke of the frustration he experienced, when trying to exercise on the train.

WISCONSIN, Milwaukee – 26 January 1917 – Auditorium

Figure 6.

Steadfast in my belief that negative opinion only serves to affirm the overwhelming positive reception of the Ballet Russe, I will describe to you the disastrous appearance of the Russians in Milwaukee; but not before telling you about some very important extraneous circumstances which seem to have escaped Milwaukeeans.

Nijinsky in America

One year prior, on its first American tour, which basically included the East Coast and the Midwest, the Diaghileff Ballet Russe appeared in Wisconsin, Milwaukee, without Nijinsky, of course. Just like in St. Paul, Minnesota, Milwaukee residents seemed to have felt that they knew everything there was to know about the Ballet Russe. Following their 25 January performance in Minneapolis, the special train was loaded as usual, and would have started on its way at one in the morning, but for the -26 degrees Fahrenheit which interfered with departure, causing considerable delay. Nevertheless, the troupe reached Milwaukee and with an hour late curtain time and was ready to perform on 26 January. For reasons that can only be conjectures, the program was altered in the last minute, to the great dismay of Milwaukeeans, but let us have an eyewitness account.

> ... as to the change from the printed program, this gave the audience the little "Le Spectre de la Rose," with M. Waslaw Nijinsky and Mlle. Lydia Lopkova in a single waltz number, in place of "Les Sylphides," in which the same two were to have been presented together in three duos and ensemble numbers, and each in a solo number...
>
> Except for "L'Apres Midi d'un Faune," which is practically not a ballet, but a mere tableau, and a more or less grotesque one at that, for Nijinsky's tights have spots on them like those on a "calico" dress, and a bob tail, Milwaukeeans had to form their judgment of this much praised star's abilities from the "vision of the rose" number. The music is Weber's "Invitation to the Dance," the waltz strains of which did not tax the routine of this Russian trained artist, nor serve to demonstrate his versatility.
>
> The bounding step, which is a feature of the number, can hardly be said to surpass that of M. Mordkin in his palmiest days in Pavlowa's early companies.
>
> ...(January, *Milwaukee Sentinel*)

Milwaukee does not seem to be pleased with the Ballet Russe. The Auditorium was only specked with people, and the applause was faint. The seating arrangement of the lower floor is as poor as ever, the same complaint as to catching sight of the stage being as true as it was during the recent engagement of the Ellis Opera Company.

The American Tour of the Ballet Rouse

How much longer will vulgarity be allowed to pass for art, is a thing for the public to decide. When it is no longer patronized, and the money does not gather in the box office - then will there be sweet pure art. While Flore Revalles and Nijinsky have both been widely advertised as wonderful dancers and high salaried artists, neither fact was brought out at the Friday night performance. Mme. Revalles danced not at all, [of course not, she was an opera singer] and Nijinsky only in La Spectre de la Rose.

...

This rather questionable ballet (Cleopatra) was followed by the delightful Spectre de la Rose, which the audience applauded. Just, however, as the audience had become accustomed to the real art of dancing, L'Apres Midi d'un Faune was put on. This is advertised as a Greek frieze, and as a frieze, is a beautiful piece of art. As a picture in action, it is hardly within the bounds of decency. A young faun, making passionate love to a piece of polka dotted chiffon as seriously as he would a thing of flesh and blood is nauseating. Nijinsky did no dancing in this ballet, that being left to a half dozen chorus girls, a few of them rather untrained. It was disappointing not to see Nijinsky dance, and Milwaukee could have done very nicely without this particular ballet, which was taken off in New York, and other of the big eastern cities... (27 January 1917, *Milwaukee Journal*)

ILLINOIS, Chicago – 28 January 1917 – Cohan's Grand

Illinois, *The Land of Lincoln*, needs no introduction, neither does Chicago, known as *Second City, Windy City*, and called by the great American poet Carl Sandburg, the "City of Big Shoulders," for Chicagoans do everything in a big way! The Russians would have been gratified to know that the Pullmans used for their itinerant slumber was first designed and built by George M. Pullman, as far back as 1858, in Bloomington, Illinois.

The arts had always played an important role in Chicago's life. During the 1880's, the noted architects Louis Sullivan and Dankmar Adler designed the Auditorium Theatre on Michigan Avenue which is still in use today. The Art Institute of Chicago is second to none. The Chicago Symphony is world renowned, the list goes on: theatre, opera, dance, Broadway plays, night club-theatre, experimental theatre groups in every shape and form. And lest we forget, Chicago has been the vanguard of architecture since the Great Chicago Fire of 1871. It was the Chicago School Architects who rebuilt the city, who developed the skyscraper. There are three examples of this, built in the 1890's, which still stand one hundred years later. But before we get too far a field, we should return to defend the Russians!

> Mr. Nijinsky found in nearly all the circumstances of his first appearance copious provocation to return soon and tarry longer: the theater was jammed; un-estimated hundreds sought unobtainable admission; the phone in the Grand was dedicated for the day to the sole service of communicating to fevered inquirers the fact that The Tribune erred in its Sunday statement that he would be back in a fortnight; and the crowd made for him after he had re-danced the finale of the "Enchanted Princess", an ovation hardly second in volume or length to Al Jolson's for singing:
>
> "You Made Me Love You; 'n' I Didn't Wish to Do It."
>
> Moreover, Nijinsky so imposed himself to the affections and imagination of the onlookers that the ex-piscatorial Miss Claire, heretofore inerrant, audibly and repeatedly vowed that she detected the suping in those items of the bill in which he was not formally cast...Nijinsky was then the excitement of the troupe.

The American Tour of the Ballet Rouse

First seen, Nijinsky is a shock and an emotional let-down: he is not like Mordkin, lovely in the item of legs. His seem to belong to somebody else: a barreling pedalist of the two-a-day, or perhaps the man who holds up all the others in the turn called the Nine Nimble Nubians...his technique (Nijinsky's) was revealed...as dazzling, matchless and unique, with brains to inform and a fine, subtle art to give it the quality of actual greatness. He offers for Mordkin's wild grace a sense of outline and an imaginative gift which place him securely on the throne. He met, in this item of his repertoire and, later, as the Faun, the test of Blake's "great and golden rule of art" the feeling for the "distinct, sharp, bounding line" inseparable from perfection. There was, in actual employment, little of Nijinsky in the program; just enough, in the first number to convey a sense of his primacy, skill, and, as the Faun, to make clear that he is, besides, a great mime. (Frederick Donaghev, 29 January 1917, *The Chicago Daily Tribune*)

Among the testimonials about the Ballet Russe, there is a press telegram from Wells Hawks, dated 28 January 1917 to Toledo, Ohio, one of the stops on the tour, about two weeks hence; sent at 8:35 P.M., it went like this:

Chicago January 28 -- Turning away twice the capacity of the theatre, The Ballet Russe played a single matinee and scored a brilliant success at Cohan's Grand this afternoon. The special train of 12 coaches, just from the coast, was sidetracked and stopping off four hours en route between Milwaukee and Indianapolis, the famous dancers appeared before one of the most fashionable audiences of the year. The street was blocked for an hour with motors filled with theatre parties. Nijinsky was cheered to the echo and called before the curtain a score of times. Lafolsova, Revalles, Gavuloff and the great Ensemble were at their best. It is probable that return matinees will be arranged after the Southern tour by special train which will include St. Louis, Memphis, Birmingham, Knoxville, Louisville, and Cincinnati.

The Russians did not have an opportunity to return to Chicago, but they did go to the above mentioned cities, save for Knoxville. Before we say farewell to Chicago, let us read an article featured on the day of the performance, for the benefit of health conscious Chicagoans, with illustrations and all.

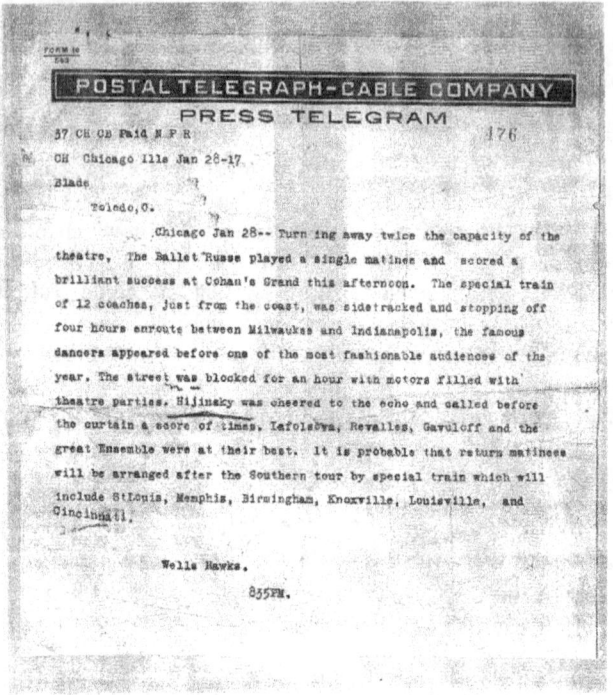

Figure 7.

Have you ever noted a woman dancer of Russia in street or home attire? If so, you have no doubt remarked her striking carriage and grace. That much of her personal attraction is due to her splendidly developed back muscles is perfectly obvious to one who has been through the rigorous training school in Petrograd.

A Russian dancer's back is like that of an Indian - strong yet supple and slender of muscle. Ballet instruction scientifically brings out those muscles which are most conducive to grace and strength.

Backs that are strongest prevent fatigue from coming. The woman whose back is strong rarely becomes worn out; her nerves are steady. The average housewife today has a weak back. If she sits at a desk or table all day long her back aches; if she goes shopping she comes home with her back aching more than her head.

This Russian dancer can sit all day in one position, can ride for twenty hours in a train seat and never grow weary across the small of the back.

The American Tour of the Ballet Rouse Should Begin Slowly

The housewife cannot practice Russian ballet methods all day long, but she can do much to harden the muscles across her back by practicing the two exercises which are pictured above.

Although they are not violent, it is better to begin practicing them slowly and to increase their number of performances gradually from day to day.

Number one is rather less simple than it looks and produces extraordinarily beneficial results if practiced a few times each day. In the beginning stand erect, both heels together, feet turned to make an angle of 90 degrees with each other. Now bend the right knee, lowering the body slowly and keeping the left knee stiff and the left leg pointed ahead, the tip of the toe touching the floor. Sink as low as possible, holding the right arm forward and the left arm backward to assist in preserving the balance. Now rise slowly, straightening the right leg, still bearing no weight upon the left leg. When erect, assume the first position, and, taking the weight upon the left leg, extend the right, and reversing the action, perform it again.

The second position is commenced in the same erect position. Slowly the right foot is moved back, the knee being unbending. The weight shifts backward as this is done. The trunk is maintained upright, the arms stretched upward. When the limit is reached shift the weight forward and rise slowly by bringing up the right foot until it is beside the left, leaving you erect once more. Reverse - moving the left foot back.

(Andreas Pavley & Serge Oukrainsky – "The Celebrated Russian dancers" 28 January 1917, *Chicago Sunday Herald*)

And now that we are feeling fit, are we ready to travel with the Ballet Russe to a weeks worth of one night stands!

INDIANA, Indianapolis – 29 January 1917 – Shubert Murat Theatre

Figure 8.

The American Tour of the Ballet Rouse

I am certain that many of you reading this book have heard of the famous Indianapolis 500 Automobile Race. Did you know that it dates back to 1911? Ford was not the only early name connected with motor cars. As far back as 1852, the Studebaker Brothers built farm wagons and schooners in South Bend, Indiana, later focusing on automobiles; building the first electric-powered ones in 1902 and gasoline-powered machines beginning in 1904. But it was Elwood G. Haynes of Kokomo who designed one of the earliest gasoline-powered autos back in 1894. Another notable name was that of Richard J. Gatling, credited with the invention of the rapid-fire machine gun, in 1862. Indiana is known not only for creative inventions however, she also boasts of a noble literary tradition, with such illustrious names as James Whitcomb Riley, Lew Wallace, Booth Tarkington, George Ade, and Edward Eggleston.

Ona B. Talbot Announces

Serge de Diaghileff's
Only and Original
BALLET RUSSE
in a Brilliant Repertory of
Ballets and Mimed Scenes

By Special Arrangement with the
Metropolitan Opera Company

SHUBERT MURAT THEATRE
For Three Performances
Thursday, Friday Eve. and Saturday Matinee
March Ninth, Tenth & Eleventh

SYMPHONY ORCHESTRA
M. ANSERMET — Conductor

DIRECTION GENERALE
M. Serge de Diaghileff and Baron Dimitri Gunzbourg
John Brown — General Manager

Figure 9.

So, when the Serge de Diaghileff's Ballet Russe arrived for a three day performance, in March of 1916, Indianapolis residents were more than ready. No, there is no mistake with the date; the Russians were in Indiana, a year earlier, without Waslaw of course. It is worth our while to examine their first time reception, not only as a basis for comparison with the second appearance, but especially in paralleling it with other cities, who had the rare opportunity to see the troupe twice within twelve months, without and with Nijinsky.

The 9-10-11 March 1916 performances included the following numbers: "Cleopatre," "Le Spectre de La Rose," "Carnaval," "Les Sylphides," "L'Apres Midi d'un Faune," "Le Prince Igor," "Sheherazade," "Thamar," "Soleil De Nuit," and "La Princesse Enchantee." Oliver M. Sayler was one of the few fortunate people who had the opportunity to see the Russian overseas, his perspective then, is of particular interest to us as to how in his opinion, the Russians fared in his own back yard?

> The glorious art of Muscovy, now wild, now chaste, won a brilliant triumph last night...

> To most of last night's audience the introduction to the real ballet Russe was entrance into wonderland - a wonderland made flesh and blood and color and sound from the strangest dreams of our childhood. To the happy but unfortunate few of us who had seen the Diaghileff ballet in Paris or London or Petrograd, last night meant something more. In anticipation there was the nervous uncertainty whether the glory we had known in other lands could really be brought to America intact and with the charm unbroken. But happy we were when we found out that the mystic ensemble...is still there...Unfortunate we were, however, for as many times as you see the ballet Russe, as often as you wonder and your affection for it mount higher and higher with each rare moment you spend with it, the strange and mystic spell of the first time you sat in its presence comes up to remind you that once you did not know and then all of a sudden you did! And that moment you carry through life like a jewel.

> The secret of this art of Muscovy and the key to its enjoyment is its absolute and childlike abandonment. Imitators or those who would disparage an art built on so seemingly easy and flimsy a basis must remember, on the other hand, that pure, genuine, unaffected abandonment is to the adult mortal of the occidental nations one of the most difficult of feats. Hedged in by the inhibitions of our hidebound existence and slapped in the face and in the heart by the rigors of our conventions and our Puritanism, we are more easily baffled by

the simple than we are by the most profound and complex. We tie our nerves up into a knot over the geometry of a primary election until, when someone points us to the sunset; we knit our foreheads and with difficulty find our way back to the simple and the real things of life.

Just so with the ballet. Its appeal is to the primitive emotions, the feelings that made of childhood a magic city built only on sacred wooden blocks - and imagination. And just as the secret of the creation of the art of ballet is abandonment, so must its appreciation come through an open heart and mind. Don't be afraid of what you feel and think. Don't think. Just feel. Let the joy in color and motion and sound surge through you and take you back to the vague imaginings of childhood when a bright red ball danced before your eyes and thrilled you with ecstasy. Don't be ashamed to feel. Rather rejoice that you have forgotten how wise you are for a moment and thank this group of incomparable artists for revealing to you what our psychologists are pleased to call the primitive emotions, but which some of us suspect are after all the most substantial groundwork of our best life of today and tomorrow. (Oliver M. Sayler, 10 March 1916, *Indianapolis News*)

Mr. Sayler continues in this same, thought invoking manner for two more, long columns. He describes the ballets, extols the glories of the production and bemoans the fact that the troupe is "compelled to suffer the handicap of the primitive lighting conditions of the American theatre wherever they go in this country," and as a finally blow he says: "What they could do on a perfect stage passes belief...!" The following day, Oliver Sayler presented his own assessment of the Faun, which some critics found so terribly controversial.

Whatever I have written about the simplicity of appeal of the Diaghileff ballet, I take it all back when it comes to "The Faun." Only thus can I protect myself from the shades of Omar and Rabelais - and even, perhaps, of Aristophanes. "The Faun" is sophisticated, make no mistake. It is not decadent, however, as many a critic has said in the last few weeks. Nor is it raw or suggestive, as "Mr. Dogleaf's" friend, the police censor of Kansas City, feared.

The satiric twist of this brief and fragile ballet is evident on the rise of the curtain. It is no wood of the childlike imagination that rises behind the rock on which the dappled form is reclining. Rather, it is a wood of the poet, used to conceiving vague fancies and amusing and whimsical impossibilities. Into this half-smiling scene come three startled nymphs, locked arm in arm like their ancient sisters of the Pantheon frieze. Another and another slip in until there are seven. I wonder whether Nijinsky, who contrived this ballet, from the Debussy music...had any sinister intentions upon Wordsworth in his mathematics!

Of a sudden the nymphs spy the faun who has been rousing his senses little by little watching the fair creatures. In the half-friendly, half-shy way of animals, the faun and his visitors approach the retreat, gradually getting better acquainted. Discretion, though, bids the nymphs flee, one of them dropping her daintily perfumed and shimmering scarf on the way. The faun watches them out of sight and then carefully, tenderly picks up the scarf, holding it in his arms like a human form. Carefully, tenderly, he makes his way back to his rock where he basks with his hostage in the sun.

Of course, there are infinite possibilities of interpretation in this ballet. You may read into it what you like. I prefer to think of it as a whimsical joke, a satire on sex. In our western Puritanism we permit no satires on sex outside "The Follies" and the Winter Garden entertainments. Possibly that is why this extremely reserved and deliciously suave and polished fable has caused so much uneasiness. Genuine art has herein found a new field of expression.

Like Nijinsky, Mr. Sayler was definitely well ahead of his time. Ten months later, "the astonishing Russians" were in Indianapolis again, but now Nijinsky was also with them.

> One acute angle of anxiety had for its point the far-sung Nijinsky - he who performed for the ballet the service which the Ingersoll has done for the dollar - while the other angle found its apex in "Till Eulenspiegel," the new whimsy devised by this same Nijinsky last summer...
>
> These Russians, though, are ever new - no matter what they dance or who dances it or how often they dance it. There were those in the theatre last night who in two seasons had seen them twenty to forty times if they had seen them once. And to this writer, on sixth observation, they held all the wonder and the zest and the mystery of some fair dream that recurs throughout one's life...
>
> One is not likely soon to forget the first time he has seen Waslaw Nijinsky dance. With a fine respect for the ensemble, there is no artificially prepared entrance, focusing on him a forced attention. If,

as last night, the ballet in which he first appears is a richly populous one, this mad elf may have been on stage for several minutes before you are convinced of his presence. Slowly, however, your eyes have been drawn to a swiftly darting figure whose bodily movements resemble those of some animal of the jungle rather than of human. A strange, uncanny pair of legs, bowed out all around both above and below a slender knee that looks as if it might snap at any moment - these and a nervous posturing that is now effeminate and now masculine, and now animal, are enough to proclaim their author and possessor as no one else but the premier dancer of the world today.

It is doubtful whether Nijinsky has ever had a more richly dramatic opportunity than he has afforded himself in the new Strauss ballet, "Till Eulenspiegel."...

Two aspects of "Till Eulenspiegel" stamp it as one of the most refreshing and admirable additions to the Russians' repertory in several years. One is its absolute independence from sex appeal - a motive which in its constant repetition has alienated many from the ballet's potential following in this Puritan country of ours. "Till" proves conclusively that there are other thrills than sex thrills, other motives for dancing and miming than sex motives, other passions and other emotions that yield just as well to the picturesque and panoramic technique of the ballet.

The other new note struck by "Till" is the comparative simplicity in design of the costumes devised by the American artist, Robert Edmond Jones...The American artist gets effects equally as rich by absolutely contrary means..."Till" throughout is conceived and executed as a monumental joke. It screams its sardonic mockery from the crags above the market place where impossible castles sprout from rock ledges like scrubby pines. It puffs out its cheeks with hardly restrained laughter in the pompous madness of the judges' robes and headgear. It is stark mad from first to last, but all with a tempering fineness that keeps its madness from becoming unbeautiful. (30 January 1917, *Indianapolis News*)

Although no author was given, the style reminds one of Mr. Sayler. In any case, the journalist continued the review, explaining the rest of the program, including how the audience "demanded" and Waslaw obliged, by repeating "La Princesse Enchantee." The *Indianapolis Star* also ran a critique, written by a Paul R. Martin, who similarly sang the praises of the Ballet Russe. He, however, by personal admission, was like most of his fellow

Nijinsky in America

countrymen, in an "elemental" attitude toward the art of ballet; preferring the "simple dances, the airy, fairy things," rather than the "grotesque 'Till' and the repugnant 'Thamar;'" all the while, not taking anything away from the "remarkable, sumptuousness" of the production.

MISSOURI, Saint Louis – 30 January 1917 – Odeon

It was some time ago that we were in Missouri with the Ballet Russe. We have covered many miles since Kansas City, but it is hard to forget the genuine enthusiasm with which its residents praised the Russians. They found the troupe inspiring under Waslaw's directorship. You may recall that it was from there that we had the good fortune of reading a little girl's eye witness account, in light of some eighty years. Then how do we explain the tepid welcome provided by St. Louis? Were they more sophisticated than Kansas City, Indianapolis or even Chicago, or did they just think so?

Albert C. Wegman, music and dramatic critic for a St. Louis paper considered Jones' design of "doubtful value." What is more, he did not care for the "Till" as a ballet. He felt that visualizing the story was "impracticable, inchoate, meaningless and ineffective." Richard L. Stokes considered "Till" "quaint and gently amusing," but "too frail to grip the attention" and a "poor vehicle for displaying Nijinsky's…talents (as a dancer.)" And then there was Richard Spamer who stated that Waslaw "never really entered his element as a great danseur, 'Till' is not in his genre." The only woman critic, Katherine Richardson agreed with her male counterparts, Waslaw's "genius in the Terpsichorean art did not become apparent in this ballet (Till)…"

So was there anything that pleased St. Louis? Yes, "La Princesse Enchantee" was the "enchanting moment of the evening." Ms. Richardson continued: "Nijinsky, who is no Adonis, but an athletically built man of below medium height, came into his own in the audience's favor. The great bounds into the air, side jumps, and a Mordkin leap at the last brought storms of applause." Exactly what Waslaw did not wish to be known for, jumps and leaps! Wegman sang the same tune: "Here Nijinsky…found opportunity to display transcendent skill. His commanding technique found expression in great graceful leaps and twirls, and many intricate steps." Mr. Stokes, not to be left out, considered "La Princesse" the "single thrill" of the evening. Finally, let us hear from Mr. Spamer: "Nijinsky leaped into the air much after the manner of Michael Mordkin, but with much less virility and

Nijinsky in America

masculine resiliency." Poor Waslaw, if he had only known that he had to be "as good" as Mordkin! But before I am chided by St. Louis residents for my cynical remarks, let me tell you about a little known fact. There was another Nijinsky tour in 1935, no, made not by Waslaw, but by Romola Nijinsky. I am deeply indebted to the Saint Louis Public Library and Ms. Ehernbergn, who discovered the following article:

> Mme. Romola Nijinsky, wife of the famous dancer, Waslaw Nijinsky and author of the best selling biography of her husband, is making a brief visit to St. Louis as a part of her lecture tour in the United States to get funds for the Nijinsky Foundation. She will speak tomorrow morning for the Junior League.
>
> Speaking fluent English with a slight trace of accent, Mme. Nijinsky talked freely yesterday afternoon of the foundation which has for its present object the care of the great dancer, who since 1919 has been living in a private sanitarium...Ultimately, the directors of the foundation, one of whom is Tamara Karsavina...hope to use the fund to care for any dancers who have in some way become incapacitated and to give scholarships to promising students of the ballet. (17 November 1935, *St. Louis Globe*)

The article continued about Waslaw's condition and the attempts made to find a cure for his mental illness. It is a sensitive and insight filled piece, giving us a good picture of Nijinsky at age forty-four. My grandmother Romola was forever hopeful that a cure would be found. Sadly, the illness that stilled Waslaw's body was as new in those days as the choreographies that propelled him into posterity.

TENNESSEE, Memphis – 31 January 1917 – Lyric Theater

The last day of January found the Ballet Russe in Memphis. The one night stands were beginning to take their toll on Waslaw. Unlike Missouri, the Russians had not been in Tennessee before, but their reputation had preceded them, especially that of Waslaw; but regrettably, he turned out to be somewhat of a disappointment for Memphis audiences.

> Sometimes we are delightfully surprised and again we are dismally disappointed when we confront a theatrical performance that counts for much. And sometimes the performance is not exactly what we expect, nor what we want it to be.
>
> The Ballet Russe as presented at the Lyric Theater last night was an exquisite, artistic performance, something superbly perfect in every sense, but the great Nijinsky, like Humpty Dumpty, fell off the wall when it came to his personal work. His artistic direction is perfect. His work otherwise does not sustain the impression that we entertained in advance. He does one thing well and the other with decided indifference.
>
> The engagement of the Ballet Russe…last night, was in a way a wonderful one. The exhibition of the ballet was complete and harmonious. It touched the mind with the mystery, with the exquisite dancing of the ages past, with the dances of the Orient, and entranced the eye with pictures of the curious but opulent…

The production numbers Memphis ballet lovers saw were "Les Papillons," "Scheherazade," and "Cleopatre," which was truly appropriate if we consider the fact that Memphis was named for the ancient Egyptian capital of Memphis (ca. 3100 B.C.,) which lay on the Nile, Tennessee matching it with the great Mississippi. It is interesting to note what Mr. Huhn, the journalist of the above piece, found to his liking and what gave him displeasure:

> The "Cleopatre" number was offered as an introduction because of a change of program. It was poignantly persuasive, in its way, and beautiful in its tragedy; gloomy and yet magnetic. To mention the principals is unnecessary. They were all so exquisite in their dancing that the only thing that can be said is that Nijinsky was distinctly disappointing, but the performance that he so admirably conducted was one of the best Memphis people have ever seen. (1 February 1917, *The Commercial Appeal*)

Nijinsky in America

What was it Mr. Huhn did not like about Waslaw's dancing? Why was he disenchanted with him? Why was Waslaw in such bad form? We may never know. But then, there was another critic who saw the very same, single performance, and whose appraisal took a slightly different bent.

> The majesty, the magnificence and the vitality of illusionary pantomime, moving to the rhythm of a wonderful musical score which almost visualized the mime-drama and ballets, was recognized in the greater sense...where a representative Memphis audience was awed and delectably pleased with what Ballet Russe presented...Headed by the great Waslaw Nijinsky...Nothing of the caliber of the Ballet Russe has ever been presented here, and its presentation marks a most notable event in artistic circles.
>
> Of the principals nothing need be said individually they are preeminent.
>
> The great Nijinsky...is as great an actor as he is a danseur. (G. E. Brown, 1 February 1917, *Memphis News Scimitar*)

In addition of the praises he showered on Waslaw, G. E. Brown also felt that Waslaw was not at his best that night. Was it just an off night or was there more to it than that? We shall talk about this later. For now, let us look at some of the obvious reasons for some of the poor performances.

Aside from the physical wear and tear of an arduous schedule as that of the Russians, the complications that arose from setting up and tearing down, often on a daily basis, was problematic at best. Frequently, the announced curtain time was delayed, sometimes by as much as an hour. It could not be helped; the stages were, more often than not, inadequate for the elaborate scenery; understandably, local stage hands were not familiar with the routine and lacked efficiency; the artists did not always have ample time for adequate rest nor warm up. But the audience, who had paid their hard earned dollars to see the "eighth wonder" of the world, cared little about that, even if they were cognizant of it. Intermissions were long too, mostly because of scenery change difficulties. Time after time, the orchestra would play an interlude or "entr'acte symphonique" as they called it, but even that was not enough. This, occasionally, colored the critic's perspective. It makes complete sense then that the longer the engagement the more successful, with heightened artistry of the dancers.

ALABAMA, Birmingham – 1 February 1917 – Jefferson Theater

Boston, Albany, N.Y., Detroit, Chicago, Milwaukee, St. Paul, Minneapolis, Kansas City, Mo., St. Louis, Indianapolis, Cincinnati, Cleveland, Pittsburgh, Washington, D.C., Philadelphia, and Atlantic City; these were the cities the Diaghileff Ballet Russe toured twice, once without and then with Waslaw. Birmingham, Alabama was not one of them, but the Russians had crossed there on the way to New Orleans, coming from Atlanta. Residents of the deep south, in the *Heart of Dixie*, recognized and appreciated a good thing when they saw it. And so it was with the Ballet Russe in Alabama.

During my research I received one of the most enthusiastic responses from a librarian in Birmingham. She wrote: "Imagine, Nijinsky for a dollar!" She continued, stating that she had known of several Birmingham residents who might have seen my grandfather dance; she was going to pursue it. And then I received a letter from a gentleman who resided in Lincoln, Alabama. Although too young to have seen Waslaw dance, he had heard of him and was fascinated by him, but let him tell you:

> *I read your quest in the magazine and was not aware that any relatives of Waslaw and Romola were in this country. It has been years since I have even heard the name Nijinsky. Personally, I had never seen him, though as a youth I was fascinated with stories about his life and dancing. In London, during the war, I saw a few performances choreographed by Nijinska. Years later, my teacher, a conductor from Budapest, told me about the fantastic leap he had seen Nijinsky perform in, (I believe) Le Spectre de la Rose. He estimated to be 25 feet, as Waslaw turned and leapt through a window. Books remark, also, about his "Entre chat dix", (though how could anyone count them accurately?)*
>
> *Nearly everyone who had seen Waslaw Nijinsky perform must be in their 70's, obviously, but I doubt there will be another with his command of the art.*
>
> *I wrote to Romola, once, (at the Sanatorium) and asked for a photograph of him. She was the most gracious lady and sent a short note with the photograph. Their life was one of the truly great love affairs...*
>
> *Sincerely yours, Rolf Thomsen*

The American Tour of the Ballet Rouse

Seventy years prior, another Alabama son had this to say:

Princes and Princesses and Genii and Magic of Old Araby Spread on Jefferson Stage by Nijinsky, Lopokova and Revalles - A Wonderful Ballet

When one was young and read of genii, princesses and princes in that treasure house of imagery, the Arabian Nights, he sighed, because vain visions never quite came up to what he would with the true power. Imagination was limited with youth.

But now men have dreamed those barbaric splendors and enchanting hours of old Araby and put them in color and music and form. Other men and women were found to translate the form of the exquisite poetry of motion, and Serge de Diaghileff's Ballet Russe was born.

Dusty volumes of childhood were opened by many at the Jefferson Theater on Thursday evening and they looked on living dreams instead of the printed imagery of youth. Nijinsky, Lopokova, Revalles and Gavrilow brought to life those enchanted creatures of long ago.

Palms, rosy with the faint dawn over the Persian Sea, which - lay twinkling into miles of fading distance, formed a background for a dream dance.

Nijinsky danced.

Magnificent Grace

He is no ethereal sprite of the imagination, but his massive body floated over the great stage, touching it, it seemed, but for an instant to rise in another sustained flight of poetic motion. Swaying like some frail reed he soared as some winging bird to end his dance with a whirling close.

Only once Nijinsky appeared, and that was in "La Princesse Enchantee," but Birmingham can say it has seen the greatest living male exponent of the dance. Reply to a sustained and imperative encore, he denied again the laws of gravity and floated across the stage. (Pettersen Marzoni, 2 Feb. 1917, *Birmingham News*)

At the conclusion of his long article, Mr. Marzoni noted that visits by artists, the stature of the Russians, was rare in Birmingham, but something to be looked forward to, and furthermore, a thing that

Nijinsky in America

Birmingham audiences duly appreciated; their admiration being rewarded with an encore by Nijinsky. He concluded by reminding his readers that "Nijinsky accepted an encore. He refused to dance at all in Atlanta." Why he didn't dance in Atlanta is still open to speculation. Nevertheless, Birmingham's esteem for the troupe did not go unnoticed by the artists.

TENNESSEE, Chattanooga – 2 February 1917 – Grand

And now for a bit of detective work. According to Romola's itinerary, the next stop was Chattanooga. When inquiring, I was told that they had no record of such a performance, furthermore, there was no theatre named Grand. Librarians in Chattanooga were kind enough to send me a 1917 city directory. The only theatres listed were the Albert, Lyric, Rialto and Superba. Chattanooga is located half way between Birmingham and Nashville. Nashville is a straight shot north, while Chattanooga is towards the northeast. Remembering that this was in the middle of winter and that Chattanooga is surrounded by the Appalachians, a fact that was more than beneficial in the early days, when "these natural mountain barriers protected settlers against their enemies," we searched for another explanation. Our intuition was justified by the following report from Ms. Raney: "The weather at that time was particularly cold; the railroad tracks were frozen for a while. Perhaps the troop had to cancel." Whatever the case may be, Chattanoogans were aware of the tour as the following article from a local society paper demonstrated:

> It was my privilege to go behind the scenes of the Russian Ballet, with a friend, at the performance in Nashville. It was an interesting experience. One very gorgeous number was over, and the confusion of rearranging the scenery, costumes, etc., for the next scene was appalling to the uninitiated. Trunks and boxes were piled in rows, and hurrying people packed the things used, and unpacked the ones needed, with too little room to do so conveniently. In the dressing rooms it was just as crowded, but an air of comradeship and good fellowship seemed to reign.
>
> We were shown into the dressing room of the two famous women dancers, and my friend interviewed them as they arranged their costumes for the next scene. They were very charming and pleasant, in spite of the hurry and confusion, and I thought it a proof of much poise and self-control for them to be calm and polite under such trying circumstances.
>
> Just before leaving, my friend asked them, "What do you think of suffrage;" One of them replied, "Oh, we do not think of anything but the art." The other dainty little dancer said: "It is to dance, to sleep, to eat, to rest, to dance again; and we do not have time to think at

all," and with a lovely smile dismissed the subject as one not to be compared with the art.

Then I realized that their lives are, after all, much like that of the busy housekeeper's, revolving around the wheel of duty, daily. With us it is to work, to cook, to eat, to sleep, to rest, just to cook and work again, and the revolution of the wheel of life goes on forever. When we are in front of the footlights, and see the tinsel and glory, we feel that actors and dancers must lead butterfly lives, but when we go behind the scenes and see the sordid disarray and confusion; the rush of the busy people, who still take time to smile upon the stranger within the gates, we realize to some extent the hardship of their lives. The sacrifice of home, home ties and loved ones. The sacrifice of time for individual pleasures; the sacrifice of assurance that they can sit down and rest awhile, sometimes, as do tired housekeepers, without being haunted with the horror of being dropped from the ranks of salary earners; the dread of old age with no abiding place, no loved ones to watch tenderly and care for willingly as one drifts to the time Death claims his own. All these sacrifices for "the art," and all the tinsel and glory, all the fame, admiration and applause will not suffice for the loss of loved ones and the loneliness of old age.

Could we look behind the scenes of the lives of those whom we think happiest and gayest, I wonder how many cares and burdens we might find, There is no life however protected, but has its trials, its burdens and its dares, and 'tis by these paths the soul for heaven prepares, so from even the dancers along the primrose way, we learn a lesson - a lesson of going cheerfully about our work whether it be "the art" or the more homely tasks of living, with the courage to still smile upon the stranger that passes by, as well as the friend that is near, and to hold to the principle that it is not to think, if the thought be unpleasant, unhappy or discouraging; it is not to theorize over the problems of life; it is not to worry over the

Inevitable, it is just to live. If we make living daily, what the little dancer makes her art daily, public acclamations and adulation may not be ours, but contentment, peace of heart and the devotion of loved ones will be our "tinsel and glory," but the tinsel will be gold. (Clara Cox Epperson, 17 February 1917, *The Lookout*. Chattanooga)

Ms. Epperson had the wisdom, sagacity, and discernment that require no further comment.

TENNESSEE, Nashville – 3 February 1917 – Vendome

It has been immeasurably gratifying to be on the receiving end of such enthusiasm about the Ballet Russe, in light of ninety years, as the one that came from the Athens of the South or Music City, U.S.A., as Nashville is known by most.

Dear Ms. Nijinsky:

...I cannot tell you what a thrill it was for me to receive your letter. In my younger days, I danced with the local dance theatre company, both ballet and modern, and have always admired the work of your grandfather, the great Nijinsky. I have enclosed the only newspaper clipping I was able to find on the performance. Evidently, the performance was to take place at Ryman Auditorium but at that last minute was switched to the Vendome. I hope that this helps and again, I must tell you that it is a thrill for me to have received your letter.

Sincerely, Laura H. Rehmert (Mrs.) The Nashville Room

P. S. The Ryman was the logical choice - had it not been in such poor shape. That wonderful old theater played host to Anna Pavlova, the Ballet Russe (in the 1940's and 1950's), the Isadora Duncan dancers, and many others too numerous to mention. The Nashville Room counts as one of its most prized collections, The Naff Collection, a wonderful treasure trove of photographs, programs, and posters from The Ryman Auditorium.

Mrs. Rehmert was kind enough to send a descriptive summary of The Naff Collection along with the only existing clipping about the 1917 stop of the Ballet Russe. It is not a review per say, rather, a keenly perceptive piece, much like the insightful article by Ms. Epperson; this too gave a behind the scenes look.

> Beautiful Russian women in queer costumes, wiry men, aquiline of face, dressed in drab and grotesquely daubed with grease; musicians in their full dress -- all crowded together or sat upon the high wicker baskets beneath the Vendome stage while the scene-shifters rumbled overhead preparing for the next offering by the Imperial Ballet Russe.
>
> It took some little courage to do it - you were so helplessly in the way. Johnny Simpson wanted to see, too, so together you edged

Nijinsky in America

through the heavy door, stumbled through twisted coils of electrical tubing back of the wings, and made for the dressing rooms below.

The excuse for living just then was to get an interview with Nijinsky. Afterwards, one might browse around - local color for your criticism - the sultan's wives - quien sabe?

There was plenty of color all right, but far from local. In the big room beneath the stage, into which the dressing rooms around the side open, were people crowded in groups and sitting on trunks and big baskets and all of them talking that laughable peddler talk? Here sat one of the corps de ballet, her yellow hair hanging in plaits like some Norseman's bride. A brown scarf was wrapped around and hung from her head, and her arms and legs and feet were clothed in what looked liked brown cotton tights. Behind her, hunched upon a trunk, was a little fellow with his face streaked with black, his costume looking like a dishwasher's in a cheap restaurant. Later, he was a Polovetsien boy in "Prince Igor," in this same costume.

Hurrying through the crowd was a man with a bushy red beard and round black felt hat - a typical Cossack, if you ever saw one. Over on the other side of the room the fellow who played the violin solo in the opening overture was now giving little funny notes on his violin that made the group of exotic men and women around him laugh at his cleverness. Nothing in that fiddling that you could see to interest those beautiful women.

Interviewing Nijinsky Easy - Just Like That.

Somebody showed you Nijinsky's dressing room and you knocked on the door. Nobody answered. The door was not locked, so you walked right in. Three men were in the room. Two of them wore street clothes, while the other - a little five-footer - was dressed in white tights and sweating like a trotter just in from a trial heat. Maybe they were rubbing him down. Nobody in there looked like the tall, muscular premier who had just finished Le Spectre de la Rose.

The two men in citizen's clothes both rushed at you with hands outstretched in holy horror.

"I'm on The Tennessean - interview with Nijinsky - only a minute -"

By that time you were outside admiring the ease and politeness with which they ejected you, and grumbling to yourself because you had not even caught a glimpse of the great Nijinsky.

The American Tour of the Ballet Rouse

You saw him later, dancing with Lopokova, and by his face you knew that he was the little fellow in white tights that you had seen in the dressing room. That Nijinsky?

The anonymous journalist continued in his inimitable style for many more paragraphs, bringing many a smile and chuckle to one's face. And while critics and curiosity seekers were back stage, trying to get an "up close and personal" view of the action, there was another "behind the scenes" crisis, not far away.

Great as was Nashville's enjoyment of the Ballet Russe Saturday night, Nashville came nearer than they knew to missing part or all the big production at the eleventh hour.

Even while the first number was being given Garland Cooper, local manager for the Nashville Society of Fine Arts, which brought the ballet here, was over at the courthouse taking out requisition papers to back down the ballet manager and force him to finish the program.

The ballet was originally booked for the Ryman auditorium, and the seat sale was made on a basis of prices for that building. Three days before the ballet arrived their advance man came and refused to allow the production to be given at the auditorium because of complete lack of facilities there. The ballet was then switched to the Vendome theatre, and Garland Cooper went through three days of torment swapping tickets and getting cussed out for something he couldn't help.

Saturday afternoon Mr. Cooper informed the manager of the ballet that because of the change to the smaller building, the seat sale at the fixed prices would not amount to enough to pay the ballet the stipulated guarantee. He offered to give them all of the receipts for the night, minus the remunerate for his own services. With the assistance of Attorney K. T. McConnico, he persuaded them to come to such an agreement.

All then looked lovely, but at 8:30 o'clock the ballet manager again demanded the full guarantee. He threatened to ring down the curtain in the midst of the first number, then being given, if the money was not forthcoming. Mr. Cooper hastened to the courthouse. It all ended by the ballet agreeing to take the receipts for the night, minus the remunerate for Mr. Cooper's services as local manager. These receipts amounted to less than the original guarantee.

Nijinsky in America

Between the first and second numbers of the ballet the crisis of affairs was reached, and in a few minutes the rumor was all over the house that the performance might not be finished.

The whole affair was the outcome of Nashville's lack of proper auditorium facilities, and may hasten the movement to remodel the Ryman auditorium, for which plans have already been drawn. The changes as now suggested would include new heating and lighting facilities, moving the platform and changing it into a stage, raising the balcony and installing opera house seats. Several men have already offered to give a personal subscription of $100 to such a project.

From Mrs. Rehmert's letter, we now know that the renovation did take place and provided Nashville audiences with many more years of pleasure and diversion.

KENTUCKY, Louisville – 5 February 1917 – Macauley

One of this country's most noble statesman, Abraham Lincoln, called Kentucky, "home." He was born near Hodgenville, not too far from Louisville. *The Bluegrass State*, one of the four official Commonwealth states, is steeped in history. Tobacco production and horse racing gave it great affluence, early on. By the turn of the century, Louisville's population had soared to 205,000.

There was much to see and do on any given day, and "amusements" were plentiful. Macauley's had the following offerings for the week beginning on 5 February: Serge de Diaghileff's Ballet Russe, presented by the Louisville Fine Arts Association - Ona B. Talbot, Managing Director; for one night only, "the sensation of the century," tickets - $5, $4, $3, $2, and $1. Preceding this engagement was "Montgomery & Stone in the Most Successful of All Musical Comedies, 'CHIN-CHIN,'" all week long, seats going for 50c to $2. Following the Russians, for four nights, Irving Berlin's "Big Musical Success, 'Stop Look Listen,'" and on Saturday, 10 February, Mme. Sarah Bernhardt gave a "farewell performance to Louisville." The most expensive ticket to see the "divine Sarah" was $3. The week after that, D.W. Griffith's "Colossal $2,000,000 Spectacle, 'Intolerance'" was available anywhere from 25¢ to $1, considerably less than the ballet!

Along with the advertisement, there was a short article about the Ballet Russe that read like a press release from the company, rather than a commentary or discourse. While we're in Kentucky, let me mention that decades later, a winning race horse was named "Nijinsky;" one wonders if Waslaw would have considered this humorous or an affront. Romola did find it humorous and even had her picture taken with the famous stallion.

OHIO, Cincinnati – 6 - 7 February 1917 – Music Hall

> By Arrangement with the Metropolitan Opera Company
>
> ### SERGE de DIAGHILEFF'S
> # BALLET RUSSE
>
> Artistic Direction, WASLAW NIJINSKY
> For "Sadko" and "Les Papillons," ADOLF BOLM
>
> ## MUSIC HALL
> *FEBRUARY 6 and 7, 1917*
> *CINCINNATI, OHIO*
>
> ARTISTS
>
> | *Madames* | *Messrs.* |
> |---|---|
> | JANINA BONIECKA | ADOLF BOLM |
> | LYDIA LOPOKOVA | ALEXANDRE GAVRILOW |
> | SOPHIE PFLANZ | IVAN JAZWINSKY |
> | FLORE REVALLES | NICOLAS KREMNEFF |
> | LYDIA SOKOLOVA | WASLAW NIJINSKY |
> | ALEXANDRA WASILEWSKA | MIECZYSLAS PIANOWSKI |
> | | NICOLAS SVEREW |
>
> and CORPS de BALLET
>
> Symphony Orchestra Conducted by M. PIERRE MONTEUX
>
> General Stage Manager . . . . . M. NICOLAS KREMNEFF
> Technical Director . . . . . M. EDWARD S. FENNELL
> Chief Machinist . . . M. MICHEL TSCHAOUSSOVSKI
>
> BALDWIN PIANO USED

Figure 10.

We are on the final leg of our journey with the Ballet Russe and Nijinsky. The tour visited four cities in Ohio: Cincinnati, Dayton, Toledo and Cleveland; not in succession however, but interspersed with two locales in Michigan. Cincinnati and Cleveland were two

The American Tour of the Ballet Rouse

of the sixteen places that the Russians had toured before. One wonders if that could have been the cause for the waning enthusiasm for the Terpsichore?

A large city even at the turn of the century, Cincinnati gave home to many of European decent. It is strategically located on the Ohio River, making it ideal for commerce. The 6 February Enquirer had reported in a tiny column, with absolute nonchalance about the Ballet Russe's pending evening performance at the Music Hall, which is still in existence today, and a splendid hall it is, if I might add. The article called Wasalw the "most widely discussed dancer of the present day." The company's efforts a year earlier were considered a "gorgeous production." Being duly impressed with the size of the group, Cincinnatians were expecting great things now that Nijinsky was there!

Let us see then what this city, once known as the *Queen City of the West*, had to report in a column called "Stage land Gossip."

> The Ballet Russe, which astounded the community last season by the gorgeousness of the settings, its dash and its spirit and its remarkable mingling of the arts of music, painting and dancing, under the personal direction of Serge de Diaghileff, returned last night to Music Hall. This time the much-discussed Nijinsky, who was prevented from appearing last year by the exigencies of war, was included in the company. His appearance was the only distinctly new feature the ballet had to offer. The standard of the productions had been definitely fixed last season. There was, to a certain extent, an absence of that element of surprise which characterized the first production. The audience was prepared and expectations were high. It is not a matter of making comparisons, for the genius of color, motion, artistic direction and spectacular grandeur is still maintained, but the program last night was not of that sweep which might be calculated to stir the languishing imagination of an audience.

It is an open question what Cincinnati audiences were expecting and why they were disappointed? Perhaps the answer is hidden in the following:

> Two new ballets were presented last night, the more important of which was a choreographic version of Strauss's fascinating scherzo, "Till Eulenspiegel." The pranks of the legendary wag, which upset

the dignity of court and church. The medieval setting was extremely atmospheric and the costuming little short of wonderful.

Nijinsky proved himself to be a dancer of artistic discrimination and a pantomimist of rare imagination. He is technically superb. Much was expected of him, which was not entirely realized in this production, because the opportunities were not afforded...

One of the most delightful things of the evening was the exquisite pas de deux danced by Nijinsky and Lopokova, called "The Enchanted Princess." It was light and airy, and displayed the dancing ability of both to full advantage. In this the dancing art of Nijinsky had a better opportunity to display itself, which was readily appreciated. The barbaric and dramatic dances from Borodine's opera, "Prince Igor,"...were an impressive climax to the evening's program.

So far, it is a bit problematic to find anything in the production that sounds terribly disappointing, but, as usual, it's up to you to decide.

To-night Nijinsky will appear in the most celebrated of his characterizations, that of the Faune...and with Lopokova in the "Spectre de la Rose." The other ballets announced are "Papillons" and the spectacular "Scheherazade." (J.H.T., 7 February 1917, *The Enquirer*)

This "most celebrated" piece of work was the cause of some concern in the department of "propriety" as we must recall that the moral standards of 1916 were just a bit more stringent than that of today!

BALLET'S LEGS BARE, ANYHOW

The Ballet Russe concluded its Cincinnati engagement at Music hall Wednesday night, giving a very beautiful series if divertissements and further imposing upon the good nature of the audience by making the intermission longer than the dances. Nijinsky and Mlle. Lopokova brought a storm of appreciation unto themselves in the "Spectre de la Rose" dance...

For an artist greatly peeved over a certain situation, Nijinsky appeared willing and cheerful. The mayor's orders forbidding the display of bare legs arouse much chagrin in the Nijinsky breast, and he is reported to have said - well, no matter what he said. The girls wore bare legs anyhow in the "L'Apres Midi d'un Faune" number.

There may have been an improvement in Nijinsky's faun over the effort of last season's creature, but, frankly, the average mind couldn't discriminate.

As on Wednesday night, everybody in the auditorium fretted himself into a state of nervous nothingness over the endless intermissions. (G.B.N., 8 February 1917, *The Cincinnati Post*)

It should be noted that ladies were beginning to don swim wear, formerly worn by men, which showed plenty of leg!

There is one more substantive article that dealt with the Russians but regrettably, it is not available unless one goes in person to the Library in Cincinnati. Even with today's technology, the newspaper cannot be copied as it is crumbling. I encourage those with an interest in the topic and a close proximity to Cincinnati to pursue this. Along with the article, the Public Library of Cincinnati also houses a significant collection of music, dance and theatre programs, including one in mint condition for the 6-7 February 1917 Ballet Russe performance.

OHIO, Dayton – 8 February 1917 – Victoria

"How I'd like to take a sock at that guy! Why doesn't he work for a living?" So declared and challenged under the same breath, a Dayton engineer, upon seeing Waslaw dance. In the heartland of America, ballet, especially as practiced by male dancers, was met with a great deal of contempt, in certain circles any case. Why such animosity? Because there was nothing like the Ballet Russe, in this country. There were many urgent problems facing this land, not to mention Dayton, Ohio. Even if we do not consider World War I looming on the horizon, the more immediate concerns were the flooding of the Mad, Miami and Stillwater rivers in 1913, killing 300 people and causing $100 million in damage. The dams that were to forever protect the city from such calamity were not built until 1918. Dayton, the Birthplace of Aviation, the world's chief producer of cash registers, a city of more than 800 manufacturing plants, had more pressing concerns than watching men in white tights dance, and then, at a cost that was twenty times what a good film like Chaplin in "Easy Street," or even a terrific vaudeville show would be! So, was there anyone in Dayton who took pleasure in terpsichorean art? We may never know, for all we have is a preview of the Ballet Russe, and an erroneous one at that. The *Dayton Journal* featured an excellent photograph of Flore Revalles and Alexandre Gavrilow, which may or may not have enticed prospective audiences, along with the following article, on the day of the performance:

> Serge de Diaghileff's Ballet Russe, which will be seen at the Victoria Theater tonight, has just completed a successful invasion of the New England states. he mimes and dancers of this celebrated troupe are headed by Waslaw Nijinsky, who has been conceded by the press of Europe and the American cities which he has visited to be the greatest male dancer of our generation. This is the first time that Nijinsky has appeared in any American city except New York. His reception throughout New England fully justifies the reputation which he has established and maintained through the six years of the ballet's existence.
>
> Nor was he the only dancer who found favor in the eyes of the New England audiences. Adolf Bolm immediately won a place by his graphic genius for pantomime and his virile personality. Flore Revalles received her share of praise for the cruel beauty of her

The American Tour of the Ballet Rouse

statuesque poses. In direct contrast to Mademoiselle Revalles, Lydia Lopokova charmed New England by her Dresden china prettiness. Olga Spesizewa, Margareta Frohman and Alexandre Gavrilow -- all earned plaudits. But -- and this has never been the case with any other ballet organization -- the New England states accorded the highest mead of praise to the regal splendor of the magic ensemble.

This entire piece sounds much like a press release, in which someone has forgotten to replace New England with the other states and towns that were toured. Before we uncover how the rest of Ohio greeted the Russians however, we will first pay a visit to Detroit.

MICHIGAN, Detroit – 9 - 10 February 1917 – Lyceum

By Arrangement with Metropolitan Opera Company
SERGE de DIAGHILEFF'S

BALLET RUSSE

Artistic Direction, Waslaw Nijinsky
For "Sadko" & "Les Papillons," Adolf Bolm

ARTISTS

Mlles.
Janina Bonievka
Ekaterina Galanta
Lydia Lopokova
Vera Nemtchinova
Sophie Pflanz
Flore Revalles
Lydia Sokolova
Alexandra Wasilewska

Messrs.
Adolf Bolm
Alexandre Gavriloff
Ivan Jazwinsky
Nicholas Kremneff
Waslaw Nijinsky
Mieczyslas Pianowski
Nicholas Sverew

and Corps de Ballet
Symphony Orchestra Conducted by M. Pierre Monteux

General Stage Manager .... M. Nicholas Kremneff
Technical Director .... M. Edward S. Pennell
Chief Machinist .... M. Michel Tschaoussovski

Baldwin Piano Used
DIAGHILEFF'S BALLET RUSSE

Management .... Metropolitan Musical Bureau

FRIDAY, FEBRUARY 9th, 1917

SCHEHERAZADE

A Persian Fable in One Act by
MM. LEON BAKST and MICHEL FOKINE
Music by RIMSKY-KORSAKOW
Choreography by M. MICHEL FOKINE
Scenes and Costumes by M. LEON BAKST

PERSONNEL

ZOBEIDE, Princess of Samarcande .... MLLE. FLORE REVALLES
LE NEGRE, Zobeide's favorite .... M. WASLAW NIJINSKY
SHARIAR, King of the Indes .... M. JAZVINSKY
SCHAH-ZEMAN, his brother .... M. MIECZYSLAS PIANOWSKI
LE GRAND EUNUQUE .... M. NICOLAS SVEREW
ODALISQUE .... MLLE. ALEXANDRA WASILEWSKA
THE SULTAN'S WIVES—Miles. Pflanz, Bonievka, Stawicka, Doris, Kochouba, Chabelska, Zamoucchovska, Sumarokova 2.
FIRST SLAVES OF THE HAREM—Miles. Sokolova, Zalewska, Mieczkowska, Pajewska, Galanta, Nemtchinova.
SECOND SLAVES OF THE HAREM—Miles. Potapovica, Kostrovskaja, Artaka, Kurtener, Sumarokova, Nemtchinova.
NEGRES—MM. Woronttow, Kawecki, Kostrovskoy, Statkiewicz, Kegler, Herman, Bromberg, Tchumakow.
VIOLIN SOLO .... FREDERIC FRADKIN

Detroit's Exclusive Corset Shop
Now in its New Location—21 Adams Avenue East

Corset Pleasures

How many pleasant evenings have been spoiled for you by an uncomfortable corset?

Doesn't it seem a shame to make elaborate preparations, and then get only about one-third the pleasure you should have, just because of the discomfort of your body, when the right corset would eliminate all this trouble? "BINNER" Corsets stand for the best in style and comfort.

I GIVE THE BEST CORSET SERVICE IN DETROIT

DORA LUDWIG
CORSETIERE

The American Tour of the Ballet Rouse

DIDN'T BEGINSKI

Nijinski, Airylike and Fairylike, in Wingski,
Practicing so Sweetly While Audience Waits and Waits.

At least one is assured of experiencing a variety of emotions when one sees the Serge de Diaghileff ballet at the Lyceum. And some of the emotions are pleasurable.

It began last night when M. Pierre Monteux took up his baton, brushed back his eight-pound brakeman's mustache and prepared to lead the orchestra on to battle with the music of Rimsky-Korsakow. Pierre tapped on his desk and uplifted his arms. Somebody sneezed. Down came his arms. A pause. More tapping. Up go the arms. A smothered cough. Another pause. Finally the spectators realized that Pierre wanted quiet, and the cougher jammed his handkerchief in his mouth, choked to death silently and the fight was on.

This Rimsky-Korsakow must have been a steam-riveter before he took up music. After Pierre had the audience cowed into silence, the orchestra let loose a blast of sound under cover of which a troupe of Hippodrome elephants might have galloped down the aisles and Pierre would never had heard them.

At times opinion was divided as to whether the orchestra had gotten out of Pierre's control. There seemed to be some feud between the brass and the strings with the drummer neutral and throwing in a lot of tympani tumult on both sides. Then things would quiet down a little, and Pierre had them pacified again.

Just Like Old Man Casey Jones

The first ballet is called "Scheherazade," and the scene is the home of Mr. Sultan, an engineer on the Petrograd-Siberia railroad. When Sultan is called to take out the 9:50, he leaves behind his wife and all the hired help. But he doesn't know that the Moscow sleeper has pulled up right at the door, and as soon as hubby has gone, Mrs. Sultan opens up the doors of the Pullman and out troop a lot of Russian traveling men and the Pullman porter.

Of course the traveling men act just like traveling men and grab off all the Muscovite chickens, while the porter, who looks a little like Al Jolson, only isn't so funny, begins playing around Mrs. Sultan. This is the part Nijinsky plays, and he is almost as good as the black man in "Birth of a Nation," who drove Mae Marsh off the cliff. But Mrs. Sultan doesn't jump; she likes it, which just goes to prove again that there is no accounting for tastes. To an outsider it appears that the weapon to use on this porter is a fly swatter.

Busy Getting the Poster Paint Off

Nijinsky made a lot of motions and Mrs. Sultan was just about to second some of them when friend husband came home, bringing a lot of huskies from the yards, who put the boots to the traveling men. Nijinsky did a great head-spin when he was stabbed, a bit of acrobatics that would get him a place on the Temple [a circus] bill any day.

The scenery for this number looked like the Germans had been using it for target practice, and the Germans are good marksmen.

At this point in the performance, an impressive man with a top hat and other expensive clothes informed this chronicler that he could now go back stage and interview Nijinsky.

The prospective interviewer dodged scenery for 35 minutes, alone on the Lyceum stage, which has the general dimensions of the Sahara desert. The man in the top hat came at intervals and reported that Nijinsky was still scraping Pullman paint off himself.

"Are you French?" he asked.

The reported blushed and at the risk of seeming a rank outsider, confessed that he wasn't.

"But Nijinsky speaks no English," said the top hat.

"I guess I can get along without talking to him," said the reporter.

And the top hat went away again.

Meanwhile the stage was set for the butterfly dance and a pretty creature with a quantity of yellow whiskers dominated the stage for five minutes while he tripped about with a saltshaker full of resin, stopping now and then, hand on hip, to view the results of his labors.

"He was brought from Russia just to do that," whispered the stage manager, as the be whiskered resin-shaker paused, and with eyelids half closed carefully viewed the general effect. He gave the shaker one flip to drop a little resin in a spot that seemed a little slippery for the divine feet of Nijinsky, and departed, exhausted.

The butterfly dance over, the stage was prepared for the enchanted princess dance. Still no Nijinsky and the interviewer became quite hopeful. Perhaps he wouldn't appear at all.

The American Tour of the Ballet Rouse

At least 15 minutes after the stage was set and fully an hour after Nijinsky had flitted away as the porter, he arrived. Meanwhile the audience had been waiting. Nobody seemed to know what kept Nijinsky so long.

And Then the Reporter Went Away

Once on the stage, he did a lot of exercises to limber himself up, waving first one hand, then the other hand, then both hands. He certainly is dainty in his calisthenics. After 10 minutes of this, he was ready. By this time several stage hands had been threatened with apoplexy. One red-faced husky with half a pound of line cut in his cheek, stood swaying in a corner of the stage, an iron bar clenched in his hands, muttering to himself. He was in no mood to be trifled with.

Nijinsky breathed on his fingernails and polished them on his sleeve; he flecked a bit of imaginary dust from his costume and gently stroked a couple of quarts of turquoise that hung on him.

Then the curtain went up and the prancing began.

Top hat appeared now.

"You may meet him directly after this dance," he said.

"Thank you," said the reporter, and in 60 seconds he was walking briskly westward on Monroe avenue. He came away from there. And so if you want to know what happened in the Lyceum last night, you must read it elsewhere in The News today. This reporter admits that he fell down on the job. There's a limit to this reporting thing. He spent the rest of the evening with two honest, hardworking pickpockets and went home much refreshed.

(10 February 1917, *Detroit News*)

The mysterious writer certainly agreed with the Dayton engineer and he wasn't bashful about it either. There were also favorable reviews, including one from the same paper, on the same day. The *Detroit Free Press* also presented an opinion that was provoking from another point of view. The journalist went so far as to sign his initials, C. S. S. All in all, C. S. S. enjoyed the ballet, having seen it the year before, still feeling that it had improved in some areas. Like in other cities that had the dubious distinction of a double Russian invasion however, Detroit too, noted the lack of "absolute novelty." Of course, how can anything be novel, the second time around? Even so, Nijinsky was certainly something new! And Waslaw once again rose to the occasion and gave an encore. Yet, not even his "wonderful" interpretation could assuage the critic when it came to the old matter of "decorum," not the bare legs this time, but something even more "unclean."

> In "Scheherazade" Nijinsky replaced Bolm. There are two ways of viewing Nijinsky's impersonation of Le Negre. As a work of art it was no less than wonderful, and realistic to a degree that can be understood only by a person who has read the prologue of the "Thousand and One Nights" before it has passed through the prudent hands of the censor. Such dancing and such miming have not been done before in this city by any man. At the risk of being considered crude and prudish by those who justify all art no matter how repulsive, we venture to express the opinion that it will be as well if precisely such dancing and miming are not seen here again. A creature having a similitude of a lecherous crouching, Negroid, man-ape, with grinning, slobbering lips, is no pleasant figure. When this creature fingers and fawns upon a woman with all the extravagances of bestial passion, a strong stomach is requisite to real enjoyment. The thing is not disgusting because it is immoral, but because it is unclean.

I must stop here and do a bit of editorializing. The first question that comes to mind is whether the illustrious C. S. S. would have made the same statement, had Scheherazade's slave been white? Secondly, such bigoted remarks clearly illustrate the tragedy of slavery and prejudice in this country.

OHIO, Toledo – 12 February 1917 – Valentine

    Oh, the Russians, the Russians,
    Their rhythmic percussions,
    Their wskis and Inskis,
    Their Nymphs and Nijinskys,
    Their Spry Lopokowas!
    With their names so like sneezes,
    Their bare feet and kneeses.
    Such curling and whirling
    And skipping and tripping,
    And dipping and tipping!
    Fairy-tale, airy-dale,
    Lady and shady-like,
    Never old maidy-like.
    And oh, what a glory
    They add to a story!

    Ah, what agility;
    Dresden fragility;
    What display of expressive ability
    For the magical toes
    And appropriate pose
    Can disclose, goodness knows.
    The swoon of a swan,
    Or the bloom of a rose,
    Till brokers and bankers,
    The gentlemen rankers,
    The dubs from the clubs,
    The wiffles and hubs,
    The dudes and debutantes,
    Matrons and maid-aunties
    Rise up in a unison,
    Praising the Benison,
    Pleased with the pirouettes,
    Praising the pepper,
    Blessing the steps
    From the steppes,
    And the stepper.

              -George S. Chappell

Nijinsky in America

This bit of verse in the *Toledo Daily Eagle* welcomed the Russians, along with some advance notice of the marvels to behold. The tone of the ensuing critiques was mildly enthusiastic. Journalist, F. Glenn Baker of the *Toledo Blade* found the program charming, but much too brief. Commentators from other papers felt the same, in particular about Waslaw. "We saw very little of Waslaw, physically or 'dancingly.'" In addition, The *Toledo News-Bee* writer was disturbed by Waslaw's attire: "The extreme weather may have induced the comfortable looking clothes, but then Nijinsky is a Russian who should be immune to the zero thing." It is hard to figure out what this critic was referring to, as Waslaw danced in "Les Sylphides," a piece whose costumes are not exactly of the Arctic Circle. "This chap…appeared only in one act, a dreamy, graceful sort of extended number…" In his opinion, although the dancing was "exceptional," it was not "quite as varied and important as that presented here frequently by Pavlowa." Baker, more or less, agreed, "Nijinsky, the embodiment of grace and agility when in motion, proved lacking in personal appeal or charm when in repose."

The Toledo commentary may not be too thrilling, but the fact that the Valentine Theater is still standing, is. Not only is it standing, but the dwelling section of the building has been restored and rented, as part of the revitalization project of downtown Toledo. The vision now is to restore the theatre as well. With Ohio's track record for having the largest concentration of historic theaters, the Valentine's chances are pretty good.

MICHIGAN, Grand Rapids – 13 February 1917 – Powers

Tuesday, the 13th of February found the Russians in Michigan one more time. The by now familiar column, "The Theaters" was covered by a Ms. Mary E. Remington. She gave her report about all artistic events of the week, decisively and succinctly:

> Additional standards for the dance drama were set by the Serge de Diaghileff Ballet Russe at Powers Theater Tuesday night. Heretofore, Mordkin, Pavlowa and her Ballet Russe have been the standards of the choreographic art in Grand Rapids, but the Diaghileff Ballet Russe is so entirely different that comparisons are impossible. The latter is far more Slavic.
>
> The dancing of the ballet is superb. There is rhythmic power, grace, abandon and a mastery of the pantomimic art. The orchestra, which was strong numerically, gave an effective if somewhat uninspired rendition of the music scores.
>
> Leon Bakst in his decorations and costume designs has brought a new idea to the art of the theater - the unity and fusion of all arts of music, dancing and costumes, and scenery. The Bakst background accentuates the art of the dancers and brings the drama into the foreground.
>
> Waslaw Nijinsky was programmed for only one dance drama, the "Carnaval," but he also danced in the "Scheherazade" and for the first time in a one-night engagement. "Carnaval" is a pantomime of the early Victorian period arranged by Michel Fokine for the Schumann music. He appeared in the role of Arlequin, and it was wonderful dancing that he gave - vigorous, athletic, with amazing leaps and bounds contrasted with the graceful poses, the expressive use of arms, hands and, in fact, entire being, in the spirit of the dance. Lydia Lopokova was as graceful as thistledown in the role of Columbine. "Scheherazade," a tale from the "Arabian Nights," to which Rimsky-Korsakov wrote a brilliant score, was a savage, sensual bit of orientalism, in which Mlle. Flore Revalles as the princess of the harem was a beautiful and seductive creature, while Nijinsky minced the role of the Numidian paramour, giving a remarkable exhibition of the dance and pantomimic art. "Prince Igor," an episode from Borodin's opera of the same title, introduced the barbaric and primitive spirit of the steppes. It was pure Slavic and splendid in its semi-savage beauty. The decoration and costumes by Roerich were in the spirit of Bakst and quite as fine. Nicholas Zverew demonstrated his splendid prowess as a dancer. Mlle. Sophie

Pflanz made an excellent impression. The leading principals with the exception of Adolf Bolm appeared once, Bolm not appearing in any of the dance dramas.

The visit of the Ballet Russe stands out as the novelty of the season. (14 February 1917, *Grand Rapids Press*)

OHIO, Cleveland – 15 - 17 February 1917 – Colonial

Culturally speaking, Cleveland residents, at the turn of the century, were well above the norm found elsewhere in America. They had seen the Russians the season before and had welcomed Pavlowa and Lopokova in years past, when they performed on their own. Charles Henderson, the fine art critic for the *Cleveland Plain Dealer* had given a delightfully intelligent preview that clearly explained it all about the Ballet Russe; how it came to be; what it was attempting to accomplish; and its importance in the world of art. Mr. Henderson had some fine words to say about Waslaw: "…it just happens that this time the company is better than it was the first time because, as was pointed out above, of the presence of Nijinsky, without whom it is difficult to think of the Diaghileff Ballet at all."

A review by a far-sighted journalist is one that can be trusted; consequently, we must come up with an explanation for some of the erratic behavior of the troupe at this point. I have some theories, but first, the article:

> Probably for the last time in Cleveland, the Russian ballet organization of Serge de Diaghileff, the greatest in all time, is giving an engagement which opened last evening at the Colonial theater. It was a splendid performance, a good program, and the right sort of an audience enjoyed it.
>
> That is, the audience was representative of intellectual and musical Cleveland. The theater was almost filled with the people who literally devoured the music and dance festival. And it all made a brilliant evening.
>
> Nijinsky, Lopokova and Revalles were the big favorites in the dances last night and Lopokova, with Nijinsky to help her, scored the biggest individual triumph. This was in the dance duet "Enchanted Princess," using the English at least as well as the program used the title in French. This dance gave the full opportunity to each dancer of making a direct appeal to the audience and it happened last evening that Nijinsky rather ungallantly took the encores away from the lady.
>
> The audience admired Nijinsky, but it wished to deliver a personal tribute to the woman, Lopokova, even if it appreciated right along that the man was the better dancer. This little bit of feeling on the

audiences part had the effect of spurring Nijinsky on to better and better dancing - but not to letting the audience recognize the lady alone. And, together with a few other things, helped to make the audience hard toward the performers. They invited it -- and got it...

Conspicuous, in a negative way...was the refusal of Nijinsky to let the audience recognize his dancing partner...

It seemed that the dance company danced when it wished, and the audience could ponder the price it had paid and wait for the Ballet Russe to get good and ready. When it was ready to dance, the audience was treated to such miracles of harmony in color and sound and motion as "Les Sylphides," the opening number, "Scheherazade," in which Mlle. Revalles was so wonderful, and "Prince Igor."

Diaghileff's Ballet had an audience last evening that was responsive and that was representative of everything good in Cleveland's social and artistic life, but the ballet, while it was perfect on the stage, did not seem to be in harmony with the audience. The orchestra, that gave symphonies startling in their majesty, and that stirred an audience well used to the best symphonies, did not have the proper respect for its auditors. There was an occasion when a player had taken more than his share of a long, tiresome wait between numbers and dashed down an aisle, during a splendid overture, leaped over the railing, grasped his instrument -- it was a horn -- and started to play as if Cleveland were used to such conduct.

It is too bad that so great a work of art should be marred by a patently contemptuous attitude on the part of a few subordinates in the company toward the public. Monteux accomplishes wonders with his great orchestra. Diaghileff has acquired a sensational equipment of dance and dancers - but somebody should teach the occasional and obstreperous member of the organization to pretend that he has respect for the audience, even if he hasn't it.

The Diaghileff Ballet Russe is a beautiful thing and it has never has been seen to better advantage than in the Colonial theater, with better dancers, with better music and with better effects. This afternoon, the organization will give a matinee and tonight it will give Cleveland a last chance to witness real Russian ballet with a good program.

The peculiar behavior found in the company may have had a number of causes. Under the review, some of the headlines read:

The American Tour of the Ballet Rouse

"U-Boats Lie in Wait In Gulf of Mexico U. S. Skipper Asserts," and "Britain Warns of Sea Danger Zones." Most members of the ballet were three cities away from returning to warn-torn Europe, by ship! Many of them did not know what was waiting on the other side; how their families and loved ones faired, and what the future held, both professionally, as well as personally. They had traveled tens of thousands of miles, performing in fifty-two cities, under all kinds of circumstances, including the tribulations of weather, poor theatre facilities, not to mention living out of a suitcase and on a moving train for the greater part of four months. It is small wonder nerves were frayed and behaviors possibly not at their well-mannered best. As to why Waslaw seemingly "stole" the encore from Lopokova, well, frankly, I only have a very biased, one sided opinion about that, therefore, you will make up your own mind and form your own conclusions.

PENNSYLVANIA, Pittsburgh – 19 - 21 February 1917 – New Pitt Theater

One of the leading industrial cities in America, Pittsburgh is also a great steel manufacturing center of the world. Like in a number of other industrialized towns in the US, this was the Russians' second trip here. Their reception was refreshingly warm, generous and erudite. And this, from a city that had as many hard working laborers as any, along the tour.

BALLET RUSSE GETS A REAL OVATION

Already a favorite in Pittsburgh because of the excellence of its offerings, the Serge de Diaghileff Ballet Russe scored another distinctive triumph in its initial performance at the Pitt Theater last night, when the management presented four numbers as the opening attraction of a three day engagement.

Much of the ovation extended the company was due to the beautiful interpretation of Nijinsky, premier dancer, who was absent from the company when it appeared here last year, and to the equally beautiful work of Lopokova. To these two go the highest meed of praise, and to them Pittsburgh lovers of the art of dancing who witness their performances ever may revert with pleasing memories.

Not the least helpful toward the success of the opening performance was the splendid work of the orchestra under the direction of H. H. Heidelberg and Pierre Monteux, the first named conducting for "Till Eulenspiegel," and the latter for the three other numbers.

"Till Eulenspiegel," the opening number which also served to introduce Nijinsky, is a ballet of his own arrangement, from Strauss' music. Whatever Strauss' music held of beauty and mirth and satire, Nijinsky accentuated it, and one almost lost the thread of music in admiration of the Till of Nijinsky, who slipped in and out of the crowds he was impersonating, and with elfish glee was mocking to their faces. As buffoon, clergyman, doctor, gentleman, soldier, he held up to the faces of each his characterization and poked all manner of fun at them until, having run his race, the gallows took its toll…Nijinsky made Till the very spirit of mischief and at the same time presented him as graceful with a smoothness that was more than pleasing.

Nijinsky made his second appearance of the evening with Lopokova in "La Princess Enchantee," surrounded by the wonderfully colorful settings by Bakst, remembered so well from last year. It is doubtful if the present generation ever will see two such perfect artists in this beautiful work as was presented for their edification last evening. Lopokova, more than popular here, whose exquisite charm has won her thousands of admirers was but complimentary to Nijinsky, so wonderful did he seem. Here the slight, lithe Nijinsky gave almost an entirely different interpretation of the dance from that of the opening number and seemed all grace and ethereal. So well pleased was the audience and so great an ovation did the stars receive, they were compelled to give an encore of the last duet...

(20 February 1917, *Pittsburgh Press*)

The above article continued with a well-informed preview of the ballets for the second evening. The review for that performance was no less laudatory.

NIJINSKY PLEASES IN SPLENDID BALLETS

De Diaghileff's Ballet Russe scored another decided hit at the Pitt Theater last night when it gave the second of its series of performances before a much larger audience than was present on the opening night. And again Nijinsky came in for additional praise and commendation due to splendid work, while Lopokova continued to win new admirers by her grace and beauty.

"Scheherazade" was the opening number of the evening, with Nijinsky in the role of chief eunuch, and Revalles as the harem favorite. Nijinsky gave to his role a far different atmosphere than that of his predecessor seen here last year. He made it fantastically droll, kept in complete touch with the music and fitted into the story of the passionate orgy so well one almost believed him the character he portrayed...The Bakst settings did not show all their barbaric beauty because of being cramped for room...

"Les Sylphides," a romantic reverie to compositions of Chopin, possessed all the delicacy and charm of last year, with the addition of the wonderful dancing of Nijinsky. In a pas seul to a Chopin mazurka, and in a valse with Lydia Lopokova, his consummative virtuosity, airy lightness and exquisite grace of movement, made it, perhaps the most finished and artistic performance ever seen here. The small stage necessitated a reduction in the number of dancers, and hampered, a little, their movements.

"L'Apres Midi d'un Faun" was presented with Nijinsky in the leading role. Comparing it with the same ballet, as seen last year, the result but adds to the extremely favorable impression Nijinsky has made in Pittsburgh. Last year there seemed to be lacking some of the pagan frankness necessary to bring out all the motif of the number. Not so this year. Nijinsky seemed to have caught the spirit of the faun entirely and made it just what one would expect of such a being. There was some who did not like this interpretation, believing it too broad, but nothing less could have made it fitted to Nijinsky or vice versa. Praise also is due to the nymphs, for they seemed to catch enthusiasm for the perfect artistry from Nijinsky, and therefore gave a splendid performance... (21 February 1917, *Pittsburgh Press*)

The *Post Gazette's* commentary, though not as extensive, was similar in tone. There is no doubt that the Ballet Russe and Waslaw had made a very favorable impression on this Iron City. What has been an even more fascinating find however, was the unearthing of another Russian troupe in Pittsburgh at the same time! Concurrently with the advertisements for the Diaghileff Ballet Russe, there was an aggressive promotional campaign, large photographs and all, for the "Imperial Russian Ballet," with Theodore Kosloff and Vlasta Maslova. They were slated for the Davis, a vaudeville theater. Kosloff had partnered Tamara Karsavina and during the early days of the Diaghileff organization, danced with Bolm, Mordkin and Waslaw.

> In the Davis Theater this week Harry Davis is to present the Petit Ballet Russe, a company of 12 Russian dancers - from Serge de Diaghileff's organization, as the extraordinary attraction in a bill of nine high-grade vaudeville acts. Theodore Kosloff and Vlasta Maslova, respectively premier danseur and premier danseuse, head of the organization, which will be accompanied by Kosloff's, own famous Russian orchestra. The dances are all to the classic music of such eminent composers as Grieg, Delibes, Brahms, Glinka, Tchaikovsky and Rusky-Korsakoff. In contradistinction to the ballet performance will be the divertissement offered by Dunbar's Old Time Darkies... (18 February 1917, *Post Gazette*)

Pity the poor dancer, especially a Russian, who had to compete with the incomparable Nijinsky! And the humiliation of it all, on a vaudeville stage, yet! One wonders if Waslaw and Theodore had an opportunity to meet, while in Pittsburgh, and reminisce about old times.

NEW YORK, Syracuse – 23 February 1917 – Empire

FRIDAY NIGHT, FEBRUARY 23 --- ONE TIME ONLY

By Arrangement metropolitan Opera Co.

LAST AMERICAN APPEARANCES

SERGE de DIAGHILEFF'S

BALLET RUSSE

With the World's Greatest Imperial Dancers

NIJINSKY   LOPOKOVA

REVALLES   GAVRILOW

IN A BRILLIANT ARRAY OF SENSATIONAL BALLETS

EXACTLY AS PRESENTED IN PARIS AND AT THE NEW YORK TRIUMPH

COMPLETE SYMPHONY ORCHESTRA   Monteux Conducts

BAKST SCENERY IN RIOTOUS COLORS AND MAD FANCIES

REPERTOIRE - SCHEHERAZADE - LES SYLPHIDES - PRINCE IGOR

SEATS -- Orchestra $5, $4, $3. Balcony, $4, $3, $2, $1.50. Gallery, $1.

The Serge de Diaghileff   Ballet Russe appeared at the Empire last evening before an audience which comfortably filled the lower floor and crowded -- the balcony and gallery. The three ballets which were given -- each absolutely different from both the others -- were applauded to the echo, and the audience which left the theater at 11 o'clock felt as though it had been transported back into modern times from the pages of an Eastern fairy tale.

There is only one adjective which fitly describes the Ballet with its marvelous ensemble of sound and color and exquisite motion, the much abused and overworked word "exotic." Even in the land of the Czar, the home of the ballet, the birthplace of Diaghileff and

Nijinsky in America

Nijinsky and Lopokova, it must appear as it does to us: something wonderful apart, like the growth of some strange tropical flower...

Nijinsky's Wonderful Dancing

The grace and wonderful posturing of Nijinsky was shown more harmoniously, however, in "Les Sylphides," where, in a garment of white silk with royal purple velvet tunic, he was the fairy prince. Nijinsky is not so faultless a type of male beauty as is Mordkin, but excels in grace. His ankles, his wrists and his neck play their part in his marvelous dances. His agility is marvelous. He skims through the air like a bird, and in "Scheherazade" you can see all of Nijinsky over the heads of all the other persons in the ballet...

And thus hailed Syracuse the Russians, who, in spite of having the formidable tour of fifty-four cities behind them, gave their artistic, best, once again.

NEW YORK, Albany – 24 February 1917 – Harmanus Bleecker Hall

Figure 11.

The kind people at the Albany Public Library left no stone unturned to search for a review of the Ballet Russe's final performance in America, they found none; so dear reader, you will have to be satisfied with a bit of preview. Albany too, had seen the Russians before, but without Waslaw. Anticipation was at fever pitch.

> An unusual attraction will be the appearance at the Hall next Saturday night of the Russian Ballet, under the patronage of the Metropolitan Opera Company, and under the direct management of Nijinsky, one of the greatest of all dancers. The company was here last season, but without Nijinsky, and this time his appearance is guaranteed. There can be no doubt about the sensation that this announcement will make, or of the importance of the engagement. The organization comes here complete, with all the gorgeous scenery, costumes, colorings, etc., that have made such an impression. In addition to these it will have its own symphony orchestra of 60 men, under the leadership of Pierre Monteux…(17 February 1917, *The Albany Evening Journal*)

Nijinsky in America

Enthusiasm and interest increase as the appearance of the celebrated Diaghileff Russian ballet draws near, and it indicates a very large audience in attendance at the Hall to-morrow night; when the organization makes its visit to Albany. There will be no matinee performance, as the company does not arrive in Albany until 12 o'clock, but a remarkably interesting program is being arranged for the evening entertainment.

```
            HARMANUS BLEECKER HALL, ALBANY
                SATURDAY, FEBRUARY 24th, 1917
                    AT 8:30 O'CLOCK P. M.

           By Arrangement with Metropolitan Opera Company
                     SERGE DE DIAGHILEFF'S
                      BALLET RUSSE
                  Artistic Direction, WASLAW NIJINSKY
              For "Sadko" and "Les Papillons," ADOLF BOLM
                Management, Metropolitan Musical Bureau

                            ARTISTS
        MMES.                                    MESSRS.
   JANINA BONIECKA                          ADOLF BOLM
   EKATERINA GALANTA                        ALEXANDRE GAVRILOW
   LYDIA LOPOKOVA                           IVAN JAZWINSKY
   VERA NEMTCHINOVA                         NICOLAS KREMNEFF
   SOPHIE PFLANZ                            WASLAW NIJINSKY
   FLORE REVALLES                           MIECZYSLAS PIANOWSKI
   LYDIA SOKOLOVA                           NICHOLAS ZVEREW
   ALEXANDRA WASILEWSKA
                         AND CORPS DE BALLET

              Symphony Orchestra Conducted by M. PIERRE MONTEUX

                        Serge de Diaghileff's Staff
   Business Manager..........................M. STANISLAW DROBECKI
   General Stage Manager.....................M. NICOLAS KREMNEFF
   Technical Director........................M. EDWARDS S. FENNELL
   Chief Machinist...........................M. MICHEL TSCHAOUSSOVSKI

            LOCAL MANAGEMENT OF BEN FRANKLIN
```

Figure 12.

The American Tour of the Ballet Rouse

In two of the ballets Nijinsky, said to be the world's greatest ballet dancer, will appear, and it is known that "Cleopatra" and "Scheherazade," two of the most successful and beautiful entertainments in the company repertoire will be given here...the entire magic ensemble that has so astounded audiences in all the cities visited will be given here. Splendid scenic effects will be produced by this company, and this and the beautiful music by the orchestra of 60 men are second only in interest to the marvelous dancing... (23 February 1917, *The Albany Evening Journal*)

Conclusion

We have come to the end of our journey; a journey that spanned the continent, for 118 days, in 55 cities and 31 states. I purposely left out New York City, since that has been covered in a myriad of books and articles and for which material is much more readily available.

You have read about America's reaction to the Ballet Russe. Throughout this book, I suggested that you make up your own mind about the issues concerning the Ballet Russe's American Tour. One final time, I will ask you to be judge and jury. In light of ninety years, did Nijinsky and the Ballet Russe win American's mind and heart?

I would like to express my gratitude to one and all who were in any way a source of support and encouragement for me; To my grandmother Romola - a spirit of gratefulness for keeping such a careful itinerary, without which the realization of this book would have been close to impossible; To my grandfather, Tatakaboy – the charge to go on:

"My heirs will continue what I have begun."

Phoenix, Arizona
June 2006

Epilogue

Dear reader, permit me to digress for a moment. In front of me are two photographs: one is of a distinctively handsome young man in civilian clothes, hands folded, looking relaxed and sure of himself; the other, a dancer in an oriental costume, using Siamese hand pose, looking somewhat androgynous and feline-like. The 9 November 1916 issue of *Boston Evening Transcript* called it "'Literal Fact and Pictorial Illusion,' Waslaw Nijinsky, From the Recent Photograph by Georg and From the Celebrated Portrait by Blanche." Yes, both images are of one and the same man, Nijinsky. The photographs are accompanied by an intimate interview with Nijinsky: "'Nijinsky On and Off the Stage,' MANIFOLD NIJINSKY." There is a library-full of theorizing about the cause of Nijinsky's madness. My grandfather, Tatakaboy (my aunt Kyra's nickname for her father), was diagnosed mentally ill early in 1919, almost two years to the date when the U.S. Tour of the Ballet Russe ended. The validity of the diagnosis was not questioned until eighty years later. For clarification's sake, I'd like to reprint here an address, given by my mother Tamara, Nijinsky's younger daughter. On 26 October 1995, Tamara Nijinsky spoke at a public forum in celebration of Waslaw Nijinsky at the Clarke Institute of Psychiatry Foundation, associated with the University of Toronto.

> [The] next day, about three in the afternoon, we drove across the bridge, on the Lake of Zurich to the hilly side, where, in the woods, a little distance the State asylum is built, a big old-fashioned building with iron barred windows. But the smiling porter and the flowers which surrounded the directorial building, where Professor Bleuler received, took away the disagreeable impression. We sat for a few moments and then the Professor came out. I introduced him to Waslaw, and they both disappeared in his study. The door opened within ten minutes, and the Professor showed out Waslaw smilingly, "All right. Splendid. Won't you step in for a second? I forgot to give you the promised prescription yesterday." I smiled at Waslaw as I passed him, following the Professor; what prescription I could not remember. As he closed the door of his study behind him, he said firmly, "Now, my dear, be very brave. You have to take your child away; you have to get a divorce. Unfortunately, I am helpless. Your husband is incurably insane. I must seem brutal, but I have to

Nijinsky in America

> be in order to save you and your child --- two lives. We physicians must try to save those whom we can; the others, unfortunately, we have to abandon to their cruel fate

So wrote my mother, Romola Nijinsky, more than sixty years ago. The year was 1919. Professor Eugene Bleuler had just diagnosed my father, Waslaw Nijinsky, a "schizophrenic." Dr. Peter Ostwald, author of a book about my father, had this to say about the Professor:

> Bleuler was one of Europe's foremost diagnosticians. He had recently coined the word "schizophrenia," literally "splitting of the mind," to describe a psychological process that he believed to be responsible for many mental diseases. "Schizophrenics," thought Bleuler, were people whose thoughts typically followed no logical sequence, veered off in unexpected directions, or got completely stuck. Such individuals tended to focus all their attention on themselves and have reduced or inappropriate emotional reactions as well as ambivalent social attitudes, Bleuler called this "autism." He believed that many additional symptoms flowed from these "primary" psychopathological processes, including delusions, hallucinations, and disturbances of speech and behavior. He had presented his theory of schizophrenia in the form of a monograph, published in 1911, and included it in every edition of his widely read *Textbook of Psychiatry*.

What had led to Bleuler's diagnosis of Nijinsky was a series of eccentric behaviors on the part of my father, following his dismissal from the Ballet Russe and the lack of opportunity to dance due to World War I.

In January 1995, the French Publisher, Actes Sud, brought out the unexpurgated diary of Waslaw Nijinsky. [since then it has appeared in 13 languages, in 16 countries]. My father wrote it at the onset of his illness, a few months before the diagnosis was made. A heavily edited version was published in 1936, but only now has the unexpurgated text been made available to the public. Often the question is asked whether Nijinsky was really mentally ill. Was he suffering from schizophrenia? Was he just acting? Well before seeing Professor Bleuler, my father wrote:

The American Tour of the Ballet Rouse

...want to weep but I cannot because my soul hurts so much that I fear for myself. I feel pain. I am sick in my soul but not in my brain. The doctor [not Bleuler but a GP who saw him earlier] does not understand my sickness. I know what I need in order to be well. My sickness is too great for me to be cured too soon. I am not incurable. I am sick in my soul. I am poor. I am a beggar. I'm unhappy. I'm hideous. I know that everybody will suffer while reading these lines because they will feel me [i.e., feel what I feel]. I know well what I need. I am a strong and not a weak man. I am not sick in my body. I am sick in my soul. I suffer. I suffer.

In the late 1980's, Dr. Peter Ostwald, Professor of Psychiatry at the University of California in San Francisco approached us with the request of examining my father's medical records. The result of his painstaking investigation and search was the 1991 publication of Nijinsky, A Leap Into Madness. Dr. Ostwald ends the book with a formal diagnosis; Dr. Joseph H. Stephens, Associate Professor of Psychiatry at the John Hopkins University School of Medicine concurred with his diagnosis: Nijinsky did not suffer from schizophrenia.

In his notebook on "Feelings" my father wrote: "People like eccentrics and they will therefore leave me alone, saying that I am a 'mad clown.'" Chapter eight in Dr. Ostwald's book is entitled: "Playing the Role of a Madman." My father was a great dancer and choreographer, but what not everyone knows is that he was a remarkable actor as well. [American audiences were sophisticated enough to sense this at once.] Commenting on one of his performances, Sarah Bernhardt said: "I'm afraid I have just seen the greatest actor that ever lived."

Was my father acting at the onset of his illness? Was he diagnosed properly? [Obviously not.] Did people in the medical field know enough about geniuses like Nijinsky? Did they understand how to deal with them? All of our answers would be mere conjecture. What we do know is this, the GP who had seen him first, wrote to Professor Bleuler the following:

> The patient's wife portrays him as always having been a strange, eccentric person. Nijinsky's valet, who knew him well, told her the same thing. Somatically I find nothing of significance. Syphilis is denied. No drinking. Nicotine very rarely. Alcohol nearly

abstinent. He does not hear voices. Sleeps generally well. Occasionally he eats enormous amounts, then again little . . . he is ironic, mischievous, argumentative, torments everyone with his remarks . . . . He claims that he does everything on purpose "in order to play the fool." His wife says that he is a comedian from A to Z.

Professor Bleuler wrote the following report after seeing my father for the first time:

I was consulted on Thursday. The man came up with a few difficulties, showed fear of being declared mentally ill [wouldn't you in 1919?] and answered my questions for the most part with a flood of words behind which there wasn't much substance, or evasion. He constantly had to ask me how I can recognize mentally ill people etc., explains that he acted like a mentally ill person in front of his wife in order to see how she reacts to that, and therefore sometimes just stared into a corner. He guarded himself against giving information about any delusions. Intelligence evidently very good in the past, now he is a confused schizophrenic with mild manic excitement.

It is significant to note that my father spoke no German and could not communicate very well in French either. His mother tongue was Polish and then he learned Russian, neither of which the Swiss Professor Bleuler spoke. We must ask ourselves what Diaghilev's dismissal meant to my father - whose very existence depended on expressing himself through his art? Did Bleuler delve deeper into the reasons for his eccentric behavior, about which not only the people around him spoke, but my father himself wrote: "people like eccentrics." My father knew he was a genius; an "autistic genius" is used to getting his way, and being the center of attention; he knew how to hold his audience spellbound. Bleuler had problems with that sort of behavior as an earlier quote illustrates. Would my father's behavior be considered "eccentric" in 1995; yes, definitely, but would that make him mentally ill?

MADNESS IS A QUESTION, NOT AN ANSWER . . .

WHAT DISTANCE SEPARATES MAN FROM GOD?

WHAT SEPARATES LIFE FROM DEATH?

MADNESS FROM TRUTH?

The American Tour of the Ballet Rouse
AND WORDS FROM SILENCE? (Dr. Peter Ostwald. Ch. 9)

You might ask why I burdened you with this. In order that the following interview, dear reader, may help you make up your mind, bring in the verdict: was Nijinsky a madman or genius?

Works Cited

"Aim of Serge De Diaghileff," New Haven Journal Courier, 28 October 1916, Connecticut.

A. L. S. W., "Supreme Dancing by the Ballet Russe," Springfield Union, 4 November 1916, Massachusetts.

"Amusements," Boston Evening Transcript, 6 November 1916, Massachusetts.

Anthony, Walter, "Ballet Russe Delights Both Eyes and Ears," San Francisco Chronicle, 3 January 1916, California.

"Apollos and Beauties Sought As Ballet Supers," Saint Paul Pioneer Press, 23 January 1917, Minnesota.

"At the Theaters," Dayton Journal, 8 February 1917, Ohio.

"At the Theatres," Providence Sunday Journal, 29 October 1916, Rhode Island.

Baer, Leone Cass, "Magic of Russian Ballet Enthralls," Morning Oregonian, 13 January 1917, Oregon.

Bagg, Ernest Newton, "Russians Invade Springfield," Springfield Union, 3 November 1916, Massachusetts.

Baker, F. Glenn, "The Ballet Russe," Toledo Blade, 13 February 1917, Ohio.

"Bakst Ballet Is Pleasing, Beautiful, Gorgeous, Bizarre," The Seattle Daily Times, 17 January 1917, Wednesday Evening, Washington.

"Ballet Corps to Arrive on Special Trains," Fort Worth Record, 30 November 1916, Fort Worth, Texas.

"Ballet Ends Boston Season," Boston Sunday Post, 12 November 1916, Massachusetts.

"Ballet's Final Program Finest," The Seattle Daily Times, 18 January 1917, Thursday Evening, Washington.

"Ballet Russe," Brooklyn Daily Eagle, 1 November 1916, New York.

The American Tour of the Ballet Rouse

---, Brooklyn Daily Eagle, 2 November 1916, New York.

---, Courier Journal, 4 February 1917, Louisville, Kentucky.

---, Evening Bulletin, 1 April 1916, Philadelphia, Pennsylvania.

---, Inquirer, 26 November 1916, Philadelphia, Pennsylvania.

---, Syracuse Herald, 18 February 1917, New York.

---, Worcester Daily Telegram, 13 November 1916, Massachusetts.

"Ballet Russe Arrives for Performance Tonight," Saint Paul Dispatch, 23 January 1917, Minnesota.

"Ballet Russe at Academy," Brooklyn Daily Eagle, 3 November 1916, New York.

"Ballet Russe at New Nixon Tonight," Atlantic City Daily Press, 16 November 1916, New Jersey.

"Ballet Russe at Parsons Theater," Hartford Daily Currant, 12 November 1916, Connecticut.

"Ballet Russe at Worcester Tonight," Worcester Daily Gazette, 13 November 1916, Massachusetts.

"Ballet Russe Beneath the Stage Gave Exotic Picture," Nashville Tennessean and The Nashville American, 5 February 1917.

"Ballet Russe's 'Cleopatre' Proves Brilliant Novelty," The Times-Picayune, 2 December 1916, New Orleans, Louisiana.

"Ballet Russe Closes," Brooklyn Daily eagle, 29 October 1916, New Jersey.

"Ballet Russe Gets a Real Ovation," Pittsburgh Press, 20 February 1917, Pennsylvania.

"Ballet Russe Here Tonight," Tulsa Daily World, 11 December 1916, morning ed., Oklahoma.

"Ballet Russe Is Animated Art Exhibit," Wichita Beacon, 12 December 1916, Kansas.

"Ballet Russe Is Gorgeous," Hartford Times, 15 November 1916, Connecticut.

Nijinsky in America

"Ballet Russe Makes Wonderful Impression at the Shubert," New Haven Evening Register, 1 November 1916, Connecticut.

"Ballet Russe Nixon Thursday," Atlantic City Daily Press, 14 November 1916, New Jersey.

"Ballet Russe Rich in Artistry," Worcester Evening Gazette, 14 November 1916, Massachusetts.

"Ballet Russe Scores Big Success in Dallas," The Dallas Times Herald, 8 December 1916, Texas.

"Ballet Russe Stars Present Few Dances," Milwaukee Sentinel, 27 January 1917, Wisconsin.

"Ballet Russe to Give Extra Performance as a Farewell," San Francisco Chronicle, 5 January 1916, California.

"Ballet Russe Travels at Loss," Desert Evening News, Friday 22 December 1916, Salt Lake City, Utah.

"Ballet Russe Unique," Baltimore Sun, Saturday Morning, 18 November 1916, Maryland.

"Ballet Russe with Nijinsky," Atlantic City Daily Press, 13 November 1916, New Jersey.

"Ballet To-Night," The Enquirer, 6 February 1917, Cincinnati, Ohio.

Barrows, Jack, "Ballet Russe Renews Success - Gives Its Second Fine Program - Last Appearance Here Tonight," The Denver Times, 29 December 1916, Colorado.

---, "First of Exhibitions at the Auditorium Is Fascinating Entertainment in All Departments; Lighting Effects in Thoro Accord," The Denver Times, 19 December 1916, Colorado.

"Belasco," Evening Star, 21 November 1916, Washington, D.C.

Borgium, A. M., "Ballet Russe Proves Exceptional Treat," World Herald, Morning edition, 17 December 1916, Omaha, Nebraska.

Bourman, Anatole and D. Lyman. The Tragedy of Nijinsky. New York: McGraw-Hill, 1936.

The American Tour of the Ballet Rouse

"Brilliant Audience Attends Premiere of the Ballet Russe, The Times Picayune, 1 December 1962, New Orleans, Louisiana.

Brown, G. E., "Dramatic News," Memphis News Scimitar, 1 February 1917, Tennessee.

Buckle, Richard. Nijinsky. New York: Simon and Shuster, 1971.

Chaplin, Charles. My Autobiography. New York: Simon and Schuster, 1964.

Chappell, George S., (A poem about the Ballet Russe, originally in Vanity Fair,) "Ballet Russe Tonight," Toledo Daily Blade, 12 February 1917, Ohio.

Cline, Louis, "Nijinsky Appeared In Ballet Russe," Atlantic City Daily Press, 17 November 1916, New Jersey.

"Columbia Art Capital with Ballet Reigning," The State: Columbia, S. C., 29 November 1916, Morning edition, South Carolina.

"Columbia Theatre," The Columbia Record, Columbia, S. C., 28 November 1916, South Carolina.

C. S. S., "Nijinsky and Lopokowa Charm Detroit Audience," Detroit Free Press, 10 February 1917, Michigan.

"Dancers Bill for Tonight," Wichita Eagle, 12 December 1916, Kansas.

"Dancers Strike but Return When Bolton Builds A New Stage," Des Moines Tribune, 16 December 1916, Iowa.

"Diaghileff's Ballet Russe Charms All with its Wonderful Grace in Theme and Movement," Worcester Daily Telegram, 14 November 1916, Massachusetts.

"Diaghileff's Ballet Russe Is Splendid," Dallas Morning News, 8 December 1916, Texas.

"Didn't Beginski," The Detroit News, 10 February 1917, Michigan.

Donaghey, Frederick, "Nijinsky Makes the Ballet Russe an Entity," The Chicago Daily Tribune, 29 January 1917, Illinois.

Nijinsky in America

"Don't Kid 'Super Captain' of the Ballet Russe; He's O'Fallon, and Backs it Up," Minneapolis Journal, 25 January 1917, Minnesota.

"Don't You Want to Get Away From the Annoying Features of Catarrh?" American, 7 December 1916, Austin, Texas.

Dooly, Louise. "Russian Ballet in "Cleopatre" Scores Triumph at Auditorium," The Constitution, 30 November 1916, Atlanta, Georgia.

Downes, Olin, "Russian Ballet Returns," Boston Sunday Post, 5 November 1916, Dramatic page: 37, Massachusetts.

Eastman, Max. "The Masses," This Fabulous Century.Vol. 2, New York: Time-Life Books, 1969.

Epperson, Clara Cox, "On with the Dance," The Lookout, 17 February 1917, Theatrical News, Chattanooga, Tennessee.

Erb, Robin, "Treasures of past hidden beneath the faded paint," Blade, 12 March 1995, Toledo, Ohio.

"Exotic and Beautiful Scenes and Dances Thrill in Ballet Russe," The Spokesman-Review, 20 January 1917, Spokane, Washington.

"Famed Ballet Russe with Exotic Music Delights Audience," American, 7 December 1916, Austin, Texas.

"Famed Russian Dancers Here Next Week," Tacoma Sunday News-Ledger, 7 January 1917, Washington.

"Famous Ballet Russe Gives an Artistic and Novel Performance," Worcester Evening Post. 14 November 1916, Massachusetts.

"Famous Russian Ballet Tonight," Kansas City Journal, 13 December 1916, Missouri.

"Famous Stars of Russian Ballet Here Thursday Night," Tacoma Sunday News-Ledger, 14 January 1917, Amusements, Washington.

Farrar, Sara, "Ballet Is Feast for Eye and Ear - Scenic Effects Are Startling," The Rocky Mountain News, 20 December 1916, Denver, Colorado.

The American Tour of the Ballet Rouse

---, "Ballet Russe Is Gorgeous in Its Grace, Its Coloring and Its Miming," The Rocky Mountain News, 19 December 1916, Denver, Colorado.

Flagg, Harriet S., "American Artist Is Designer of Setting for Russian Ballet," Minneapolis Journal, 21 January 1917, Amusement Section, Minnesota.

Flandrau, C. M., "The Auditorium," Saint Paul Pioneer Press, 24 January 1917, Minnesota.

"Footlight World," Observer, 31 December 1916, Oakland, California.

F. W. W., "Russian Ballet," Denver Post, 19 December 1916, Denver, Colorado.

"Gallery Gods Lucky Enjoy Ballet Russe," The Seattle Daily Times, 18 January 1917, Evening edition, Washington.

G. B. N., "Ballet's Legs Bare, Anyhow," The Cincinnati Post, 8 February 1917, Cincinnati, Ohio.

Glover, Mary F., "Striking Proportions Attained in Part of Program Designed to Mark Rhythm; Orchestra Plays With Understanding," The Denver Times, 19 December 1916, Colorado.

Gordon, Douglas, "Russian Ballet Presented on Magnificent Scale," Richmond Times-Dispatch, 28 November 1916, Richmond, Virginia.

"Great Ballet Russe Here for Engagement Thursday Evening," The Dallas Daily Times Herald. 7 December 1916, Dallas, Texas.

Greene, I. Newton, "Russian Dancing," The Town Crier, 27 January 1917, Seattle, Washington.

Hale, Philip, "Bostonians See the Ballet Russe in 'Sadko,'" Boston Herald, 10 November 1916, Massachusetts.

---, "Four Ballets Produced at Opera House." Boston Herald, 7 November 1916, Massachusetts.

"Hartford to Have Russian Invasion," Hartford Daily Courant, 14 November 1916, Connecticut.

Nijinsky in America

"Has Unique Place in Europe and New York," Sunday Herald, 5 November 1916.

Hawks, Wells, Telegram, 28 January 1917.

H. C. "Cleopatra Will Be Played at Opera House," The Vancouver Daily Sun, 15 January 1917, B.C., Canada.

Henderson, Charles, "Diaghileff's Ballet Russe," Cleveland Plain Dealer, 17 February 1917, Ohio.

---, "Nimble Nijinsky and Niblo – Welcome," Cleveland Plain Dealer, 11 February 1917, Drama Sections, Ohio.

Huff, Theodore. Charlie Chaplin, a Biography. New York: Pyramid Books, 1951.

Huhn, Hugh H., "Amusements," The Commercial Appeal, 1 February 1917, Tennessee.

N. B., "Ballet Russe in Brilliant Performance at Coliseum," Des Moines Register, 16 December 1916, Iowa.

"Jack Rabbit Dinner Is an Occasion for Eulogies of Bunny," American, 7 December 1916, Austin, Texas.

J. H. T., "Stageland Gossip," The Enquirer, 7 February 1917, Cincinnati, Ohio.

Kingsley, Grace, "Dreamlike Ballet," Los Angeles Daily Times, 29 December 1916.

---, "News and Gossip Plays and Players," Los Angeles Daily Times, 30 December 1916.

Kirstein, Lincoln. Nijinsky Dancing. New York: Knopf, 1975.

"Libretto to Read Dancing Will Be Work of Nijinsky," Fort Worth Record, 28 November 1916, Fort Worth, Texas.

"Many Present on First Night of Russian Ballet," Boston Sunday Herald, 1 November 1916, Women's section, Massachusetts.

Marshall, Frank A., "Diaghileff Ballet Gorgeous Picture," Kansas City Journal, 14 December 1916, Missouri.

Martin, Paul R., "Russian Ballet Seen at Murat," Indianapolis Star, 30 January 1917, Indiana.

Marzoni, Pettersen, "At the Theaters," Birmingham News, 2 February 1917, Alabama.

Mason, Redfern, San Francisco Examiner, 3 January 1917.

"Master of the House and the Boudoir Robe," The Vancouver Sun, 1 January 1917.

McNally, William J., "Entertainments." Morning Tribune, 25 January 1917, Minneapolis, Minnesota

"Men Here Overfed, Lazy; Says Dancer," Minneapolis Journal, 25 January 1917, Minnesota.

Milton, Richard, "Being a Russian Ballet Girl Is a Hard Life; Food Denied From 2 p.m., until the Show Is Ended," The Denver Times, 19 December 1916, Colorado.

M. K. P., "The Real Russian Ballet," Kansas City Times, 14 December 1916, Missouri.

Moore, Frederick B., "Glorified Ballet Art," Los Angeles Sunday Times, Morning edition, 24 December 1916.

---, "Virility Its Essence," Los Angeles Daily Times, 28 December 1916.

"Muscovite Host Invades Back Bay," Boston Post, 6 November 1916, Massachusetts.

"Meals Will Fit! No Indigestion, Gas or Acidity," Statesman, 5 December 1916, Austin, Texas.

"Music of the Ballet Russe," Atlantic City Daily Press, 9 November 1916, New Jersey.

---, Statesman, 5 December 1916, Austin, Texas.

"Music of the Week," Boston Sunday Post, 12 November 1916.

"News of the Stage and the Play," Post Gazette, 18 February 1917, Pittsburgh, Pennsylvania.

Nijinsky in America

"News of the Theatres," Bridgeport Evening Post, 2 November 1916, Connecticut.

Nijinsky, Vaslav. Notebooks. 1919.

"Nijinsky," The News Leader, 28 November 1916, Richmond, Virginia.

"Nijinsky and Russian Ballet," The Albany Evening Journal, 17 February 1917, New York.

"Nijinsky and Strauss' 'Till' Novelties of the Ballet Russe," Indianapolis News, 30 January 1917, Indiana.

"Nijinsky Creates Spiritual Response to His Art," Fort Worth Record, 29 November 1916, Fort Worth, Texas.

"Nijinsky in Own Ballet," Boston Post, 9 November 1916.

"Nijinsky in the Ballet Russe," Atlantic City Daily Press, 15 November 1916.

"Nijinsky Pleases In Splendid Ballets," Pittsburgh Press, 21 February 1917.

Nijinsky, Romola, Letter to Rolf Thomsen, January 1940.

Nijinsky, Romola. Nijinsky. New York: Simon and Schuster, 1937.

"Nijinsky Thinks Genius No Bar to War Service," Boston Herald, 6 November 1916.

"Nijinsky Will Dance Here December 8 and 9," Fort Worth Record, 8 November 1916, Fort Worth, Texas.

"Nijinsky Wins New Yorkers on First Appearance," Fort Worth Record, 2 November 1916, Fort Worth, Texas.

"On with the Dance; Finances Are Fixed," Nashville Tennessean and the Nashville American, 5 February 1917.

Pakulski, Gary T., "Renaissance Ready for Pioneers," Blade, 31 July 1993, Toledo, Ohio.

Parker, H. T. "An All-Russian Evening," Boston Evening Transcript, 8 November 1916.

---, "Nijinsky On and Off the Stage," Boston Evening Transcript, 9 November 1916.

---, "Old with New," Boston Evening Transcript, 11 November 1916.

---, "The Russians' Climax," Boston Evening Transcript, 10 November 1916.

---, "The Russians in Full Glory," Boston Evening Transcript, 7 November 1916.

---, "Week-End Music," Boston Evening Transcript, 13 November 1916.

"Parson's Theater," Hartford Daily Courant, 13 November 1916, Connecticut.

Pavley, Andreas, and Serge Oukrainsky, "How Would You Like Never To Become Tired? Here Is Dancers' Secret for a Strong Back," Chicago Sunday Herald, 28 January 1917.

Player, Cyril Arthur, "Russian Ballet Closes Season in Great Program," The Post Intelligencer, 18 January 1917, Seattle, Washington.

---, "Russian Ballet Transcends Art of Best Critic," The Post Intelligencer, 17 January 1917, Seattle, Washington.

Poe, Edgar Allen. Lenore, 1843.

"Program Announced for Ballet Russe," Dallas Morning News, 7 December 1916.

"Program Announced for Ballet Russe," Statesman, 6 December 1916, Austin, Texas.

Rehmert, Laura H. Letter to author, 7 March 1989.

Reid, Grace Fealy. Letter to author, 5 January 1989.

Remington, Mary E., "The Theaters," Grand Rapids Press, 14 February 1917, Michigan.

"Revel In Anarchy of Art," Wichita Eagle, 13 December 1916, Kansas.

Nijinsky in America

R. M. K., "News of the Theatres," Bridgeport Evening Post, 16 November 1916, Connecticut.

Robinson, Harlow. The Last Impresario: The Life, Times and Legacy of Sol Hurok. Viking: New York, 1994.

"Russian Ballet," Hartford Times, 11 November 1916, Connecticut.

---, Hartford Times, 13 November 1916, Connecticut.

"Russian Ballet at Opera House," Providence Journal, 31 October 1916, Rhode Island.

"Russian Ballet Glory of Color, Music and Motion, Red Blood and Savagery," Houston Chronicle, 5 December 1916, Texas.

"Russian Ballet Heavy Movement," The Columbia Record, Columbia, 28 November 1916, South Carolina.

"Russian Ballet Is Genuine Treat," Hartford Daily Courant, 15 November 1916, Connecticut.

"Russian Ballet Manager Engages Local Attorney," Saint Paul Pioneer Press, 21 January 1917, Minnesota.

"Russian Ballet Music Feature," Tacoma Daily Ledger, 13 January 1917, Washington.

"Russian Ballet Program," Public Ledger, 26 November 1916, Philadelphia, Pennsylvania.

"Russian Ballet Tonight," Kansas City Times, 13 December 1916, Missouri.

"Russian Dancers Coming to the Davis," Pittsburgh Gazette Times, 18 February 1917, Pennsylvania.

"Russian Dancers Seen at Empire," The Syracuse Herald, 24 February 1917, New York.

"Russian Invaders," Hartford Times, 14 November 1916, Connecticut.

"Sadko Feature of the Ballet Show," Inquirer, 25 November 1916, Philadelphia, Pennsylvania.

"Salt Lake Theatre," Salt Lake Tribune, 23 December 1916, Utah.

Sayler, Oliver. M., "Diaghileff Ballet, Up to Mark Set in Europe, Wins Triumph," Indianapolis News, 10 March 1916, Indiana.

---, "'The Faun' and 'Scheherazade' Escape the Censorial Eye – Diaghileff Ballet reaches new Heights," Indianapolis News, 11 March 1916, Indiana.

Schallert, Edwin, "Ever-Varying Moods," Los Angeles Daily Times, 27 December 1916, California.

---, "Its Sweep Powerful," Los Angeles Daily Times, 26 December 1916, California.

"Scheherazade One of the Ballets," Atlantic City Daily Press, 8 November 1916, New Jersey.

Scott, Harold George. Lelia: The Complete Ballerina. Pelican, 1975.

Scott, Marion A. Letter to author, 6 February 1980.

"Seats on Sale for the Ballet Today," Atlantic City Daily Press, 11 November 1916, New Jersey.

"Seats on Sale for the Ballet Tomorrow," Atlantic City Daily Press, 10 November 1916, New Jersey.

"Second Night's Ballet Even More Charming than First," New Haven Evening Register. 2 November 1916, Connecticut.

"See Little of Russian Dancers; Keith's New Bill Has Much Merit," The Toledo News-Bee, 13 February 1917, Ohio.

"Serge de Diaghileff's Ballet Russe," The Columbia Record, Columbia, Sunday Morning, 26 November 1916, South Carolina.

"Shoppers May See Ballet Tomorrow; Pay Roll Here," Saint Paul Dispatch, 22 January 1917, Minnesota.

"Six Americans Killed in Sinking of Steamship Marina; Wilson Directs All Haste in Ascertaining the Facts; Sec. Lansing Asks Germany for Complete Information,"
New Haven Journal-Courier, 31 October 1916, Connecticut.

Nijinsky in America

"Slav Dancers Win Hearty Applause," Tacoma Daily News, 19 January 1917, Washington.

"Spectacular Ballet Tonight," The Constitution, 29 November 1916, Atlanta, Georgia.

"Stage," Los Angeles Sunday Times, Morning, Literature – Society, 24 December 1916, California.

"Stage," Milwaukee Journal, 27 January 1917, Wisconsin.

Stover, John F. American Railroads. Chicago: University of Chicago Press, 1961.

Sully, Harry L., "Ballet Russe Recreates Tone Poems of Composer," Oakland Tribune, 10 January 1917, California.

"Super Human Agility of Nijinsky Attributed to Diaghilev's 'Magic'," Kansas City Star. 18 April 1950, Missouri.

"Talk with Nijinsky," Brooklyn Eagle, 1916, New York.

"Theaters," The Albany Evening Journal, 23 February 1917, New York.

"Theatrical," Pittsburgh Press, 19 February 1917, Pennsylvania.

"The Ballet Russe," Houston Daily-Post. 3 December 1916, Sunday Morning, Texas.

"The Incomparable 'Ballet Russe' City Auditorium Tomorrow and Tuesday Nights, Dec. 4-5," Houston Chronicle, 3 December 1916, Sunday Morning, Texas.

Thompson, Oscar, "Grace, Not Lurid Color, Triumphs," The Tacoma Daily Ledger, 19 January 1917, Washington.

Thomsen, Rolf. Letter to author, 31 November 1989.

"Three Ballets Tomorrow Night," Tulsa Daily World, 10 December 1916, Tulsa, Oklahoma.

T. M. P., "The Ballet Russe," New Haven Journal-Courier, 1 November 1916, Connecticut.

"Two Special Trains Carry Russian Ballet," World-Herald, Evening, 16 December 1916 Omaha, Nebraska.

The American Tour of the Ballet Rouse

"Two Thousand See Ballet Russe Here," Tulsa Daily World, 12 December 1916, Tulsa, Oklahoma.

"Unique Celebration," Los Angeles Daily Times, Monday Morning, 25 December 1916, California.

Upshur, Vincent, "Discriminating Audience Witnessed Ballet Russe," Houston Daily Post 5 December 1916, Tuesday Morning, Texas.

Ward H. Baldwin, ed, Year-Mid-Century Edition: 1900-1950. Los Angeles: Year, 1950.

World Book Encyclopedia. Chicago: World Book, 1986.

Young, Art. "Cartoon," This Fabulous Century. Vol. 2. New York: Time-Life Books, 1969.

Aalto, Madeleine, Director, Vancouver Public Library, Canada.

Alexander, Sarah H., Special Collections, Atlanta-Fulton Public Library, Atlanta, Georgia.

Beihl, Renee, Music and Performing Arts Librarian, Detroit Public Library, Michigan.

Brady, Susan, Archivist, Yale University Library.

Brin, E. J., New Orleans Public Library, Louisiana Division.

Campbell, James W., Assistant Librarian, New Haven Colony Historical Society.

Craven, R. Jayne, Head, Art and Music, The Public Library of Cincinnati and Hamilton County. Ohio.

Dobson, Joan L., Texas/Dallas History, Dallas Public Library.

Finley, Patricia, Librarian, Local History/Special Collections, Onondaga County Public Library. Syracuse, New York.

Gaudette, Nancy E., Librarian, Worcester Collection, Worcester Public Library.

Gehres, Eleanor M., Manager, Western History Department, Denver Public Library.

Nijinsky in America

Geisler, Barbara, Librarian, Archives for the Performing Arts, War Memorial Opera House, San Francisco, California.

Gillmer, Jean, Northwest Room, The Tacoma Public Library, Tacoma, Washington.

Glasser, Doris, Manager, Texas and Local History Department, Houston Public Library.

Greenwald, Evelyn, SCAN Director, Los Angeles Public Library, California.

Gregels, Gerard A, Librarian Assistant, Grand Rapids Public Library, Michigan.

Gregg, Martha, Local History, Wichita Public Library, Wichita, Kansas.

Harpole, Patricia, Chief of the Reference Library, Minnesota Historical Society, Saint Paul, Minnesota.

Hobin, James R., Reference Department, Albany Public Library, New York.

Kearl, Biruta Celmins, Assistant Curator, Austin History Center, Austin Public Library. Texas.

Kent, Frederick James, Head, Music Department, The Free Library of Philadelphia, Philadelphia, Pennsylvania.

Kinney, Marjorie, Missouri Valley Special Collections, Kansas City Library, Kansas City, Missouri.

Knutsen, Sheila, Librarian, Fine and Performing Arts, Seattle Public Library.

Kritemeyer, Ann, Reference Librarian, New Haven Free Public Library, Connecticut.

Librarians and their assistants in fifty-six cities in the Continental US & Vancouver, Canada.

Logan, Kathryn, Music/Art Department, The Carnegie Library of Pittsburgh, Pennsylvania.

Loughlin, Beverly A., Administrative Assistant, Hartford Public Library, Connecticut.

The American Tour of the Ballet Rouse

Lowell, Clinton, Magazines Division, The Dayton and Montgomery County Public Library. Ohio.

Maccary, Dianne, History Subject Specialist, SCAN, Los Angeles Public Library, California.

Marshall, James C., Manager, Local History and Genealogy Department, Toledo, Lucas County Public Library, Ohio.

McQuillan, Valerie, Connecticut Valley Historical Museum, Springfield, Massachusetts.

Milwaukee Public Library. Wisconsin.

Mosiniak, Judith, Library Assistant, Special Collections, Minneapolis Public Library and Information Center, Minnesota.

Mulligan, John.

Multnomah County Library, Portland, Oregon.

Nelson, Judy, Periodicals, Spokane Public Library, Washington.

Nijinsky, Romola.

Nijinsky, Tamara.

Nichols, Madeleine, Curator, New York Public Library for the Performing Arts - Dance Collection, Lincoln Center, New York.

Norton, Margaret K., Executive Director, San Francisco Performing Arts Library & Museum.

Pawlowski, Jennifer, Periodicals, Tulsa City-County Library System, Oklahoma.

Raney, Suzette, Local History and Genealogy Department, Chattanooga-Hamilton County Bicentennial Library, Tennessee.

Ray, Kathryn C., Assistant Chief, Washingtonian Division, Martin Luther King Memorial Library, Washington, D.C.

Scannel, Henry F., Reference Librarian, Micro text Department, Boston Public Library.

Shelkrot. Elliot L., President and Director of the Free Library, The Free Library of Philadelphia, Philadelphia, Pennsylvania.

Shook, Suzanne, Art/Music Department - Interlibrary Loan, Richmond Public Library, Richmond, Virginia.

Shults, Carol, Portland, Oregon.

Sleeman William E., Reference Librarian, Maryland Department, Enoch Pratt Free Library, Baltimore, Maryland.

Smithsonian Institution, Public Inquiry Mail Service, Washington, D.C.

Sorger, Joan L., Head of Main Library, Cleveland Public Library, Ohio.

Stewart, Alan, Art/Music/Films, Memphis Shelby County Public Library & Information Center, Tennessee.

Strow, Mary R., Librarian for Reference Services, Main Library, Indiana University, Bloomington, Indiana.

Tanaka, Kirsten, Head Librarian, San Francisco Performing Arts Library & Museum, California.

Taylor, Lynn, Western History Department, Denver Public Library, Colorado.

Thelma (?) At the Phoenix Public Library, Phoenix, Arizona.

White, Elizabeth L., Local History Librarian, Brooklyn Public Library, New York.

Webb, Rebecca, Agency Head - Fine Arts/Audio Visual, The City Library System, Salt Lake City, Utah.

www.ingramcontent.com/pod-product-compliance
Lightning Source LLC
Chambersburg PA
CBHW070052080526
44586CB00013B/1024